ALPINE CLIMBING

Bruce Goodlad

First published in Great Britain 2025 by Pesda Press
Tan y Coed Canol
Ceunant
Caernarfon
Gwynedd
LL55 4RN

© Copyright 2025 Bruce Goodlad

ISBN: 9781917182034

The Author asserts the moral right to be identified as the author of this work. All rights reserved. No part of this publication may be reproduced, stored in a retrieval system, or transmitted, in any form or by any means, electronic, mechanical, photocopying, recording or otherwise, without the prior written permission of the Publisher.

Maps by Bute Cartographics

Contains Ordnance Survey data (c) Crown copyright and database right 2025

Printed and bound in Poland, www.hussarbooks.pl

Acknowledgements

When starting any book, the scale of the project is never really as apparent as it should be; by this stage, having written two and edited one other book, I should know better. What started as a project, and an excuse to go and climb a few routes and take some photographs, quickly morphed into the book you are reading today. Mountaineering is not really an activity that is best done on your own. You can go solo, but it is more serious and not as much fun. Writing a book is a bit like climbing a big mountain, in that you need a strong team around you to support you through the difficult sections and keep you going when your legs are tired, and your concentration is waning.

Since my first project I have married, had two children and renovated a chalet, so *Alpine Climbing* has been a team event. A massive thank you to:

Franco and Pesda Press for believing in me, and their patience in pulling the book together then working around my schedule of parenting, guiding and climbing, to manage all the edits.

Don at Bute Cartographics for taking the time to pull all the map info together from multiple different countries, scales and rough scribbles.

Kate, my long-suffering wife, for supporting me with time to climb, time in the mountains together, and time behind the camera.

Mike Austin who has been a regular partner in the mountains for more than 25 years. When asked if he fancied doing a route and taking some photos, would just get his diary out as he knew it would be an adventure. It is unlikely the book would have been finished if it wasn't for Mikes efforts, both in climbing the routes and taking many of the photographs.

I owe a debt of gratitude to Mark Charlton and Martin Chester who gave their time to technically edit the book. We have enjoyed many great days in the mountains together.

Photographs

Photos by Bruce Goodlad, Mike Austin, Kate Scott, Mark Charlton and Martin Chester.

About the Author

Born in Ayrshire with both parents employed as teachers, Bruce spent most of his childhood in the outdoors. Summer holidays were spent sailing the west coast of Scotland, exploring the coastline and islands. After studying geography at Glasgow University, Bruce spent a year at Glenmore Lodge (the national outdoor training centre in the Scottish Highlands) on the night-watch scheme as a trainee instructor. He has worked in the outdoor industry ever since, guiding and instructing all over the world. Bruce qualified as an IFMGA (International Federation of Mountain Guide Associations) guide in 2001, he is a former Technical Director of the British Mountain Guides and was involved in guide education for 18 years.

Away from the mountains Bruce has been a regular contributor to Climber Magazine, he has authored / edited three other books: *Alpine Mountaineering*, *Ski Touring* and *Alpine Ski Touring*, all published by Pesda Press.

Bruce lives in the Alps with his family.

Introduction

As a climber we are always looking for the next challenge, the next adventure, wondering what is over the next ridge and around the next corner. Many of us sate this desire by trying harder and longer routes on our home mountains, but sometimes we need a bigger challenge. The Alps, with so many mountains and routes of greater length and complexity than we can find at home, are the perfect place to expand your horizons.

This book is for the climber who is comfortable in the mountains in summer and winter and wants to bring these skills together into a glaciated mountain environment. The concept behind the book is to take the knowledge and skills you already have and adapt them to the alpine environment.

We start this by checking some assumptions that are laid out in the first chapter, along with a skills check that will make sure we are starting from a level playing field. The book is then split into two distinct sections.

The first is all about the skills you will need to go alpine climbing, building on the skills and techniques you have already. We will look at everything from route finding, equipment selection, glacier travel, moving together and how to move quickly and efficiently through the mountains both in ascent and descent.

The second section is a guidebook, and the selection of routes is unashamedly personal. I have climbed all the routes in the book, some of them many times, and enjoyed every one of them enough to want to share them. We have kept the routes in the PD+ to D range, so the routes all require a blend of skills – efficient pitching and moving together being the hallmark of the alpinists craft. Some of the routes involve glacial approaches and descent, some are on snow and some purely on rock. The selection has been made to reflect the change that global warming has had on the Alps. I have grouped the routes geographically so there will be a few great climbs in each area.

Contents

Acknowledgements	3
About the Author	4
Introduction	5
Contents	6
Participation Statement	8
Alpine Climbing and You	9
How to Use this Book	13
Alpine Climbing – What Makes It Different?	17
Styles of Alpine Climbing	21
Alpine Approach	25
Choosing the Right Route	29
Acclimatisation	35
Terminology and Situational Awareness	39
Glacier Travel	47
Equipment	65
Climbing Up	91
Going Down	107
The Alpine Progression	115
Spending the Night Out	117
When It All Goes Wrong	121

GUIDEBOOK

Introduction	127
How to use the Guidebook	129
Monte Viso	131
Punta Udine 3,022m	133
East Ridge	133
Monte Viso 3,841m	135
East Ridge or Voie Normal South Face	135
Valle dell'Orco	139
Becco Meridionale della Tribolazione 3,360m	140
Malvassora	140
La Vanoise	145
Aiguille de la Vanoise 2,796m	146
Traverse of the Aiguille de la Vanoise E-W	146

Mont Blanc Massif (Chamonix)	149
Aiguille du Midi 3,842m	151
Cosmiques Arête	151
Aiguille du Peigne 3,192m	154
Voie Normal	154
Les Perrons de Vallorcine	159
Les Perrons 2,673m	160
Traverse of the Perrons East - West	160
Mont Blanc Massif (Cormayeur)	
Routes from the Torino Hut	163
Aiguilles Marbrées 3,535m	164
Aiguilles Marbrées Traverse NW to SE	164
Aiguilles d'Entrèves 3,600m	166
Aiguilles d'Entrèves Traverse SW to NE	166
Dent du Géant 4,013m	169
South West Face	169
Aiguille de Rochefort 4,001m	172
Rochefort Arête Traverse	172
Cabane D'Orny	175
Aiguille d'Orny 3,150m	176
South Ridge Direct	176
Aiguille de la Cabane 2,999m	179
Bon Accueil	179
Aiguilles d'Arpette 3,059m	182
South Ridge	182
The Aravis	183
Pointe Percée 2,750m	184
Arête du Doigt	184
Pointes de la Blonnière 2,369m	188
L'Arête à Marion	188
Val d'Hérens	191
Dent de Tsalion 3589m and Aiguille de la Tsa 3668m	194
West Ridge	194
Aiguille de la Tsa – East Face	196
Mont Blanc de Cheilon 3,870m	198
Traverse East to South West	198

Le Miroir d'Argentine – Alpes Vaudoises	201	Gletschhorn 3,305m	255
Le Miroir d'Argentine		*South Ridge*	255
(Haute Corde 2,326m)	202	Läckihorn 3,068m	258
Traverse of Miroir d'Argentine	202	*Traverse of the Chli and Gross Läckihorn*	258
Miroir d'Argentine Direct Route	204		
		Grimsel Pass	261
Zermatt	207	Gross Diamantstock 3,162m	262
Dufourspitze 4,634m	210	*East Ridge*	262
West Ridge	210		
Breithorn 4,164m	213	**Tessin and Lombardy**	267
East Ridge half traverse	214	Poncione di Cassina Baggio 2,860m	268
		South Ridge	268
Saas-Fee	217	Pizzo del Prévat 2,557m	271
Lenzspitze 4,294m and Nadelhorn 4,327m	220	*North East Pillar*	271
ENE Ridge of Lenzspitze and		Monte Disgrazia 3,678m	275
SE Ridge on Nadelhorn	220	*North West Ridge*	275
Weissmies 4,017m	222		
North Ridge	222	**Bernina**	277
Dri Horlini 3,209m	225	Piz Morteratsch 3,751m	279
SW Ridge traverse	225	*Morteratsch Skyline North Ridge*	279
Joderhorn 3,035m	227	Piz Bernina 4048m	281
South East Ridge	229	*Biancograt North Ridge*	282
Jegigrat 3,368m and Jegihorn 3206m	232	Piz Palü 3,900m	286
Jegigrat, SE Spur of Grand Gendarme		*Traverse of Piz Palü*	286
and traverse	232		
		Bregaglia	289
Bernese Oberland	237	Spazzacaldeira 2,487m	290
Jungfrau 4,158m	239	*North East Ridge*	290
South East Ridge	239	Piz Balzet 2,869m	292
Eiger 3,970m	241	*South Ridge*	292
Mittellegi North East Ridge	241	Punta da l'Albigna 2,825m	294
		Via Meuli	294
Furka Pass	245	Piz Badile 3,308m	297
Gross Furkahorn 3,169m	247	*North Ridge*	297
East South East Ridge	247		
Klein (Chli) 2,900 and		**Index**	301
Gross Bielenhorn 3,210m	249		
Klein (Chli) Bielenhorn	250		
Gross Bielenhorn	251		
Galenstock 3,586m	253		
South East Ridge	253		

ALPINE CLIMBING

The Author and Publisher of this book agree with the British Mountaineering Council (BMC) Participation Statement that:
"The BMC recognises that climbing and mountaineering are activities with a danger of personal injury or death. Participants in these activities should be aware of and accept these risks and be responsible for their own actions."
Every effort has been made to ensure that the content and instructions in this book cover all aspects of personal safety skills and techniques required in Alpine mountaineering at beginner and up to intermediate level. The Author and Publisher cannot accept any responsibility for any accident, injury, loss or damage sustained whilst following any of the techniques described within.
If you feel that you need additional instruction in order to use this book then it is advised that you employ a suitably qualified and experienced mountain guide.

Alpine Climbing and You

Mark Senior climbing on the Cosmiques Arête, Chamonix.

You love climbing and want to start climbing in the bigger mountains. You want to climb in the Alps but don't have the skills to move on a glacier. You want to climb longer routes but feel you are too slow and don't know how to climb exposed terrain quickly and safely. This is the book for you!

We are going to walk you through all the techniques and tips you need to take the skills you have developed on your home mountains into the higher ranges. We will look at the equipment and skills you need to move efficiently on alpine terrain, be it on rock, snow and ice or, as is often the case in the Alps, a blend of all three.

One of the many fun things about alpine climbing is this blend of skills often required in any single day. You may sleep in a mountain hut, cross a glacier wearing crampons, climb a snow slope, cross a bergschrund, climb 20 pitches of amazing rock, and then descend the other side of the mountain. There are a lot of skills in that one sentence, and to learn them all from scratch could take many seasons. However, given that you have picked this book up at all, you will almost certainly have many of the fundamental mountaineering and climbing skills. We are going to take these skills and build on them to allow you to move safely and efficiently on larger mountains, both glaciated and unglaciated. The skills we will look at are transferable to any mountain range; be it in the Mont Blanc Massif, Greenland, Alaska or the Himalaya, the techniques we will use are all the same.

ALPINE CLIMBING

Sam Davison-Webb on the traverse of the Breithorn, Zermatt.

The bigger the mountains, the bigger the challenges. Stepping up to alpine scale mountains increases the hazard both physically, due to the scale and the effects of altitude, but also in terms of seriousness, where objective danger is a feature of most alpine days.

Where it all began

One of the driving forces behind this book is to help the reader avoid the many mistakes that I have made in my alpine career. The early days of my alpine climbing can be characterised by being in the wrong place at the wrong time, every time. My climbing partners and I thought that because we could climb E1-E2 rock and grade V in winter, we could go straight onto routes of similar grades in the Alps. The mountains can be a hard schoolroom and in our first season we did not summit a single mountain; but we learnt a lot, nobody got hurt (other than their pride) and we applied those lessons going forward. If we had been more humble and listened to those around us, we would almost certainly have been more successful. Moderating our ambition and matching it to our experience, ability and the conditions would have undoubtably made us more successful. I will focus on helping the reader to avoid these pitfalls and climb routes in the Peu Difficile – Difficile (PD-D) grade range.

Important assumptions

I am going to make some assumptions about the skills you already have, to give us a starting point. These are that you have done some climbing and mountaineering in the past and have the fundamental movement and safety skills that will allow you to operate in your domestic mountains. When I talk about domestic mountains, I am thinking about sub-alpine mountains,

Alpine Climbing and You

in winter and summer, where routes can be completed in a single day. In these smaller ranges there is rarely any need for moving-together techniques, descents are generally uncomplicated, and there are no glaciers.

To make things easy, here is a skills check list. If you aren't happy with any of the skills outlined, then we would suggest referring to *Alpine Mountaineering* by the same author or consider taking a course. A course is a great way of developing the skills you are missing in a focussed way, effectively short-cutting the learning process. Most climbers come from an amateur mountaineering background where the idea of employing a guide to help them is alien, but with limited holiday and time available perhaps employing someone to help you bridge the gap and develop your skills will speed you on the road to independence in the mountains. It may help you avoid a first season like the one I had. If you are under the age of 30 then there are some amazing, subsidised courses run by the Jonathan Conville Memorial Trust. www.jcmt.org.uk

Skills check list

The climber is comfortable scrambling on grade 1 and 2 scrambles without feeling the need for a rope. On grade 3 scrambles the climber may use a rope and has the skills to do this using basic techniques.

On rock the climber is comfortable climbing on pitched terrain up to VS (Very Severe), making solid belays and placing good running belays. They will have done some abseiling to descend.

In the winter environment the climber is comfortable with the use of crampons to move about on steep snow, mixed (rock, snow and ice) ridge, and winter climbs up to Scottish grade III. They can also build belays and take those key skills from summer rock climbing into the winter environment.

We must also add in some other key mountain skills like navigation. Although we generally go climbing in good weather in the Alps, you still

Kate Scott climbing at Shiegra in the NW highlands of Scotland.

ALPINE CLIMBING

Gavin Pike climbing
Orion Direct on
Ben Nevis.

need to be able to navigate. You will almost certainly start most of your days in the dark or the dawn light, and if the weather comes in and you are on a big, wide-open glacier you need to be able to navigate.

If you are comfortable with the skills outlined above then you are ready, we will now build on those skills to take them into the alpine environment. If you are not, please don't write off the Alps – there are still many amazing routes suitable for you to develop those skills on. In *Alpine Mountaineering* I walk the reader through the acquisition of those skills, with the routes to develop your techniques on. When you feel comfortable with those skills you will be ready to move onto the more advanced skills and more difficult routes in this book.

How to Use this Book

Approaching the summit of the Aiguille Verte.

In order to make this book, *Alpine Climbing*, useful and accessible, I have broken the topic down into sections.

Together, you, the reader, and I are going to set the scene and then look at the approach we need to adopt to successfully climb in the Alps, which involves thinking about conditions and choosing the right route. This leads smoothly into alpine weather, how it works, where to get the information and how to interpret it.

We will then look at alpine terrain, styles of route, and physical considerations. This is all intertwined with how climate change has and will affect what we do in the Alps.

Once we understand how the Alps work, we will look at the specific techniques that allow us to move efficiently and safely through the mountains.

A big part of any alpine climb is having the correct kit – take too much and it will slow you down, take too little and it will slow you down – so we will look at how to tailor your kit to your objectives. Along with kit, how you prepare for an alpine climb in the months as well as the days before any route is important and we will help you to make sure you are ready.

Inevitably, at some point, it will all go wrong. Hopefully not to you but maybe to someone nearby on the mountain, so knowing what to do and how to manage any situation is equally important.

The second half of the book is a guidebook, with all the information needed to go and climb a selection of amazing routes. They are grouped together geographically so that there are a few routes in each area. All the

ALPINE CLIMBING

routes have been climbed recently by the author or a trusted colleague (IFMGA Mountain Guide), so the information is as up to date as possible.

While all the topics are interlinked, the book is designed so that you can dip in and out and find the topics you are most interested in. All the routes in the guidebook section are brilliant, the information up to date and you won't find them all in another collection.

A typical alpine day – Galenstock

To give some context to the chapters to come I thought it was worth talking through a classic alpine day. A day that requires a blend of skills to be achieved comfortably, but also a day that gives great climbing on all sorts of terrain.

I have chosen the Galenstock, the highest peak in the Swiss canton of Uri, easily accessed from the Furka Pass close to Andermatt. We can break the day down into the different elements that are important in any alpine ascent. While no day is typical, I think this highlights the different skills that blend together to make for a brilliant day of mountaineering.

The Galenstock seen from the Furka Pass approach.

The Sidelin hut with the Furka Pass in the background.

Where to stay

Many of the huts in this part of the Alps have fairly easy approaches, so it is possible to climb some of the routes in a day. Huts provide incredible facilities close to our chosen objective; however, they can be busy, noisy, and expensive. If I choose to use one, the decision will be based on an equation of the above factors plus the proximity of an alternative option.

In this case the options are: the Sidelin hut, which is a great spot but small, often busy and only an hour's walk from the road; a bivvy by the car; a van night if you have one, the Tiefenbach hotel (10 minutes' drive away) will provide breakfast at whatever time you like; or accommodation in ReAlp or Andermatt.

Let's say for the sake of argument that you were staying in ReAlp. The plan is to get up early enough to have breakfast and walk in past the hut so you are on the route ahead of those staying in the hut.

Approach to the route

You can scope most of the route and some of the descent from the hut on your way past (if you do decide to stay there, you can do this the night before). You want to start early so that the glacier will be frozen and the snow on the upper part of the route will be in good condition. Passing the hut at first light will let you scope out the approach but means you will need a headtorch to navigate the track on the approach to the hut.

The route now climbs a moraine before ascending a small glacier, it may look small on the map, but it does have some crevasses.

Having climbed the glacier to a point under the Obere Bielenlücke (col), you leave the glacier and follow an easy via ferrata to gain the Obere Bielenlücke.

You have now been through; an approach on a track, glacier travel and a simple via ferrata to gain a col. You aren't really on the ridge yet, but the top of the Tiefengletscher which you follow, crossing a small bergschrund, brings you to the SE ridge proper. You can now put away your crampons for a while.

Sam Davison-Webb on the approach to the Galenstock via ferrata.

Sam Davison-Webb on the South East Ridge of the Galenstock.

The route

Climb the ridge via a series of pitches of up to (French) 5b to reach easier angled rock. You can then move together to the end of the ridge, where it merges into easier angled terrain.

You now need to change back into crampons and climb the increasingly exposed South Ridge to the summit.

The descent

Do not dally too long on the summit, as the snow will now be in the sun and softening fast. Retrace your steps down the ridge, then head north-west, descending broad snow fields to find a cairn at the top of the abseil descent.

This well-equipped descent takes you in 8 x (20-25m) abseils onto easier ground; you then descend steep snow and the Sidelengletscher. Where the snow and glacier run out, pick up a small track that leads you down to the path you used to approach the hut earlier in the day. Walk down the path back to the road.

In that simple description we encompass everything that is great about alpine climbing. It initially involves a skills blend where you are using crampons and an ice axe, and navigating on a crevassed glacier using the rope to protect yourself. You then route-find and climb technical pitches, move together on rock followed by a narrow snow crest. The descent involves down-climbing on snow, a multi-pitch abseil, then more down-climbing on snow, and a small glacier.

It is this skills blend that makes alpine climbing so special.

Alpine Climbing – What Makes it Different?

Gareth Hughes climbing on the ESE ridge of the Lenspitz.

What do we mean by alpine climbing? At its simplest it's going climbing in the Alps, but what makes them different?

Scale

The main factor is a question of scale, as the vertical interval on some Alpine peaks is as big as anything else in the world. The vertical interval on the Weisshorn from the car park at Randa to the summit is 3,077m – that's almost as much as Everest base camp to the summit (3,485m). The mountains are big, and the distances can be large – a peak like the Dufourspitze (second highest mountain in the Alps) being a round trip of over 10km from the hut to the summit and back. This scale, height and distance offers some great challenges, both logistically and physically.

If you have a problem, this can mean that you are a long way from help. Consider a route where you have walked for five hours to a hut then climbed for six hours above the hut – if you have an accident, it will take a long time for anyone to walk in and help you. This is why helicopters are generally used for rescue, though if the weather is bad and they can't fly it is unlikely anyone will be coming for you until the weather improves.

Hut network

We are very lucky that in the Alps we have an incredible network of huts. It is unique in the world's mountains in that every major peak is serviced by at least one mountain hut. The huts provide a bed and half board, allowing the climber to travel with relatively light rucksacks, saving energy for the climb.

Huts are expensive, as the food and fuel is flown in by helicopter, so another option is to camp or bivouac close to the start of your climb. The down side is that you will pay the penalty of having to carry that equipment with you on the approach, and maybe up and over your route.

Almageller Hut

Objective danger

No adventurous activities are without risk. The fun and excitement we get from an activity are some of the things that make it worthwhile, as well as the opportunity to climb in some incredibly beautiful places. The Alps inherently involve more risk than our domestic mountains. The most obvious difference is the presence of snow and ice in the summer months, and glaciers. You need to consider the snow conditions in relation to what you are climbing. You also need the skills and techniques to manage moving around on glaciers, so minimising the chance of a crevasse fall. Should one happen, you need the skills to deploy the rope in an appropriate way to manage the situation.

Rockfall is the second most obvious issue. The mountains are big and can tower a long way above you, but they are also young, and the rock does not have the maturity of older mountain ranges such as those found in the UK. In the more mature mountain ranges the rock has been weathered for longer, so much of the loose rock has gone. As a result of global warming, we are losing the permanent snow and ice that glues the mountains together both internally, with the melting of the permafrost, and externally, with the melting of what was permanent snow and ice, and the glacial retreat.

Alpine Climbing – What Makes it Different?

Descending the Monte Rosa-Gletscher after climbing the Dufourspitze.

The effect on the mountains is that as the season progresses and the winter snows melt, fresh rock is exposed, and loose rock previously held in place is more likely to fall. You can address this by crossing any threatened areas early in the morning, when things are more likely to be frozen together, and you can monitor the area by speaking to local hut guardians and mountain guides. However, once the snow and ice are gone, there is nothing left holding the mountain together, and flowing water from melting snow can increase the chance of rockfall. Ultimately you must decide whether it is safe enough to cross through an area.

As the season develops, certain areas have more pronounced rockfall due to the recent loss of permafrost and deglaciation. The Gouter route on Mont Blanc is a classic example of this. Once the majority of the snow has melted out of the Grand Couloir, rockfall is a regular occurrence. The way I deal with this as a guide is that I would not guide Mont Blanc beyond early July. Even within that period I will gather local knowledge to decide if it is safe enough to make it worth our while to go to the hut, and then carefully observe the couloir to see if there is any rockfall. I will then plan the ascent to make sure we only cross at the coldest times of the day.

Altitude

The human body will start being affected by altitude from about 1,800m. The body's reaction to the reduced oxygen concentration is to produce more red blood cells (this is why many athletes uses high ski resorts like Val d'Isere 1,800m to train). The body is very clever and can adapt to extreme altitude remarkably well. The problem for the alpinist is that until you have been at altitude several times, you will have no idea how your body will adapt to the lack of oxygen. When you are well acclimatised (your body is adapted to the lack of oxygen) climbing can feel as easy as at sea level, but if you are not well acclimatised, everything can feel difficult and you may become ill, maybe even seriously ill. We will talk more about this in a later chapter.

Glaciers

We haven't had anything approximating a glacier in the British mountains for at least 10,000 years, in the United States they have nothing bigger than a pocket glacier in the lower 48, but in the Alps, we have some incredible glaciated terrain. The Aletsch Gletscher is the longest at 24km, an incredible piece of ice. This glaciated terrain provides us with a stunning landscape and some unique mountaineering challenges. They also have the hazard of crevasses and the risk of falling into them.

Seracs

A serac is an ice cliff. There is a common misconception that these are safer at night when it is cooler, this is not the case. Seracs collapse or have sections collapse when gravity overcomes their internal strength. They can collapse at any time of the day. The only way to manage them is either to avoid them all together, or move underneath them really quickly.

A serac on the Monte Rosa-Gletscher.

Weather

One of the great things about climbing in the Alps is the continental climate. While no mountain range is immune to bad weather, the Alps are far enough from the sea that they generally get pretty stable weather in the summer months. The potential issue is when it gets hot, especially in August – think 35°C on the valley floor, where the nights are too short to cool the air temperature properly – there is the chance of thunderstorms. These are relatively predictable as they build up over several days and generally happen in the afternoon. If there is any chance of thunderstorms you do not want to be anywhere exposed when one arrives. Being hit by lightning is not something many people recover from.

Styles of Alpine Climbing

Mark Dearnley emerges into the sun at the top of the North Face of Gran Paradiso.

There are many different types of alpine climbing. Some are defined by the time of year, where snow and ice will predominate, and some by rock type, where the quality of the rock will force us onto ridges. These different styles of climbing that you may choose to undertake will almost certainly be influenced by the climbing you are most comfortable with. If you have never worn crampons before, then the East ridge of the Weisshorn (very exposed) is not the place to learn, but if you have done a lot of multi-pitch rock climbing, then a big rock climb with a snow or even glacier approach may play to your strengths.

Snow and ice climbing

I think when everyone pictures the Alps this is what they think of, moving along a narrow snow crest with a short rope between you, standing on lofty summits, crampons biting into perfect névé. There is no doubt about it, some of the most memorable routes I have done in the Alps have been routes in exactly this style. One of the many tragic things about global warming is that it has become increasingly difficult to get these routes in good condition. Routes that rely on snow and ice need the spring to bring in liberal quantities of wet snow that sticks onto the mountains, and that then goes through several melt-freeze cycles to create perfect névé that is a joy to climb on. The reason the spring snowfall is so important is that in the winter the weather is too cold and windy at altitude for the snow to stick. When you look at the mountains, if they are nice and white then you have a chance for good conditions but if your route or descent has a grey / blue sheen to it, there is a good chance it will be cold, hard ice. This can be incredibly difficult and time consuming to climb as it is really difficult to get good crampon and ice axe placements. It can also be so hard that it is difficult to protect as you can barely drive an ice screw into it.

Many of the classic snow and ice climbs like the North Face of the Courtes or Les Droites have become late winter or spring routes, as the lower parts melt out in the summer months.

With this type of route, conditions are everything. So don't become too obsessed with a specific objective but come prepared with a list of routes of different styles you would like to climb.

Mixed climbing

This epitomises the skills blend that I love in alpine climbing, a glacier approach, some movement on steep snow to establish yourself on an exposed ridge, then moving together and short pitches leading to an airy summit. The descent is usually a mix of downclimbing, maybe together, maybe one at a time, and possibly some abseiling. You need to keep moving, and your ropework and route finding need to be slick, so that you can arrive back on the glacier before the rock-hard surface you moved quickly over this morning turns into porridge. Not only does this make the day go on forever, as the snow is much more difficult to walk on, but it also becomes more dangerous as crevasse bridges that were well frozen in the morning weaken in the sun.

Mixed routes can come in all shapes and sizes, from classic ridges where you might have crampons on your feet and be climbing with your bare hands

Mike Brownlow climbing on the North Ridge of the Olan.

to giant mixed routes like those found on the north face of the Grandes Jorasses, where the difficulty means that you will be climbing most of the face in pitches, using ice tools. This requires the largest range of skills. You will need to be able to move quickly over technical terrain in exposed positions, and maybe spend multiple days on a single climb and descent.

Rock

The range of skills required to go rock climbing in the Alps is not as great as for mixed climbing. You still need a high level of skill and competence, it just means they don't need to be quite so diverse. The skills of traditional rock climbing using leader placed gear are the perfect basis for rock climbing in the Alps. The key element to consider is the scale and the need to move quickly. At home you may be able to take most of the day climbing four pitches followed by an easy descent. You cannot adopt the same leisurely pace on a route with twelve or more pitches, especially if there is a complicated descent.

One of the best ways to manage this is to choose objectives that are not towards the top of your technical grade. It is better to climb with a few grades in hand. This way you will move quickly, you won't feel the need to place so much protection and you will generally enjoy the experience much more.

One of the other differences found in the Alps is the amount of fixed equipment. Many routes will be entirely bolted, while others have bolts where there are no other protection options, and some will have the belays in place. This will vary a bit from region to region and rock type to rock type. For example, compact limestone is quite difficult to protect so all the protection will probably be in place unless the route follows a crack system, whereas granite offers more natural options.

Kris McCoey on the SW Pillar of the Dammazwillinge.

ALPINE CLIMBING

Graeme Ettle climbing Motorhead at Eldorado.

Certain areas may have bolts that were originally placed on the lead, so while the bolts may have been replaced since the first ascent they may only be in places where the leader could stand to place them. A classic for this would be Eldorado near the Grimsel Pass, where the run outs can be huge and the bolts are often just above ledges. In the guidebook section we will give you plenty of information about the routes we have featured.

While some climbers with traditional ethics may struggle with this mixed approach, having the belays in situ can make the climbing faster. On many of the classic Swiss routes they use large ring bolts that look like door knockers, where you don't even have to equalise the anchor, just clip in.

Many big rock routes in the Alps have an abseil descent. This allows you to climb unencumbered by approach shoes / boots or glacier travel equipment. However, other routes will require you to carry everything up and over the top of your route. There is something really satisfying about a journey where you approach a climb using a set of skills, switch mode to climb a route, then use a different set of skills to descend a different way.

Alpine Approach

Kate Scott on the traverse of Gross Diamantstock.

How we approach climbing in the Alps is different to how we operate in smaller mountains. The mountains are bigger and more serious, so we need to adapt how we plan, consider carefully what we take with us and make sure we are at the right place at the right time.

Speed is safety – fast and light

There is an old saying in the mountains that speed is safety, if you are moving quickly and efficiently then it is easy to be at the right place at the right time. You approach your route or cross a glacier at the optimum time of day, so that the snow is well frozen both for the approach and the descent. I remember going to traverse Liskamm, one of the most famous snow crests in the Alps. The hut guardian would only do breakfast at 0500. Given how warm the forecast was we felt this was too late, so we skipped breakfast, drank some water and ate some grain bars, and left the hut at 0300. This way we spent all day on hard frozen snow on the approach, across the route, and then on the descent as well. We were drinking coffee in Gressoney by 11 in the morning. We also had the benefit of having the route to ourselves.

If you leave things too late in the day, the timing of the day starts to spiral. If the surface of the glacier is too soft, you can't move so quickly. Then you are out in the heat of the day for longer, so you get more dehydrated. Dehydration means you won't move so quickly, so you are out in the heat for longer, so you become more dehydrated – it's a vicious cycle. The snow bridges on the glacier will start to weaken in the afternoon sun, so the glacier becomes more dangerous.

You can see how a simple thing like getting out of bed a few hours earlier can make a huge difference to how the day pans out. If you are back at the hut early you can just hydrate, have something to eat, then go to bed for an afternoon nap.

Fast and light

Mark Twight, in his seminal book *Extreme Alpinism*, talks about climbing 'light, fast and high'. The idea of climbing light and fast is that by pairing down the weight on your back you will be able move more quickly, so increasing your margins of safety. If you get the weight right, this can help you move onto potentially harder or longer routes, as you will have the speed to climb them safely and efficiently, and have the energy left to manage the descent.

I have a favourite saying 'light is right, until its wrong'. With this lightweight approach, you must be able to match it to the speed you can move at. There is no point in leaving all the emergency bivouac equipment at home if you climb so slowly that you end up spending a night out. The reverse is also true, if you take lots of bivouac equipment with you then there is a good chance you will end up using it. So, everything is a question of balance. In the equipment chapter we will look in detail at choosing the right equipment for your objective and in the guidebook section we will look at what's appropriate for each route.

The alpine season – when to climb

You can climb in the Alps at any time of the year, if you get the right weather. Predicting it has become more complicated as global warming has affected the time of year that certain routes are in condition. When I first climbed in the Alps in winter, icefall climbing around La Grave in December, morning temperatures were regularly -15c / - 17c, but we rarely see morning valley temperatures as cold as this anymore, even in the middle of winter. This warming has influenced all aspects of alpine climbing, and while the winter temperatures are indicative of this warming, it's the summer temperatures, both average and maximum, that has had the biggest effect on conditions.

Those of you who have visited the Alps over a number of years will have noticed the retreat of many of the major glaciers, one of the most sobering examples is the Mer de Glace in Chamonix.

It is more difficult to access many routes, as the glacier retreat has left smooth glacial slabs that are impossible to climb. It has exposed loose moraines – where you used to access on snow there is now a pile of unstable rubble. Gullies that used to be full of snow are now full of loose rock waiting to fall on you when you cross underneath. North faces that used be climbable through the early part of the summer melt-out much earlier,

The author climbing on the North Ridge of the Piz Badile. Photo: Mike Austin

Alpine Approach

The retreating Tré-la-Tête Glacier, Mont Blanc Massif.

making many of them spring or winter routes only. This sounds all pretty depressing but as climbers we are nothing if not adaptable. The seasons for certain routes have changed and we must move our plans and objectives to match this evolution. The Alps is still an incredible place to climb; I would just suggest that if you want to climb big snow ridges and north faces, August is no longer the month to do it in.

Traditionally, we thought of the Alpine season as being July and August, but with the changes in global temperature I would consider the season to have moved forward at least a month.

If snow and ice are your focus, I would think about coming in the earlier part of the season. This will vary from year to year. In some seasons, early June may have good snow cover but it may be unconsolidated and it can be difficult to move around; whereas in other years stable weather has already allowed the snowpack to settle, allowing fast travel on the glaciers and great snow and ice on ridges and faces. In one unusual summer recently we had an incredibly unsettled May, June and July which meant that the snow ridges were still in condition well into August, when we would usually be climbing on rock.

Classic snowy mixed terrain on the traverse of the Breithorn.

ALPINE CLIMBING

If there was such a thing as an average season in the high mountains (3,700-4,000m+), I would think about June through to mid-July as being the best time for snow and ice, July through to early August for mixed ridges, and August through to early September for more rocky objectives. On the lower peaks the evolution happens earlier in the season.

The conditions on any route are incredibly dependent on its altitude as well as its orientation and location within the Alps. The lower, south-facing routes will always come into condition more quickly after bad weather, and those routes in the southern areas of the Alps, like the Ecrin and Monte Viso, will clear more quickly than the northern mountains in the Bernese Oberland. On the flip side, when the snow and ice is melting in the southern Alps, the conditions will generally last longer in the northern Alps and the snow and ice conditions on the higher 4,000m peaks will last longer than on the lower peaks.

With this knowledge you will be wondering, if we want snow and ice why don't we just climb in the winter months? We can climb in the winter, but the problem with a lot of the higher routes in the winter months is that the temperatures are very cold, and access is difficult, requiring skis or snowshoes. Many of the routes that are climbed in the winter months are those with abseil descents so skis can be left at the base.

In an ideal world we would be tracking the conditions by looking at websites, forums, social media and following the weather conditions. Then, when the weather and conditions aligned, we would drop everything and go.

However, the world does not work like that. We all have jobs, families, and commitments. So, in my view it is best to look at the time you have available to climb, then plan a number of different options considering the possible conditions outlined above, then consider a number of options in different areas. That way, in the run up to the trip you can be watching the weather and conditions, so you will have a good idea about what you will find when you arrive. Once in the Alps, you can head for the area with the best conditions and weather.

Getting to the Alps – where to stay

There are a number of options when you travel to the Alps – planes, trains, and automobiles. In an eco-aware society, where we are concerned about reducing our carbon footprint, coming for longer trips and sharing transport will reduce our emissions. Travelling by train and using public transport is a real possibility if you want to stay in Switzerland, as their public transport system is so incredibly good. Unfortunately, outside of Switzerland public transport is significantly more limited and you will need to consider a car to get around. In many cases, arriving by car shared with a few climbing partners allows you to bring plenty of kit and camping gear, and be flexible with where you climb.

When in the valley, camping has always been the preferred option, with campsites being cheap and a great way to meet other climbers and share information about routes and conditions. In bad weather, or if you would like a bit more comfort, renting an apartment from a website like *airbnb* or even a cheap hotel from a comparison site, like *booking.com* can be a welcome relief from camping in the rain. You can dry out and rest, so that you are well fed and hydrated ready for your next route.

While most of us need to be cost conscious, sometimes spending a little bit more on somewhere comfortable in the valley will pay dividends when you are in the mountains.

Choosing the Right Route

Arriving at the summit of the Dufourspitze, the second highest mountain in the Alps.

It is really easy to overstretch yourself early in your Alpine career. Confusing ambition and ability is something that we are all guilty of at times, so play to your strengths. If you are a strong rock climber, consider a route that is predominantly rock and well within your ability. The technical difficulty will not be an issue so you can focus on the newer techniques of moving on a glacier on the approach, climbing quickly and efficiently, moving together on the easier sections, and then managing the descent. It will be more fun, and as your confidence and experience grow you can move onto styles of climbing you are currently less comfortable with.

Routes are generally longer. So, if you climb E1 5b regularly on two or three pitch crags, when you move onto a route with 20 or more pitches choosing a route with a maximum grade of Very Severe (VS) will allow you to move more quickly.

Traditionally, UK climbers would have served a classic apprenticeship, hill walking and climbing in the summer, then moving onto winter walking and ultimately winter climbing. This gave a solid grounding in all the movement techniques. However, the reality these days is that the reliability of weather and conditions in the domestic mountains means that many climbers first time with an ice axe and crampons will be in the Alps.

A steady approach, moving through the grades will set you up for success; rather than trying to learn how to use crampons in an exposed and potentially dangerous situation.

One of the key differences in the way we use the rope in the Alps, is moving together and using short rope techniques to safeguard our ascent

29

and descent. This is very new to many climbers who are brought up with a pitched climbing background on smaller crags. At the highest technical levels of alpinism, routes are climbed in a pitched style; but most classic alpine routes require some moving together to allow the team to climb, ascend and descend in a safe and timely fashion.

It is really difficult to learn these techniques on a big route at 4,000m, whereas developing these techniques before we come to the Alps, then cementing them on shorter, lower altitude routes will set you up for success on longer, higher ascents.

How to prepare at home – techniques

Many of the techniques we are going to discuss in this book can be learnt and practised at home. This can be really simple things like practising taking coils, so you know how much space to leave between each person on the rope and how to tie-off the rope.

Practising the rope systems associated with crevasse rescue means that you have the rope systems dialled in and memorised before you practise on snow or go anywhere near a glacier.

Go scrambling and practise using the rope. We look at the specific techniques in a later chapter, but having familiarity with different approaches will pay huge dividends when you arrive in the Alps.

When you go climbing, go to a multi-pitch venue, drop a few grades and see how many pitches you can achieve in a day. Concentrate on climbing efficiently, and having slick change overs and transitions from ascending to descending. Practising multi-pitch abseils will make any abseil descent situations that you come across seem familiar, and you will know what to do straight away.

If you are UK based there are not many alpine-style routes available to practice on, but linking together scrambles and easier climbs in North Wales or the Lake District is the perfect preparation. If you can go to Scotland, then the Cuillin mountains on Skye are the nearest thing the UK has to the Alps, as there is no easy way down and efficient movement over rough exposed terrain is the order of the day. In winter, there is no greater preparation than Tower Ridge on Ben Nevis; a perfect blend of length and seriousness where good moving together, route-finding, and pitched climbing are essential to make a smooth ascent.

Taking a course or using a Mountain Guide

Traditionally, climbers and mountaineers learnt by our mistakes, learnt from each other, and if we were lucky, were mentored by more experienced climbers and alpinists. This is still the case for many people, but it is worth considering taking a course or hiring a mountain guide, especially at the start of that first season.

Learning from a professional with many years of experience is a great way to short cut much of the learning. It will also make sure you are armed with the key skills and some suggestions about appropriate routes before you head out on your own.

There is something incredibly satisfactory about doing it yourself and learning as you go, but not all of us have the luxury of time, and ending up in the wrong place at the wrong time can be incredibly frustrating, not to mention dangerous.

You can access a mountain guide either by joining a course, where you are likely to meet like-minded climbers, or hire one directly. The mountain guide can tailor any time you spend together to your specific ability and aspirations.

As a guide, I have regularly helped alpinists develop their skills to move safely and efficiently in alpine terrain, then helped them choose objectives before they head out on their own. I have enjoyed a great sense of satisfaction when they phone me up to tell me all about what they have done and how it all

Choosing the Right Route

Mountain Guide, Swedish Mike, and guests arriving on the summit of the Dufourspitze.

went. We have often kept in touch over the years, with folk coming back to climb with me for a more serious objective they may not feel comfortable climbing on their own, or for a technical tune-up at the start of a season.

What is a Mountain Guide?
To work in the Alps as a mountain professional, you need to be an internationally qualified guide (International Federation of Mountain Guide Associations - IFMGA). IFMGA Mountain Guides have been trained and assessed in rock climbing, snow and ice climbing, alpinism and skiing (off-piste and ski touring). It takes many years of climbing, mountaineering, and skiing to even be able to start to train. There are 27 member countries around the world that ensure common standards of training and assessment across all the different countries. www.IFMGA.com

Alpine grades

The grading system most commonly used for Alpine routes is the French adjectival grading system. It takes into consideration the seriousness and commitment required to climb and descend a route.

The grade will consider factors such as accessibility, length, altitude, technical difficulty and objective dangers. If there is any rock climbing on the route the grade is then augmented by using a rock climbing grade to indicate the difficulty of the hardest pitch. The Union Internationale des Associations d'Alpinisme (UIAA) system is used in the Alps; this is an international system, designed to let climbers from around the world know what grade a climb will be. It is explained in more detail in the following section.

Conditions will often make a difference to how a particular grade will feel; the grade in the guidebook is for average conditions, so find out what those are. Study the book, speak to people who have done the route, and ask the hut guardian about the current conditions.

ALPINE CLIMBING

Overall grades

In this book we will look at routes up to D (Difficile) but it is worth knowing what's in store if you carry on up the grade ladder.

F (facile): Routes are usually glacial or snow routes which may be up to 40° steep. There may also be some easy scrambling.

PD (peu difficile): Routes with some difficulty, crevassed glaciers which may be steep, snow to 50°. Ridges may have some exposed scrambling that will require protection from the rope and there may be the odd pitch of grade I/II rock.

AD (assez difficile): Expect to find snow and ice up to 55° with rock climbing to grade III, with the possibility of the odd move of IV. These sections are not usually sustained but may be located within longer sections of scrambling. Expect long exposed sections on snow and rock on ridges; mountains with classic AD ridges do not normally have an easy way off so you must be confident in descent as well as ascent.

D (difficile): Expect routes of up to 60° on snow with possibly steeper sections. You may have to climb mixed sections on ice-covered rock in your crampons. Expect long exposed sections of snow or rock on ridges; if rock, then you may have climbing at IV+ and the odd bit of V.

TD (très difficile): You are now on serious terrain. Routes will have some objective danger and sustained difficulty with steep ice and rock of IV, V and occasionally VI, often with complex route-finding. You may find that much of the ground is hard enough that it is pitched, rather than using a mixture of moving together and short pitches as you would on easier routes.

ED (extrêmement difficile): As for TD but more of it, and harder.

Grades may be augmented with a + or – which effectively adds grades to the system (you would expect a PD+ to be quite a bit harder than a PD–).

Mark Dearnley descending the classic route on the Signalkuppe (F).

Climbers approaching the summit of the Weissmies on the classic South Ridge (PD).

Rich Parker on the north ridge of the Weissmies (AD).

Mark Chadwick climbing the south buttress of the Argentera (D).

Technical grades

On snow and ice, the average angle is usually used to indicate steepness, but this may hide the fact that there is the odd steeper section.

When you move onto steeper ground, some guidebooks will use the WI (water ice) grading system, and some may use Scottish grades.

Make sure you check which one is being used as they are a full grade different (Scottish grade IV is WI III).

The UIAA system is used in most guidebooks for rock. It equates roughly to the UK system as outlined below, but remember you will probably be climbing in mountaineering boots and be wearing a rucksack (and maybe climbing at altitude). On routes that are predominantly rock climbing, you may choose to wear rock boots and carry your mountaineering boots.

On routes that are generally pitched climbing in rock shoes we have used the French numerical system which uses an open-ended system starting at 1 and currently going to 9b (the hardest rock climbs in the world). In the alpine environment we have used this in 4a, 4b, 4c and 5a, 5b, 5c – while

ALPINE CLIMBING

this may appear confusing it works pretty well in reality and matches the system used in most other contemporary guidebooks. A comparison with other commonly used grading systems – UIAA, United Kingdom and USA grades can be found in the grade comparison table.

I: Easy scrambling.

II: Short sections of moderate to difficult (D) climbing.

III: Climbing very difficult (VD) with the odd move of easy severe (S).

IV: Expect climbing at S to easy very severe (VS) with the odd move of British 4a.

V: VS to hard very severe (HVS) climbing moves in the British 5a grade.

VI: HVS–E1 (extreme level 1) with climbing in the British 5a and possibly 5b grade.

Rock climbing grade comparison table

France	UIAA	US		GB
1	I	5	3a	
2	II	5.1/5.2	3b	
3	III	5.3/5.4	3c	
4a	IV	5.5	4a	VD
4b	IV+	5.6	4b	S
4c	V	5.7	4c	HS
5a	V+	5.8		VS
5b	VI-	5.9	5a	HVS
5c	VI	5.10a		E1

Acclimatisation

Sunset over Saas Tal, seen from the Hohsaas hut.

An important factor to consider when going to the Alps is that they are high enough for the altitude itself to be an issue. You will need to allow your body time to adapt.

What is acclimatisation?

The human body will begin to feel the effects of altitude from around 1,500m. If you are reasonably fit, you probably won't begin to feel the effects until you are between 2,500m and 3,000m. Above this altitude it is possible to develop altitude-related illnesses, regardless of your level of fitness. The reason your body feels the effects of travelling at altitude is that, as you gain height, the air pressure drops. Each time you breath in, the reduced partial pressure of the air means less oxygen enters the bloodstream. Your body needs oxygen to move and keep climbing, but also to perform all the daily tasks of keeping this complex organism alive. It needs oxygen to keep your brain working efficiently and to make good rational decisions; it also needs oxygen to keep your digestive system working in order to fuel your muscles.

The human body is a very clever thing and will begin to adapt to any changes in altitude. It will increase the rate and depth you breathe at, and it will make more red blood cells to carry what oxygen there is around the body as efficiently as possible.

ALPINE CLIMBING

Nick Waite outside the Margherita hut.

This adaptation, which we call acclimatisation, takes time. If you try and rush the process you may suffer from an altitude-related illness. Unfortunately, we all react differently to altitude and there is no way of knowing how well you will cope with the effects of altitude unless you put yourself in that position. In the Alps we rarely sleep above 3,000m as there are few huts at that height, so you are less likely to have the extreme effects that you may find in the greater ranges. There are of course exceptions like the Gouter hut on Mont Blanc 3,800m, the Gnifetti hut 3,600m and Margherita hut 4,500m on Monte Rosa, the highest building in Europe.

A rough guideline is, above 3,000m you should not plan to sleep more than 300m higher than the night before; you can climb to greater altitudes during the day but drop down in the evening. This is the beauty of the scale of the Alps; it is easy to climb high and descend in order to sleep lower down.

Although it is possible to acclimatise to fairly high altitudes, the rate at which you acclimatise is not something that you can speed up or train. If you have been slow to acclimatise on previous trips, you will probably be slow each time you go to altitude. At altitude, the air is drier than it is at sea level and dehydration can magnify the effect of altitude on your body; it is therefore even more important to stay hydrated when climbing at altitude than it is at sea level. If you are climbing on snow routes you can stuff extra snow in your water bottle to create more fluid, but if you are on rock there may be no opportunity to top-up on fluid all day. Start the day hydrated and take enough water with you.

The effects of altitude

As you gain height, especially for the first time, when you don't know how your body will adapt to acclimatisation, it is very likely that you will feel the mild effects of acute mountain sickness (AMS) such as a headache, feeling out of breath, sleeping badly and loss of appetite. An alarming but common effect is Cheyne-Stokes (or periodic) breathing, which occurs while you are asleep. Your body will take several deep breaths, then stop breathing before starting again with a huge breath and often a feeling of panic. This is caused by an imbalance in the amount of carbon dioxide and oxygen in the body.

Although fairly alarming for the sufferer, and those lying next to them, it isn't harmful other than disrupting your sleep. Although you may feel pretty bad, none of these symptoms are life threatening in their own right. However, if these symptoms become worse and you keep gaining altitude, you could develop swelling of the brain (high-altitude cerebral oedema or HACE) or fluid in the lungs (high-altitude pulmonary oedema or HAPE). Both these conditions are life threatening and can develop very quickly. They are relatively uncommon in the Alps, but people are rescued every year from Mont Blanc with these conditions because they have not acclimatised sufficiently before they attempt the summit.

Altitude sickness

It is unlikely that you will see the effects of altitude sickness below 3,000m. However, I have seen AMS and both of the more serious conditions at lower altitudes, so it is worth knowing the signs and symptoms and how to deal with them. Talking to your climbing partners about how you feel is the best way to monitor how you are all coping with the effects of altitude.

If you hide the effects because you don't want to turn round or let the team down, you may put everyone in danger if your condition worsens.

Acute mountain sickness (AMS): signs and symptoms
- Headache
- Nausea (feeling sick)
- Vomiting
- Feeling tired (more so than normal, given the level of exertion)
- Disturbed sleep
- Dizziness

Treatment
- Monitor how the symptoms develop; are they getting better, worse or staying the same?
- You can take a pain killer for any headache, but do not take any drugs that may suppress your breathing (especially not sleeping pills).
- If you get worse, the best solution is to lose altitude.

High-altitude cerebral oedema (HACE): signs and symptoms
- Severe headache
- Change in behaviour
- More clumsy than normal
- May develop serious vomiting
- Blurred vision
- Confused
- May sense odd things
- Reduced level of consciousness

Treatment
- Monitor the person.
- Descend immediately; the following morning may be too late.
- Sit them upright and keep them warm.
- If oxygen is available, give to the patient. If a pressure (Gammo) bag is available use this as well (the Gouter hut on Mont Blanc has one). This will only buy you time; the person still needs to descend to get better.
- Give appropriate drugs (e.g. dexamethasone and acetazolamide).

High-altitude pulmonary oedema (HAPE): signs and symptoms
- Trouble breathing
- Very tired
- Coughing
- When the lungs are listened to, they may sound crackly.
- Possible frothy breathing
- Lips, tongue, and nails become blue.

ALPINE CLIMBING

Treatment
- Monitor the casualty.
- Descend immediately; the following morning may be too late.
- Sit upright and keep them warm.
- If oxygen is available, give to the patient. If a pressure (Gammo) bag is available use this as well. This will only buy you time; the person still needs to descend to get better.
- Give appropriate drugs (e.g. nifedipine and acetazolamide).
- If you are climbing in the Alps, you are unlikely to carry any of these drugs. Guides or hut staff may have some available, so it is good to know what they are and what they do. Avoid the problem in the first place by climbing peaks of increasing altitude and keeping well hydrated. If you suspect any altitude-related illness, descend as quickly as possible.

Sleeping at altitude

The first hut night at altitude in any season can be a torrid thing. While 80% of acclimatisation happens when you are asleep, persuading your body to actually go to sleep is not always that easy. It is really common for your first night at altitude to feel like you didn't actually sleep at all. You lie awake, and every rustle in the room, every cough, every snore stops you from going to sleep. Don't worry, this is just your body's reaction to being at altitude and not really knowing how to handle it.

Unfortunately, the first hut night of the season doesn't seem to get any easier, after more than 30 alpine seasons, the first night is still often really grim.

The worst thing you can do is get stressed about it as this will guarantee that you don't get any sleep. Even if you don't get to sleep, just by lying there your body is resting, producing red blood cells and recovering from the day's activities. Whatever you do please don't be tempted to take sleeping tablets. Research done by ENSA (Ecole Nationale de Ski et d'Alpinisme) and the CAF (Club Alpine Francais) where they tested the cognitive ability of alpinists who have taken a sleeping tablet then got up before it has worked its way through their system, (as you would when getting up early for an alpine route) versus being sleep deprived, is really interesting. You will make much better decisions and be safer in the mountains if you are sleep deprived than if you have forced your body to sleep with drugs, then get it up early.

Nick Waite climbing on the Zumsteinspitze, 4563m.

The effects were so marked that CAF have been running a campaign to educate and encourage people not to take drugs at altitude, specifically sleeping tablets.

The other drug that people consider taking is Diamox. There is a lot of research that confirms that Diamox will help the acclimatisation process. Personally, I have used it in the Himalaya when I have been suffering from altitude sickness. The drug will help you sleep and your body to adapt. I used it when I was suffering from AMS and it helped. Some doctors recommend that you use it prophylactically before a trip to help your body adapt. I would suggest that this is not what alpine climbing is all about. If you discover it takes you a bit longer than others to acclimatise, take the time to climb some routes at a lower altitude and let your body adapt. When you feel ready you can push higher.

Only ever take these medications under medical advice.

Terminology and Situational Awareness

Gary Veitch on the traverse of the Portjengrat.

When you know what things are called and can relate the guidebook and the map to the features in the landscape, we can start to think about how these features interact with the weather and the conditions. So we'll start by examining the terminology, and then move on to situational awareness.

Alpine terrain

Alpine terrain can appear complex and a bit daunting. When you try to match the terrain features that are mentioned in the guidebook to the ground in front of you it can all be a bit confusing, especially if the environment is new to you. We will now look at the main Alpine features that you may come across, and the risks or dangers that they may present.

Understanding how these features work, and their use in identifying hazards is part of being able to appreciate the bigger picture – an essential part of becoming an alpinist. Being too focused on the climb and not looking around to make yourself aware of all the factors that may affect you is a sure way of getting yourself into trouble.

Orientation

Before we start looking at rock and ice features, it is worth considering the orientation of a mountain and how the orientation of any particular aspect can affect the form of the mountain and the conditions on it at any given time. In the northern hemisphere, north faces are usually the aspect of the mountain that is the steepest and often give the most serious climbing. This is because it is the aspect that gets the least sun and is most affected by snow and ice. This lack of sun also makes these faces feel more serious.

If we flip to the south side, many southerly aspects will be stripped of snow in the summer months. These faces usually clear first after bad weather.

East-facing routes get the morning sun, so the snow will soften earlier in the day than west-facing routes (which get the sun later but keep it for longer).

North and south faces of the Grandes Jorasses, both photographs were taken in summer.

Glacial features

Glaciers are what make the Alps so special; they add a certain majesty to the mountains. These rivers of ice have some unique features which can be dangerous and add challenge to the mountain experience. The glacier itself is ice confined by rock; it moves by internal deformation of the ice and by sliding over the bedrock. Where the ice can't deform around a corner or over a step in the rock it will crack, forming crevasses or, on a larger scale, an ice fall.

The Pers glacier in the Bernina.

Terminology and Situational Awareness

Where a glacier becomes too steep or hangs over a drop then a serac (ice cliff) will form.

Due to climate change, the glaciers in the Alps are unfortunately retreating. This means that while the glacier itself is moving forwards, the whole ice mass is being melted back. We may even come across a situation where the glacier is still in the same place, but the depth of ice has been significantly reduced.

We refer to glaciers as being wet or dry. A dry glacier has no snow covering the ice, so it is easy to spot the crevasses and other dangers. When the ice is covered in snow it is known as a wet glacier; here we would always use a rope to protect ourselves in case of hidden crevasses.

Other features that we may find on a glacier are river courses that are created by meltwater at the height of summer, which may be difficult to cross if too large. Moulins are holes in the ice where rivers flowing on the surface drop inside the glacier. Slipping while crossing a stream on a glacier and being swept into a moulin is an end too grim to contemplate.

Climbers on a wet glacier after climbing the Piz Palü.

Climbers on a dry glacier near the Rotondo hut.

ALPINE CLIMBING

A bergschrund

Where the glacier pulls away from the mountain at its head or sides, a different type of crevasse is formed. This is known as a bergschrund (in German) or rimaye (in French). One of the most difficult sections of a route can be making the transition from the glacier onto the mountain across the bergschrund. They can be easy to cross when full of snow early in the season but, as the snow melts throughout the season, they can become increasingly difficult. With the reduction of the depth of glacier ice due to climate change, some of the bergschrunds on certain routes have become impossible to cross.

Moraines

In addition to features made of ice the glacier will have created features made of ground rock and boulders, the most obvious of which is a moraine. A moraine is a ridge formed by the movement of the glacier. There are three types of moraine: lateral, medial and terminal.

A classic lateral moraine in the Vanoise.

Lateral moraines are ridges that can be found at the sides of a glacier. They are often very obvious in areas that no longer have a glacier. Paths very often take the crests of these moraines, as they are raised above the jumble of boulders left by a retreating glacier.

Medial moraines are formed where two glaciers come together; the ridge of rock and debris is the coming together of the material from the edge or lateral moraines of the two glaciers.

A terminal moraine is a ridge of debris that has been left at the snout of a retreating glacier. This ridge may have a lake behind it where meltwater has collected.

Terminology and Situational Awareness

The SE ridge of the Nadelhorn, a classic arête.

Classic horns, the Obergabelhorn with the Matterhorn behind.

Mountain features

You will probably know what most mountain features are called at home, but some have different names in the Alpine environment due to the different languages spoken; others you may simply have not heard before.

A **ridge** is the eroded crest of a mountain and may be formed of snow, ice, rock or a combination of these.

An **arête** is a steep-sided sharp-edged ridge.

A **cirque** is a semi-circular or amphitheatre-shaped feature also known as a cwm, coire, coomb or basin.

A **col** is a low point on a ridge, also known as a saddle.

A **horn** is a mountain that has been eroded on all sides to create a sharp peak that usually stands separately from the mountains around it (used a lot in German mountain names).

An **aiguille** is a sharp-pointed pinnacle of rock (used a lot in French mountain names).

A **rognon** is an island of rock surrounded by glacier ice. Some of these mountain features may have been named when they were surrounded by ice, but the ice has now gone.

A **gendarme** is a pinnacle or isolated spire that sits on a rock ridge.

A **couloir** is a gully on the mountain which is sometimes filled with snow.

A **cornice** is a section of overhanging snow which can form on the lee, or downwind, side of a ridge. They can be unstable and may collapse if walked on, breaking off some way back from the edge.

A classic aiguille – The Aiguille du Peigne.

The Gros Rognon in the Vallée Blanche, Chamonix.

43

ALPINE CLIMBING

Rock types

The Alps features many different types of rock. They are all different to climb on and we all have our favourites. My personal favourite is granite, and I will go out of my way to climb on high quality granite rather than any other rock type. In the guidebook section of this book, I have highlighted at the start of each route description what the rock is. The three main types found in the Alps are granite, (which is intruded under an existing rock then the mountains are eroded to reveal it), limestone, (a sedimentary rock which is fossilised seabed) and metamorphic rock (which is sedimentary rock which has been changed by heat and pressure).

The Alps, like the Himalaya, are fold mountains, created when two continents collide and 'fold' the rocks into mountains. This creates a huge amount of heat and pressure which can allow molten rock to be intruded into pre-existing rock, the process which created granite such as we find in the Mont Blanc Massif and the Andermatt area. The heat and pressure of folding creates metamorphic rock like schist, such as we find in the Valais and the Bernese Oberland, then around the edges we find limestone which has not been affected by this heat and pressure. We find limestone mountains in the Prealps like the Aravis, Gastlosen and Miroir d'Argentine but also on the edges of the bigger mountains, on peaks like the Eiger.

The different rock types have different characteristics. Generally, granite will feel solid and there are excellent cracks and features for protection. Metamorphic rock is often of poorer quality, and routes stick to ridge crests where the rock is best; it is often best because this is the line that is most

Mike Austin enjoying the excellent granite close to the Orny hut.

Kate Scott climbing on the limestone of Miroir d'Argentine.

Terminology and Situational Awareness

travelled. Limestone can be of incredible quality, but it can also be shattered and broken. Generally, the limestone rock in the Prealps is great for climbing on but is not so good in the bigger mountains. The only big limestone mountain we have included in the guidebook section is the Eiger and the routes covered are both on ridge crests.

Situational awareness

Tuning in to the environment you are in, and developing a situational awareness of what is going on around you, is incredibly important in terms of keeping yourself alive and making the most of your time in the mountains.

This tuning in should cover all aspects of what you see and feel in the mountains. How cold is it? What direction is the wind blowing? Does what you see fit with the weather forecast? If what you see doesn't fit, is the forecast wrong and how will this impact on your day?

Situational awareness is an incredibly difficult thing to teach as it requires a level of understanding of the environment you are operating in that can only be developed over time. However, going into that alpine environment for the first time gives you a unique advantage; because as everything is new, you question everything. This can obviously lead to information overload, but it can also lead you to question things that seasoned alpinists may miss.

Some key examples would be a route approach that walks under a serac. If you spend your life in an area with a serac, you may not notice that it is getting bigger and more overhanging with every week, as the incremental

Ian Loombe approaching a crevassed and serac-threatened section on the approach to the Marco e Rosa hut on Piz Bernina.

changes are so small. When you arrive with fresh eyes and question what you see, you may look and see the overhanging serac and question whether walking under it is a good idea. This is particularly challenging in the current fast-changing environment in the Alps. The nature of guidebooks is such that the minute someone presses print, the book is out of date. Being armed with as much information as you can gather about a route, its approach and its descent, makes it easier to ask the important questions about what the conditions are like today and how that may affect your ascent.

They say time spent in reconnaissance is seldom wasted, and this is never a truer statement than in the Alps. Getting to a hut early so you have the time look and study the route for the following day is incredibly valuable. Dialling in your situational awareness to what is happening around you, seeing if there is any rockfall, what time the sun will hit the face, what time it will leave, where the path goes, etc, will all make your ascent the following day smoother and much more enjoyable.

Glacier Travel

Glacier travel on the Trient Plateau.

Travelling on a glacier is one of the special things about moving into bigger mountains. Glaciers add a certain majesty and grace to mountains, but they also offer unique challenges for the alpinist.

There are four key elements to glacier travel. If you focus on the former, hopefully you will not need the latter, and if you do, you will be prepared.

1. If you can avoid falling into a crevasse in the first place, then everything else is just good practice, so good planning and preparation is key.
2. If you rope up carefully and deploy good rope discipline, then any crevasse fall will be easier to manage.
3. If someone does fall into a crevasse then knowing how to hold a fall and stabilise the situation is vital, if you cannot hold the fall then everything else is academic.
4. Once you have held a fall, being able to create an anchor and pull someone out of a crevasse, or climb out yourself, is the next phase.

Understanding glaciers

Glaciers are just snow that has accumulated over a long period of time, turned into ice, and started to move. Glaciers move downhill with gravity, and they move by two different mechanisms.

In one mechanism they flow over the bed surface, lubricated by water. In really thick glaciers, where meltwater may not be available, the pressure of the ice above can cause melting – pressure melting at the base – which lubricates the flow of the glacier.

The other mechanism of movement is by internal deformation of the ice; as the ice moves it slowly morphs and bends. The problem being, if it moves too quickly or any change in direction is too rapid, it fractures. This is why we get crevasses, seracs and icefalls; the terrain forces a change in direction in a horizontal or vertical plane.

The beauty of knowing this is that by looking at a map we can get a fair idea of where we can find crevasses on a glacier. If the glacier goes round a bend, you may find crevasses on the outside of the bend, if the underlying bedrock drops steeply then the glacier will not be able to deform, and you will find a serac / ice cliff, or in the case of a large change, an icefall. There are of course many subtleties, and just when you think you have got a handle on where crevasses are to be found something will catch you out. I remember finding a crevasse field in the middle of a large flat glacier in Antarctica. I couldn't work out why they were there, until someone pointed out that it was so cold, and the glaciers moved so slowly, that the crevasses had formed hundreds of kilometres away and had not yet closed up.

Planning a route on a glacier

When you are planning a route, have a good look at the map and try and glean any mention of crevasses from the guidebook. Though it is worth considering the age / publication date of the map or guidebook as the mountains are changing quickly with climate change. If you can avoid any crevassed areas then you have immediately reduced the chance of anything bad happening.

Try to avoid the outside of bends on the glacier and any steepening's, as these areas are almost certainly crevassed. As an alpinist we spend the early part of the day in the dark so the snow will be well frozen, crevasse bridges stronger, travel easier, etc, but navigation is more challenging. The night before your ascent, spend time studying the glacier and work out where your route is for the following day.

John McCune on the Glacier du Triolet.

Roping up for glacier travel

Glaciers are described as either wet or dry. Dry glaciers have no snow on them, so you can see all the crevasse danger. Moving on dry glaciers can be great fun as you can see all the crevasse dangers and your crampons bite wonderfully into the blue ice. A wet glacier is covered in snow so you cannot see the crevasses; if you are on a wet glacier, you should always use a rope.

Dawn on a snow covered Trient Plateau.

A dry glacier on the way to the Monte Rosa hut.

Spacing on the rope

The amount of space you have between each person on the rope is a function of how many people there are and how crevassed the glacier is. On one trip in Greenland we were travelling through an icefall to get off a peak and we had five people with 75m of spacing between us. The terrain was heavily crevassed, and we felt having that many people on the rope gave us the security we required. Do not be afraid to have more rope out than any other team on the glacier.

The reason we spread out was so that if one person fell into a crevasse, then the next person was not pulled in. Conversely, if we had the whole rope spread out, we would find it difficult to communicate, the rope would snag on things all the time, and we would not have any rope available to create a haul system and pull someone out of a crevasse should an accident occur. Hence, the length of rope is always about finding an elusive balance – between safety (long enough) and management (short enough). The advice below gives you a good starting point to work from.

When measuring out the space between each person, I find it really difficult to visualise a number of metres when the rope is lying in a pile; it is much easier to think about arm spans. I am an average-sized adult male, so my arm span is about a metre and a half.

ALPINE CLIMBING

Two people on the rope

With two people on the rope, a spacing of 12–15 arm spans works really well in most situations. To measure this out, find the middle of the rope, measure out six or more arm spans in each direction and tie a little knot in the rope to mark the point. You both tie into the end of the rope and take coils (described in detail below) until you reach the knot, then tie off the coils.

With two people on the rope, I would then tie knots in the rope, this makes it easier to hold a fall. As the person falls in the rope tends to cut into the lip of the crevasse. As the rope slides through the knot will jam against the narrow slot cut in the snow. We will call this a brake knot. While this makes any extraction more complicated the most important thing is holding the fall in the first place; if you both end up in the crevasse then everything else is pretty academic.

The best knot for this is either an alpine butterfly or what has become known as the ENSA (École Nationale de Ski et d'Alpinisme) knot, the advantages of these knots over a figure of 8 on a bight or an overhand on a bight is that they sit in line with the rope as opposed to at one side, as a result they are more effective. Remember when calculating the spacing that the brake knots will take up some of the rope length.

Two people on a rope with knots in it.

My preference is for a brake knot in the middle of the rope, then one in each direction, one and half arm spans from the middle. This allows the rope to cut into the edge before jamming on the knot.

Knots obviously make any crevasse rescue more complicated, so we will look at techniques to manage this in the crevasse rescue section.

Brake knot

Tie a figure of eight knot on a bight of rope then take the loop and pass it right round the knot, then back through itself, leaving about 20cm of tail.

Tying a brake knot.

Glacier Travel

Three people on a rope.

Three people on the rope

With three on the rope, you have more stopping power, so you don't need such a large gap between each person. The middle person doesn't carry coils; they tie into the middle of the rope then measure seven arm spans in each direction and mark the point with a knot. The other two tie in and take coils to this point, where they tie their coils off. I find a minimum of 7 arm spans between each person works well.

More than three people on the rope

You can operate with more than three on the rope, but you just need to spread people out. I wouldn't suggest coming any closer together than five arm spans. With more than five people on the rope, the whole thing becomes a bit unwieldy, and you would be better splitting into multiple teams, perhaps coming together should the glacier be particularly challenging.

Taking coils

In most alpine situations you are unlikely to have all the rope in use, so you will need to use some method of storing the unused rope. This is usually done by taking coils around the upper body. Some people prefer to store the excess in their rucksack, so they don't have the bulk of the rope round their body. Either way, you need to ensure you are properly tied into the rope. Having coils round your body makes it easier to change the length of rope when you need to, so this is what I recommend.

Carrying extra rope in coils isn't unique to glacier travel; it is an essential alpine technique which you will use on most alpine terrain (unless you are climbing long pitches).

Tie into the rope as normal with your rucksack on. (If the coils are under your sack, they will be difficult to adjust and can also be really uncomfortable.) There are two basic ways of making the coils: one with a wrist flick and one with a static hand, personally I prefer the wrist flick as I think the coils sit more comfortably on my shoulder, but it does require more practise.

Taking in coils using the flick method.

ALPINE CLIMBING

Taking coils using the hand spacer method.

Tying off coils.

Take the rope from your harness up the front of your body and round the back of your neck (if I am wearing a top with a hood, I will pull this up before putting on coils, this prevents the coils from snagging the hood and being inconsistent in length). The most comfortable length of coil is about halfway between your armpit and your waist; any longer and coils will fall off your shoulder, any tighter and the coils feel constrictive and uncomfortable.

Once I am happy with the length of the first coil, I use my right hand to flick the rope round my neck to make more coils. With each flick I put a little twist in the rope which helps it sit nicely.

Alternatively, once you have decided on the length of your coil and have made a few, take the rope out from under your shoulder and place the palm of your hand inside the coil as a spacer and wrap the coil round your neck and hand. This is much easier to learn but I don't think gives such a neat coil.

Once you have finished putting on an appropriate number of coils – in my case over my left shoulder – put your right hand across your chest, behind the coils coming down your front. Take hold of a bight of rope of about 30cm in length from the tail of the rope, and pull it back through so it is now in the centre of the loop of coils. Using the bight, tie a hitch round the rope leading to your partner. Take the small loop that is left as a tail and clip it with a screw-gate krab into your knot loop at your waist.

This locks the coils off so they cannot tighten around your body, however the position of the pull on the coils is quite high so you can easily be pulled forward off your feet in a crevasse fall. It is better to lower the pull point

Glacier Travel

Lowering the pull point.

Orientation karabiner.

using another overhand knot or a clove hitch. This makes it easier to hold a fall as the load point is lower.

You may even want to consider using a specialist karabiner that will keep its orientation and make it easier to adjust this extra knot.

Moving on the glacier

Once you have all tied on it is time to start moving; you want to spread the rope out so it is tight enough that in the event of a crevasse fall there is not enough slack in the system to create a shock load. This can pull your partner off their feet and make it difficult to hold a fall. It is also important not to have the rope too tight as this is really annoying when moving together.

I find the perfect tension is with the rope descending from the harness, arcing down touching the snow, then coming up to the harness of your

Looking along a rope while travelling on a glacier.

partner. If you are in a heavily crevassed area, then I would tighten the rope so you are ready should someone fall in a crevasse. I would **never** carry the rope in hand coils on a wet glacier; the shock loading you would introduce will almost certainly make it impossible to hold a crevasse fall.

When moving, I am looking for any horizontal cracks in the snow or dips that may signify the edge of a crevasse or sagging snow bridge. If there is any doubt, I will walk around the area of concern. If I come to any point where I am concerned, I will ask my partner to keep the rope tight while I move forward prodding the snow with a ski stick.

Crevasse rescue

In 30 years of alpine climbing, I have been lucky enough to only fall in a crevasse to my waist. The sensation of your feet dangling in space is scary enough, and a tight rope from my partner and belly flopping motion, a bit like a seal climbing onto a rock, got me out.

A bit like avalanche rescue, I like to think of crevasse rescue as a low probability high consequence event. You practise dealing with it regularly, so that if you need to do it things will go smoothly. No two rescues will ever be the same, they will all involve the same elements, holding a fall, creating an anchor, hauling the victim out, first aid, etc. Having practised all those elements, they can be put together to solve any rescue scenario that you may come across.

I think we should start with easy scenarios and build from there; we will describe the overall system then break it down into individual techniques.

Holding the fall

This is the key to everything. With multiple people on the rope, it should be relatively straight forward to hold the fall. The load will come on to the person closest to the crevasse, they brace themselves, and perhaps drop to

Holding a crevasse fall.

the ground. It is much more comfortable to stabilise the situation from the sitting position, as the rope will be pulling you down into the ground.

With less people on the rope, it is more difficult to hold the fall. With three people you will feel a load, but unless you are travelling steeply downhill and the snow is very hard, the fall should still be relatively easy to arrest. The good news is that, whilst we may practice on open and icy crevasses, *real* falls tend only to happen where soft snow hides the crevasse – so in reality, the rope cuts in and makes it easier to hold. Drop to the ground, a self-arrest technique will help.

With two people on the rope, you will almost certainly need a self-arrest technique to hold the fall, and you will have knots in the rope to help.

Rescue – more than three on the rope

If you have more than three people on the rope, they may be able to pull the victim out of the crevasse by just walking back on the rope. If there is another team close by, they may be able to help pull the victim out. This is the quickest and simplest rescue, but if there are a number of people involved remember to ensure that someone is keeping an eye on the victim as they approach the lip of the crevasse. There have been some very nasty accidents (a number of fatalities, in fact) where people have been crushed into the underside of the crevasse lip, as enthusiastic rescuers try to haul them through the narrow slot cut by the rope.

If the person who has fallen in is on your rope, the easiest way to manage the situation is for the person nearest the crevasse to attach a sling to the loaded rope using a Klemheist knot. They then untie from the rope while the others on the rope hold the victim, this will only be possible if they have tied in on an isolation loop. They can then slide the Klemheist along the rope towards the edge. The Klemheist ensures that, should there be a crevasse between them and the edge where the victim is, they are protected. It also protects them as they approach the edge which is almost certainly undercut. Be careful as you approach the edge. I will use an ice axe or a ski pole as a probe to look for the edge. As I approach, I keep some tension in the sling that is attached to my harness – if the edge collapses, I will not have introduced slack in the system that could cause a shock load.

Having chopped away as much of the lip as possible, to make it easier for the victim to climb out as the team pulls out the victim, they can use the Klemheist to reposition themselves next to the edge and communicate with / manage the victim. If two teams are involved, it is essential to have someone positioned close to the edge so they can communicate and coordinate the pull. Place something under the rope near the edge of the crevasse to stop the rope cutting deeper into the snow.

The biggest danger with this type of rescue is overzealous rescuers who may injure the victim by pulling them out too quickly or hurting them if they get caught under a lip.

ALPINE CLIMBING

Rescue – three people on the rope

With three on the rope, when one of the climbers at the end of the rope falls in usually the person in front in the direction of travel (the middle person) holds the fall. Once everything has stopped moving the middle person kicks their feet in and makes sure they are happy that they have the weight of the victim.

The back person can then put a French Prusik onto the rope (this can slide in both directions, so is easy for the climber to move the knot). They can then move down to the middle person, using the Prusik to keep the rope between themselves and the middle person snug in case the victim and the middle person start to slip.

Three people on the rope, there are two to hold the fall.

Using a Prusik to move down the rope.

Once close to the weight bearer, they can dig a snow anchor and transfer the load from the climber onto the anchor. The middle person can now escape the system and the back person can clip themselves into the anchor as a backup. If they are totally comfortable with the anchor they can then assist with the extraction.

Setting up the anchor and transferring the load.

Once out of the system, the middle person can use a sling or a Prusik on the loaded rope and move down to the edge of the crevasse. They can communicate with the victim, check if they are injured and need any immediate care, and prepare the edge to make extraction easier.

Glacier Travel

Moving to the edge to prepare for extraction.

The two rescuers can now haul out the victim.

Not recommended
You may see some people using the slack tail of the rope with a Prusik to move down to the edge, this does make movement more comfortable but using the system I propose, you are in the system should the anchor fail, and you may be able to hold the secondary fall. If you are using the loose end of the rope as your only back up and the anchor fails, you will be shock loaded and almost certainly pulled into the crevasse.

If all is well you can set up a 3:1 haul system and pull the victim out.

Rescue – two people on the rope

This is the most challenging of rescue scenarios, as it is more difficult to hold the fall, and you will need to dig the snow anchor with the rope from your waist still under tension. With good rope management you should not be shock loaded, so once you have held the fall and are stable, dig an anchor. This is really awkward with a loaded rope. It is much better if you can dig it just in front of your hips as it will be easier to transfer the load onto the anchor.

Crevasse rescue, two people on the rope.

Once you have dug the anchor and transferred the load, improve the anchor, if possible. You may dig a second anchor, if you have another ice tool, or back it up using ski sticks or a buried rucksack. If the snow is good, you may not feel the need for this. With damp snow, which is one of the contributory factors to someone falling in a crevasse, backfilling the ice axe slot and compacting the snow for your snow anchor improves its strength.

You can now attach a Prusik to the load rope, go down and communicate with the victim and prepare the edge. You can then set up a haul system and pull the victim out.

ALPINE CLIMBING

Setting up an anchor

A crevasse fall situation will almost certainly occur on a wet glacier, where your only anchor option is a snow anchor. In certain situations, where the snow is very thin, or the glacier is in the transitionary phase between wet and dry and there are patches of bare ice poking through you may manage to reach or dig to ice. If this is the case then an ice screw anchor is the preferred anchor, as it is easier to construct and stronger than a snow anchor.

The strongest snow anchor is a buried horizontal ice axe. Dig a slot at right angles to the direction of pull. Regardless of the slope steepness, the front wall should be vertical or angled slightly back to keep the axe in place. This wall should be as smooth as possible to ensure as much of the ice axe has contact with the snow as possible.

You then need to cut a slot at right angles to this in the line of pull. This is to allow a sling to be attached to the axe and then run along the slot to where it can be attached to the rope. This slot should be as narrow as possible so as to not weaken the front wall.

Once this has been done, attach a sling by tying a clove hitch onto the ice axe shaft at a point with equal surface area of the ice axe being either side of the sling. The clove hitch is orientated in a such a way that when loaded it tightens on the shaft of the axe. The axe is then placed in the slot with the pick pointing down into the snow, this stops the axe from moving about in the slot.

If you have a second ice tool you can reinforce the buried axe by driving it vertically into the snow in front of the horizontal axe. Put the axe between the two strands of the sling before driving it into the snow, touching the horizontal axe.

Building a buried axe belay.

Glacier Travel

Transferring the load

You now want to transfer the load from you, or the person who has held the fall, onto the anchor. Tie a French Prusik onto the load rope, then clip an HMS karabiner into this with the narrow end pointing towards the victim (we call this an autobloc). It is imperative that you clip the HMS karabiner around the rope as well – as this will become the top pulley in our Z or 3:1 hoist. Clip this into the sling coming from your buried axe. Slide this as far down the rope as you can, then slowly shuffle forward allowing the weight to progressively load the anchor. When you are happy it is holding, you can untie your coils and tie off the rope, in case the Prusik slips. Make sure you do this as the French Prusik is a knot that is easily released.

Transferring the load.

Prepare the edge

Inspecting and preparing the crevasse edge.

You can now attach yourself to the loaded rope with a sling and Klemheist, as described above, and go down to the edge, where you can check on the victim and prepare it as best you can to make it easier to pull the victim over the edge.

ALPINE CLIMBING

Pulley system

You will then need to set up a pulley system. Take a short Prusik and attach it to the loaded rope and clip in a karabiner, the type with a small roller on it like the DMM Revolver or the Edelweiss Axiom are brilliant for this as they greatly reduce friction. Then take the slack rope that comes from the unloaded side of the autobloc and clip it into the Revolver. You have now created a 3:1 pulley, release the locking safety knot and start pulling. The best way to pull if you are on your own is to tie the rope into your harness using a Klemheist knot on a Prusik loop. This makes the system really easy to reset. On all fours, use your whole body to drive forward; your legs are your biggest muscles, so this is the most efficient way to pull. Try and keep everything in a straight line while pulling as this will reduce friction.

Once you have moved the victim have a break and reset the system. Just be careful to manage the Prusik grips each time you release it to reset.

If you cannot move the person due to weight difference, then you may need to increase the mechanical advantage, see next page.

Autoblock and 3:1 pulley system.

Passing the knots

Set up the haul system as described above. As the first knot approaches the autobloc, attach a sling to the anchor then a French Prusik to the load rope beyond / below the knot. Now slowly release the autobloc until the load is on the sling and not on the rope, you can now untie the knot. You can then start hauling again. Systematically pass each knot in turn.

Glacier Travel

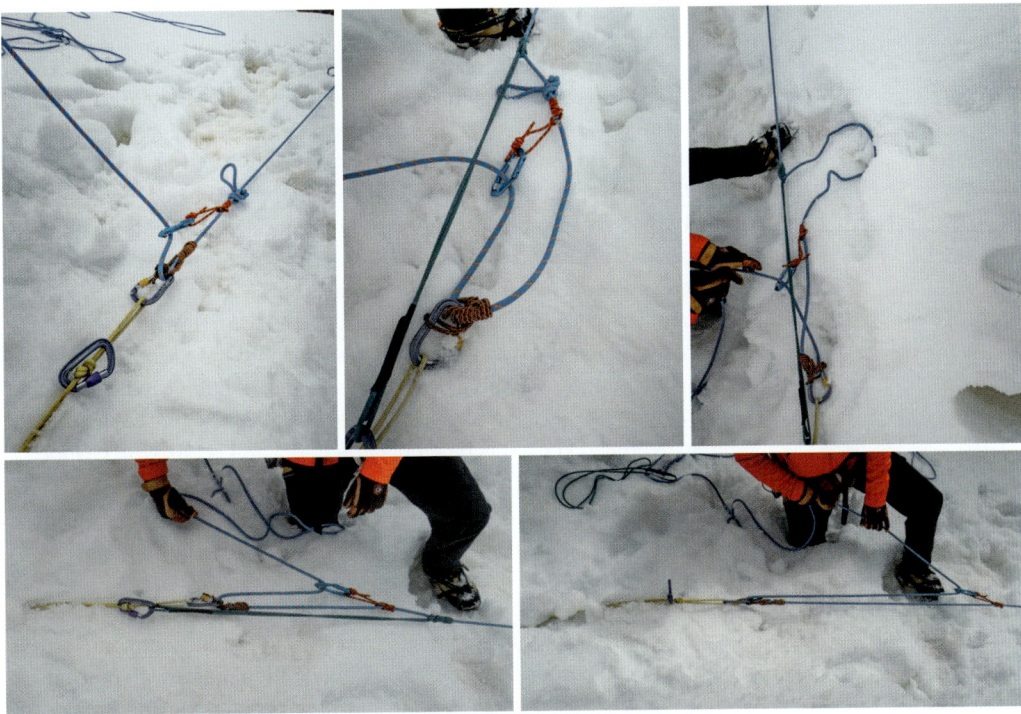

Passing a knot.

Increasing the mechanical advantage.

Increasing your mechanical advantage

If for some reason you are having trouble pulling the person out, (maybe there is a big weight difference between you, maybe you have a bad back, or hurt your leg holding the fall, or other crevasses limit the space you have to haul), it's useful to have a system where you can increase the mechanical advantage.

Those of us who like systems have to be careful, as it really easy to get carried away and go for the extra mechanical advantage as it makes the hauling easier. However, increasing the mechanical advantage means that you will have to pull twice the amount of rope to move the victim by the same amount as you would achieve with a 3:1 system. You must also remember, with this amount of mechanical advantage, how easy it is to hurt someone or overload your belay, causing it to fail if they get stuck on the crevasse lip. If you are not careful, you won't realise how hard you are pulling until it is too late.

Assuming you have set up a 3:1 system as described above and tried to haul your partner out of the crevasse, go back to the anchor and tie the rope that is tied to your waist into the anchor using a clove hitch. Leave yourself enough slack that you can move about and haul when required.

Take the rope that comes out of the opposite side of the clove hitch from the side you are tied into. Unclip the Klemheist from your waist (you are tied into the end of the rope for safety). Take a bight of rope and clip this into the Klemheist, slide the Klemheist down the original pulley system. There is now a loop of rope running from the anchor, through the karabiner next to the Klemheist and back to you. You can now start pulling, remembering to keep things in as straight a line as possible to minimise friction.

ALPINE CLIMBING

A Petzl Micro Traxion, Edelrid Axiom and Petzl Tibloc.

Crevasse rescue using a mechanical device and a Prusik.

> **Prusiks on the rope?**
> You will often see people travelling on a glacier with one Prusik on the rope clipped into their harness, so that they are ready to set up a crevasse rescue system or climb out of a crevasse unaided. This also has the advantage of lowering the pull point from the tie-off loop on your chest coils to the waist belt on your harness, making it easier to hold a fall. The disadvantage is that it is difficult to change the rope length as you have to remove the Prusik each time. This is particularly the case when you are moving from glacier travel onto more technical ground. Ironically, having a loaded Prusik already on the rope, actually makes it more awkward to transfer the load onto the anchor.
> The issue of lowering the pull point is a valid one, but it can be solved by using the extra tie in as described earlier, either with a clove hitch or an overhand knot. This has the same effect and is easier to change than a Prusik.

Mechanical devices

I have described all of the techniques above using Prusik loops, but you can make the whole process easier by substituting the Prusiks with mechanical devices. These have a small weight and cost penalty, but they make the system work more efficiently.

As a replacement for the autobloc I would look at the Petzl Micro or Nano Traxion – these have a ball bearing pulley as well as a toothed cam to lock off the rope. The difference between the two is that the Micro has a catch to hold the cam open, whereas the Nano is lighter but has no catch. The catch makes it easier to lower / let out rope. The Edelrid Spoc is very similar.

You can replace a Prusik on the load rope using a Petzl Tibloc, this works particularly well on icy or skinny ropes, it does not reduce friction just makes life easier.

The final piece of kit to consider is a karabiner with an integral pulley, the DMM Revolver is really good, but a Tibloc does not sit very well using this karabiner due to its shape. It does work, but the Edelrid Axiom works much better and has a bigger radius on the pulley, so it further reduces friction and increases efficiency.

You also may consider using a Micro Traxion as an autobloc then a Prusik for everything else.

Climbing out of a crevasse

If your partner does not have the skill level to rescue you, then the only solution is to climb out of the crevasse yourself. This is really hard work so it is worth practising.

If you have fallen into a crevasse and everything has come to a stop, you are dangling, everything feels stable, but nothing is happening, there

Glacier Travel

is no sign of rescue so you had better do something. There are a couple of possible systems you can use to climb out. We will cover two systems, one with Prusiks and one with mechanical devices.

With Prusiks

I usually use Klemheist knots as they grip well and are also easy to release. I would suggest not using a French Prusik, because if you grab the knot it can release prompting you to slide back down the rope.

You will need to attach two Prusiks to the rope. Attach a sling to the bottom one, this is to be used as a foot loop. Attach a screwgate karabiner to the other. Take the foot loop and larks foot it round one of your feet, slide the Prusik as high up the rope as you can reach. The longer the gap between your attachment and the Prusik, the further you can move, and the easier it is to get started. Stand up in the foot loop and hook your arm round the rope to keep yourself stable, now clip the second (top) Prusik with the screwgate on it into the belay loop on your harness. Slide this up until it is tight on your harness then sit down into your harness weighting the Prusik. You can now slide the Prusik with the foot loop up again, stand up in the foot loop and slide the waist Prusik up again. You are now climbing the rope. Repeat until you reach the lip of the crevasse.

Climbing out of a crevasse using Prusiks.

ALPINE CLIMBING

Climbing out of a crevasse using Prusiks, rucksack dangling below.

Climbing out of a crevasse using mechanical devices.

Having a rucksack on makes this more difficult so you can take it off and clip it into the loop you are making in the rope below your harness. It is also worth tying a clove hitch into your belay loop just below the bottom Prusik, you can feed this through as you gain height. The clove hitch will catch you should your Prusiks fail.

Climbing over the lip of the crevasse can be really difficult if no one has prepared the edge, you will have to push yourself out with your feet to get the Prusiks clear of the snow so you can slide them upwards.

With mechanical devices

Using a Petzl Tibloc and a Micro Traxion, attach the Tibloc to the rope with a sling to use as a foot loop, and attach the Micro Traxion below this with a screwgate karabiner. Stand up in the foot loop and clip the Micro Traxion into the belay loop on your harness with a screwgate, then pull as much rope through the device as possible and sit down. You can either climb out using this system, like the method with Prusiks, or clip your Revolver or Axiom into the karabiner on your Tibloc, then clip the rope coming from your Micro Traxion through the pulley. You have created a 3:1 system but also made it easier to pull the rope through your device. You will almost certainly not need the foot loop, as you pull down on the rope coming through the revolver, the rope will automatically pull through the Micro Traxion. As well as being efficient, this system makes it easier to climb over a lip. If the rope is cut into the edge, it is even possible to push the Tibloc up through this slot using an ice axe.

I would again suggest clipping the rucksack below you and using the clove hitch back-up as described above.

Equipment

Robin Clothier climbing on the Wichelplanggstock.

In the years since I started alpine climbing, kit has changed dramatically. It is more functional, easier to use, and most importantly, it has got lighter. I wrote a magazine article comparing the kit I was alpine climbing with in 2014 to what I was using when I first went to the Alps in 1991. The saving was 2.6kg which equated to food for two people for at least two days.

Since then, things have kept on getting better, enabling us to climb faster and harder, or just have more fun, as your rucksack will be lighter.

If you are new to alpine climbing it is easy to think that you will need a set of new equipment. In fact, you will almost certainly have everything you need already. The key to having a light sack is not spending money but packing thoughtfully with what is appropriate for the route you are planning.

I will walk you through my thoughts on kit, looking at everything from clothing to Prusik length. As you are a climber, I'm sure you will have most things, but I will help you weed out the non-essentials.

Personal kit

This is the kit that comes with me every time I head out in the Alps. We will then go on to look at clothing and footwear options, before getting to hardware, ropes and group kit.

ALPINE CLIMBING

Harnesses

You need some way to attach yourself to the rope, assuming you are not going really lightweight and tying onto the rope directly.

There are two harness design options. One is a classic rock-climbing style harness with leg loops, these can be fixed or adjustable. This style has the advantage that it is much more comfortable should you need to hang or abseil in, and it usually has better gear racking options. A model with slots for ice screws and racking for karabiners is also very useful.

The other style is much lighter and more minimalist, often featuring leg loops that wrap round and pass between the legs. These are really light in your rucksack and comfortable to wear but have minimal padding and are usually really uncomfortable to hang in. Many light models are also very minimal with gear loops.

I use a light leg loop style harness for any routes of AD upwards and on easier routes I will use a lighter model.

Climbing harness

Lightweight harness

Helmet

Helmet design has come on so much in recent years that there is no reason not to wear one. Rockfall is more prevalent in the Alps with the change in climate, so I wear a helmet whenever there might be a threat of rockfall. Some people also advocate wearing a helmet on a glacier in case of crevasse fall.

It is worth making sure you can easily attach a headtorch to your chosen helmet.

Lightweight helmet

Helmet with headtorch attached.

Sun cream

I would suggest using SPF50 all the time, for maximum protection. Put on a liberal coat before leaving the hut in the morning and keep topping up through the day.

Lip Cream

Lips are not good at dealing with prolonged exposure to the sun and wind, so a high SPF factor lip cream is invaluable. I always carry an after-sun product for lips, to use in the evening when you have inevitably forgotten to put on any lip cream during the day.

Water bottle

In the mountains we are always fighting dehydration. If you are dehydrated you will move more slowly and make poorer decisions. You can start your day by drinking as much as possible before heading out and using rehydration tablets when out and when you get back. When on the mountain I would suggest a litre is the minimum for a day and accept that you will be dehydrated when you get down. If you carry too much water, it is heavy and you will move more slowly. In the warmest part of summer, I will carry 2 litres, but seldom any more than that.

I will often use a 1 litre Nalgene bottle and take a 1 litre flexible container with me as well. I will usually have drunk the flexible container by the bottom of the route. I can then fold it up and put it in my pack where it will take up little room, and then use the wide necked alpine bottle.

In the colder parts of the season, I will often take a flask and a flexible water container which works as a great combination.

Overnight extras

Headtorch

Headtorches have changed immeasurably in the past few years, and the improvement in their power for weight ratio is incredible. It is tempting to go for the lightest model, but having once almost failed to find my way through the bergschrund on the way to the Whymper Couloir on the Aiguille Vert, I will not go 'under torched' again. If you have plenty of time for your route and you just want something on the off chance you get caught out, there are some really light models available; but if you have to climb or navigate an approach to a route in the dark then you need something with more power.

The strength of a torch is measured in lumens and I like a torch which has about 900 lumens. This strength can be adjusted, as on maximum power you will use the battery pretty quickly. I will save the full power for any complicated sections or when actually climbing.

The big change in headtorch technology in recent years, apart from the power to weight ratio, is the introduction of rechargeable units. I was initially resistant to this change as I was worried about not being able to resolve a flat battery in a hut or other area. This concern has proven unfounded, and as long as the torch is fully charged when you head into the mountains, you should have no issues. Units that have a lock on them have proven less prone to losing charge in a rucksack. I would still consider taking a charging cable to the hut, especially if going for a couple of routes.

ALPINE CLIMBING

Power bank
It sounds ridiculous but the reality is that we carry far more electrical products than ever before: digital navigation, cameras, headtorches, etc. Most huts will have charging stations but if a hut is busy or they have limited power (the hut may run on solar) you may not be able to plug in, so an alternative is a good idea. If you are returning to the hut after the route then you could leave it and collect later.

Sheet sleeping bag
It is a requirement in huts for hygiene reasons to use a sheet sleeping bag liner, the best ones are made of silk as they pack really small in your bag.

Clothing

I would suggest that a layering system is the most versatile option for alpine climbing; allowing you to adapt to the changing temperatures.

A system of a base layer followed by a fleece / softshell, then a waterproof / windproof layer, topped off by an insulating layer that goes on top of everything is a good place to start.

On the bottom half, unless it is the shoulder seasons when morning temperatures are very cold, I will not wear base layer leggings as it is too difficult to take them off when the sun comes out and the day warms up, but I will carry some over trousers just in case I need to add a layer.

Base layer
A breathable, wicking base layer top is the start of any system, long sleeves are most versatile, and I prefer a zip neck to allow for venting, a small collar helps keep the sun off your neck. When walking on a glacier on a hot day, having long sleeves on saves a lot of sun cream. It also means that in the event of a crevasse fall you won't scrape your arms if you are dragged across the surface of the glacier.

I will often walk to the hut in a wicking, base layer T-shirt. I can then put a long sleeve on top to protect my arms the following day.

Layering system

Base layer, long and short sleeved.

Equipment

Sun shirt

This may be a new idea to those coming from a homeland where sun is less frequent and arrives from a lower, less powerful angle. Sun protection in the Alps is incredibly important and a thin, breathable long sleeve top with a hood is incredibly useful. I will usually wear this on top of a short sleeve base layer as a standard piece of kit for most of the season as it is so versatile. The hood combined with a peaked cap is perfect for keeping the sun off my neck. I will then just layer on top of this. This will only add a small amount of insulation but will keep off a light breeze.

Sun shirt

Fleece

A thin fleece with a hood, that will layer on top of my sun shirt, adds some insulation, but not so much that it will bring on a sweat. A hood is useful, especially one that you can wear under a helmet, as you don't have to stop and dig out your hat when you start to get cold. I really like a chest pocket for a route description or phone which will have a photograph of the route description on it, my digital mapping and camera.

Softshell jacket

A lot of the time I find a softshell and a thin fleece are almost interchangeable, they may not provide the insulation of a fleece but will be flexible, windproof and breathable. There were many years when the outdoor industry was pushing softshell really hard and there are some great products as a result. Having had many years of using a softshell I have found that using a wind shirt, a thin fleece and then a windproof (see below) will actually give you more versatility for a very similar weight.

Softshell trousers

A pair of trousers that are windproof, warm enough and stretchy are essential on all alpine days, I have 2 pairs – one for warmer days and another for cooler weather – this makes it easier to stay comfortable. Pockets for a route description and a zipped pocket for car keys are really useful. Lighter colours are great on warm days.

Left to right:
Fleece
Softshell jacket
Softshell trousers

ALPINE CLIMBING

Windproof

When deciding to head out for a big route you need a good weather forecast, so given the accuarcy of modern weather forecasts I would question if you always need to be carrying a 3 layer Gore-Tex jacket. If you are trying to squeeze a shorter route in with marginal weather, then that's a different discussion.

A windproof keeps the wind out which will stop you getting cold. The difference between this and a waterproof is that a windproof will be much thinner, more breathable, softer, more comfortable, and significantly lighter. When choosing a windproof it's all about comfort. If you think you might climb without a rucksack, a chest pocket which the jacket can invert into with a karabiner loop is a really nice feature, as you can clip it onto the back of your harness. A hood that will fit over your helmet is also really great, as you can squeeze some extra insulation out of the garments you have on without stopping and taking your rucksack off.

Windproof

Waterproof smock-type jacket

Waterproof jacket

Keep it light. If my waterproof is on during the alpine summer, it either means I am walking to a hut in the rain to be in position for the weather clearing the next day, or I am running away. I may take a heavier garment for the former and a significantly lighter jacket for the latter. In any garment I want a hood that will fit over a helmet. I have been a fan of the smock design for many years. The design is inherently lighter, as there are less seams and a smaller zip. It is easy to get dragged into the marketing around high-end 3-layer products, but I would question if you need that level of protection and durability in a garment that will spend most of its time in your rucksack. There are other lighter and cheaper products on the market that would suit the alpine summer environment.

Waterproof trousers

If the weather forecast is really good these are the first thing that gets left behind; but if you are going to take them, I would take as light a pair as possible. The three occasions I may use them is:

1. Walking to a hut in the rain, so that you are in position when the weather improves.
2. You have been caught by the weather and are escaping.
3. When the wind gets up and it is really cold on the final section of your route to the summit and the start of the descent.

Waterproof trousers

Equipment

Waterproof trousers worn over the rope and harness.

All these occasions don't require heavy 3-layer fabric, but they do call for a trouser that is easy to put on and off, especially over a pair of mountaineering boots. Models with full-length side zips work really well, and those with a fly at the front allow you to put the trousers over everything including your harness; you can just have the rope coming out through the fly rather than it popping out the top. This allows you to keep moving and not faff about taking your harness off. As soon as the weather improves and you get too hot, you can easily strip the over trousers off again.

Insulation

When it gets cold towards the summit, or when you are abseiling off a route, or have been caught out and have to endure an unplanned bivouac, an insulation layer that you can pull on top of all the other layers is a fantastic thing to have in your rucksack. You have two options: down or synthetic. A thin down layer offers much more insulation for the weight in your rucksack – amazing! However, you need to spend more time looking after it. If you do not make sure you dry the down regularly it will just get damper and damper through the trip and offer less and less insulation. A synthetic insulated layer can be left in the bottom of your rucksack for the season. Obviously a dry garment will offer better insulation than a damp one, but synthetic insulation keeps on insulating when wet. As a result, this is my choice as an insulating layer, I stuff it in my bag at the start of the summer and don't even have to think about it unless I need it. When I am looking at products, I want to make sure it fits comfortably on top of all my other layers and the hood will fit over a helmet while my waterproof hood is up as well.

If the conditions are warm, for example in mid-summer when climbing on big rock climbs, it's worth considering a gilet. It offers your core lots of insulation but is lighter and less bulky in your rucksack than a full jacket and hood.

Synthetic insulation that fits over everything.

Synthetic gilet

Hats

You need a warm hat that fits under a helmet and a sun hat. For the latter I like a peaked cap that will fit under a helmet, as this will keep the sun out of your eyes when looking up.

71

ALPINE CLIMBING

Well-fitting, dark sunglasses.

A well-packed alpine rucksack.

Sunglasses

Good quality sunglasses are an essential piece of kit, as there is a huge amount of reflected light when you are moving on snow. I always use a pair of glasses with a category 4 lens then have a spare pair in my rucksack that are not as dark. This way, if the light is a bit flat or poor I can use the less dark lenses, and if I break my main pair, I have a spare.

Buff®

Buffs are incredibly versatile. Keep your neck warm, pull up over your face, use as a headband to keep the sweat out of your eyes, ears warm, thin hat ... the list goes on.

Rucksacks

You have to put all your kit in something to carry it to, and up your route. Comfortable rucksacks are heavy, there is no getting away from it, and if you want it to last it will weigh more.

Rucksack selection

The selection of a rucksack has to match the climbing objective. When going to a big rock climb with a glacial approach and an abseil descent back to the starting point, you can approach the climb with any kit that won't fit in your bag hanging on the outside. At the bottom of the climb leave your crampons and ice axe at the base, along with any extra kit, as you won't need them on the route. You only need a light sack to carry your extra layers, first aid, emergency kit, food and water to the summit.

    I have three rucksacks, one which is so light I can stuff it into another sack for the approach then climb with it. On a long, high route where every gram counts, I will take that with me. It sits really well on my back and doesn't interfere with gear loops on my harness, and it is big enough to carry a windproof, insulation layer, water, food and some abseil tat. This sack isn't big enough to get all my stuff to the mountain, but assuming I am abseiling back to my large sack, everything I don't need for climbing can stay at the base of the route.

    I then have a larger, light pack, which with careful packing I can take on most routes. The fabric is really light, so I have to be careful with sharp objects like crampons. I keep it for more technical routes when I have to carry everything over the top of the mountain and every gram counts.

    I then have a larger, heavier and more versatile sack for everyday outings.

Size

I think that, when operating in the summer, if you cannot fit everything into a 30-35 litre sack, you need to have a look at what you are taking on the hill.

    My perfect bag is one that fits the length of my back (most bags come in multiple sizes), and has a tube of about 30-35l. A bag with multiple

Light, route-specific sack.

Equipment

compartments will weigh more, whereas a single tube is lighter and easier to pack. A lid that can extend, allowing the sack to be packed high for the approach, then compressed for the ascent is a great advantage.

The lifting lid on the sack means that it can be removed or stuffed inside the bag for the ascent, the lifting lid can also hold the rope in place if it won't fit inside.

> **Carrying a rope on the outside of your rucksack**
> You can either flake the rope back and forward across your hand and tie off the middle then drape it across the top of your sack. An alternative method is to coil the rope in a classic coil and drape it over the top of the sack. With any external carrying system you need to make sure it isn't going to rain, as a wet rope will not dry at a hut unless the sun is out. A rucksack cover can help here.

A flaked rope carried under a rucksack lid.

A coiled rope draped over a pack.

Rucksack cover fitted on a pack.

Rucksack cover
I used to think a rucksack cover was for ramblers, looked terrible, and would blow away. I have now changed my view. Even if your clothes are all in dry bags inside your rucksack, the bag itself will get wet and take a long time to dry out. A lightweight cover that stretches over the whole bag keeps everything dry. I will still use the dry bags inside, but it means that if I do have to walk to a hut in the rain, I can arrive with everything, except what I am wearing, dry.

> **Umbrella**
> An extra tip that works really well is walking to the hut using an umbrella. This keeps everything dry and means that you will not get hot and sweaty like you would if you were wearing waterproofs.

ALPINE CLIMBING

Boots

Boots are the piece of kit that connects you to the mountain, and poorly fitting boots can ruin any day in the mountains. In fact, this is the only piece of kit I will not go looking for a deal or special price on. I will buy them at a specialist retailer, that has a good range both of styles and sizes. I will then make sure I actually take home the pair I tried in the shop. While fit and sizing should be standard, this avoids any surprises.

One of the keys to comfortable boots is a good quality Merino wool sock. In all my years of mountaineering I think most of the times I have suffered from sore, blistered feet have been down to cheap or poorly fitting socks. You are going to spend a lot of money on a pair of boots, so buy socks to match. Once you have the boots, make sure they are well broken in before heading for the mountains.

In the summer I will use three pairs of boots: rock boots, a heavyish pair of B2 / B3 boots that are stiff enough to use with crampons all day, and a lighter pair of B2 boots that will take a crampon.

A selection of alpine boots from lighter B2 boots to full winter alpine boots.

Boot and crampon ratings

Boots and crampons are rated for stiffness and compatibility.

Boot Rating

B0 and B1 boots are too soft and flexible to use with anything but the most of flexible of crampons and I would not use for anything other than very easy route approaches.

Equipment

B2 boots are semi-rigid and are great for mountaineering, scrambling and easier angled snow and mixed climbing, but not for any sustained front-point crampon use where the flexibility makes them very tiring to use. These are what I will use for most of my alpine climbs.

B3 Fully-rigid mountaineering boots suitable for all types of snow, ice and mixed climbing. I will use these on routes where I will have crampons on for most of the day.

Crampon Ratings

C1 flexible strap-on crampons.
C2 semi-rigid crampon with a strap at the toe and a clip at the heel.
C3 Rigid crampons suitable for technical snow, ice and mixed climbing.

Compatibility Table

Boots	Crampons
B1	C1
B2	C1, C2
B3	C1, C2, C3

Rock boots

When choosing a rock boot for use in the mountains, all day comfort is as important as precision. I would consider a boot that has torsional stiffness, as this will protect your foot when climbing a crack. A boot with torsional stiffness is also less tiring on the foot, an important consideration as on a big route you may have the boots on for 6 or 7 hours. Another reason for considering a boot rather than a shoe design is that it will protect your ankle.

Scrambling, rock-focused boots (B2)

These are the boots I will spend most of the Alpine summer season wearing, as they are reasonably light and precise for moving on easy rock climbs and technical rock ridges. They will have a smooth area under the big toe and at the front of the boot to give extra grip when rock climbing, and will then have a classic grip pattern on the rest of the sole. This is often not as deep as a heavier boot as this trims some weight. The boot will have some flex to make walking more comfortable but will be stiff enough to allow the boots to use a crampon that has a clip at the heel and a strap at the toe (C2). The lightweight construction usually means that they are not that comfortable to use with crampons all day.

Climbing all day with a rucksack is more fun in a comfortable pair of stiff rock shoes.

Scrambling, rocky B2 Boots.

ALPINE CLIMBING

Heavy boots that will be comfortable when using crampons all day.

Short, ankle-only gaiters.

Short gaiters *(right)*

Fold-up walking poles.

Heavy crampon-focused boots (B2 / B3)

The difference between these and the boot mentioned previously is that the support and insulation they offer will keep your feet warm when they are in the snow. The sole will be much more rigid so you can attach any pair of crampons, they will also have a welt at the toe so that more specialist crampons with a wire toe bail can be attached.

When you are wearing crampons all day, these will feel much more comfortable. They are the type of boots that you would use for snow and ice climbing in the winter months at lower altitudes.

If you get cold feet or are mountaineering in the shoulder seasons, I would consider using a warmer boot with more insulation. These usually have a built-in gaiter to keep the snow out and the heat in.

Gaiters

A gaiter is designed to keep snow, mud, and water out of your boots. They never seem very successful in the water department, but they are definitely worth having. The traditional gaiter covers the leg from the boot to just below the knee, this is too warm to wear in the Alps and is very rarely necessary.

I use a really short pair of elasticated gaiters that just seal the top of my boots. This stops small stones, mud, etc, from getting into the top of the boots. They seem ridiculously expensive for what they are, but they do work. I then have a longer pair of gaiters that come to my calf. This is usually long enough to keep snow out if I am breaking trail in fresh snow but are not as hot and sweaty as a traditional long gaiter. I will usually replace the cord that goes under your foot with some electrical wire, as this is much harder wearing.

Poles

Walking poles protect your knees and aid stability. Studies suggest that using poles can reduce the strain on your knees by about 20%. On a long descent or over many years of mountaineering this is a huge amount.

The best poles are ones that fold up nice and small and use a tent pole type system to lock in place. This feature means that they will actually fit inside your rucksack, and don't get in the way when climbing.

Models with a long grip are more comfortable as you can slide your hand up and down. I do not use wrist loops after a friend was injured using them in a boulder field. He slipped, the pole got jammed between two boulders and he dislocated his shoulder.

Equipment

I use two poles most of the time, then on a wet glacier I will use one pole and an ice axe. This allows me to test the snow ahead of me for any crevasses and still have an ice axe in my hand should I need one. It is almost impossible to arrest a crevasse fall without an ice axe in your hand, so don't be tempted to copy those brave people who walk on a wet glacier using two poles and no axe.

Hardware

When thinking about hardware we can split this down broadly into protection and items that allow us to make progress on snow and ice.

Snow and Ice

Ice axe

It is really easy to be lured into thinking that what you need is the most technical looking ice axe. While this may be the best thing for steep technical climbing, they are actually limiting when engaged in most forms of alpinism. They are a hindrance if you have to make a snow belay, for example in a crevasse rescue situation. So generally speaking, a more classic, all round mountaineering design is a better choice.

Classic ice axe

Ice axes are strength rated either B (also referred to as type 1, which are designed for winter walking and general mountaineering) or T (also referred to as type 2, designed for technical climbs and have a stronger construction). While I have broken ice axe shafts climbing, I don't know anyone who has broken a shaft mountaineering, so I wouldn't get too hung up on this when deciding what axe to take.

A classic axe has a curved pick and a straight or gently curved shaft with a spike at the end. The curved shaft allows a more relaxed wrist position when driving the axe into the snow, my personal preference is for a head made out of single piece of metal as this is stronger but also more comfortable to hold. An adze that isn't too steeply inclined is more versatile. I find a length of about 60cm works in most situations. It is the ideal balance between being useful when holding the head and plunging the shaft into the snow and being able to swing the tool above your head on steeper terrain. Shorter climbers may prefer a shorter axe.

One of the plusses of the move to leashless climbing, where your ice tool does not use a wrist loop, is the design of an adjustable pommel which can slide up and down the shaft. This allows you to grip the axe more easily when in climbing mode. You can then slide this towards the head of the axe for more general mountaineering. We very rarely see people using wrist loops anymore.

Classic ice axe

Adjustable ice axe pommel

ALPINE CLIMBING

Lightweight models

If I am planning a route that only needs an ice axe for a short section of snow on the approach to mainly rock or just glacier travel, I will think about taking a lightweight ice axe. These have been developed for ski touring and occasional use, and can make your rucksack lighter. I would recommend a model with a steel pick. This way if you do have to use the axe it will actually bite into hard snow and ice rather than just bounce off. Most models come with an adjustable pommel, or you can fit one yourself.

Hammer

When you move onto steeper, more technical terrain where you would like the security of a second tool, a hammer makes a lot of sense. This will give you the versatility of being able to hammer anything as well as the extra security.

On a lot of classic alpine routes, with snow that is steep enough to want a second tool but not technical climbing, a classic axe and a light hammer can be a great combination. I will keep the hammer between my shoulder blades while climbing with one axe, that way it is really accessible when I need it.

Technical tools

On more technical routes, you may want to use a pair of technical tools. I would not go super technical as these tools are difficult to plunge into snow and often do not have a hammer or any real adze. A pair of tools with a reasonable curve to protect your hands and give a good swing that are designed for leashless climbing are ideal.

Although I don't advocate wrist loop type leashes, I would pair any set of technical tools with an elasticated spinner style leash, this will save any dropped tools and the spinner version ensures less tangles.

Left to right:
Lightweight ice axe
Light hammer
Technical tools
Technical tools used with a spinner leash.

Equipment

Crampons

A bit like with ice tools, it is easy to be seduced by the most technical model. Mono points and vertical frame models are great for ice climbing and the most technical alpine routes. However, a classic 12-point crampon with an anti-baling plate will work in almost every situation. More technical C3 crampons often ball up really badly, and being rigid are not comfortable to walk in. If you do need something more technical, consider a model that has a classic frame and vertical front point or points. This will reduce the chance of balling up.

When choosing a 12-point crampon, you have three choices of attachment system: strap-on, heel clip with toe strap, and heel clip with wire toe bail. You have to match these to your boots – see Compatibility Table (page 75). A model with straps is most comfortable as there are no pressure points on the boot uppers and they will fit most boots, although they can be bulkier in your rucksack. Models with a wire toe bail will only fit on the stiffest boots with a toe welt. The most versatile models are those with a heel clip at the rear and a strap at the front, they will fit on the largest variety of boots and clip well in most situations. Be careful when adjusting the heel tension, as too much pressure can result in a blister. If your foot can feel the pressure from the clip, it is too tight.

12-point crampons

Lightweight 'string' (Dyneema®) crampons

Lightweight crampons

If you are just approaching a route on easy snow and the crampons will spend most of the day in your rucksack, I would consider a lightweight model. A model with 10 points is lighter, but in certain conditions I would go as far as using a model that uses string (Dyneema® actually) to join the front and back of the crampon. A number of brands offer completely flexible crampons, using webbing, cable or string.

Ice screws

While more in the protection department they are the only specific snow and ice protection that I carry. If I am ice climbing, I would carry a selection of lengths to cover different ice thicknesses. I would always make sure I have a long ice screw (22cm) for belays and making a V-thread anchor. It is unlikely that you will be climbing technical ice in the summer months, but if you are, all the same things apply as would in the winter in terms of kit.

ALPINE CLIMBING

Most of the time I am only carrying two ice screws for glacier travel, crossing bergschrunds, short icy sections on a ridge or the likes. I like to keep these as light as possible so carry the models that have an aluminium tube and steel tip. I usually carry a 16cm and a 22cm model. Ice screws work best with really sharp teeth so I will always keep the protecting cap on the screw, this also stops your trousers from getting ripped. It is also worth keeping the stretchy mesh that comes with the screw to protect the threads, the aluminium threads are easily damaged and won't be as easy to place in hard ice. I will always use a model with a flip out handle so they are easy to place quickly.

The last thing I will add is a V threading tool, to hook the cord or sling that you are going to thread. You can make your own using a wire coat hanger but having a specific tool with an integrated blade is really useful. The Petzl Mulithook is the best model I have found as it folds in half to keep the length minimal and protect the blade, and it stores inside one of your ice screws.

Left to right:
Lightweight ice screws
Petzl multihook folded out.
Petzl multihook stored inside an ice screw.

Protection

I will now go through the different pieces of climbing hardware that you will need to consider when protecting an alpine route, and I will take all the different items and look at the pros and cons of each. As a climber you may have most of these things already, but if you are buying some new kit then this will give you a few things to think about.

Karabiners

The basis of any climbing rack is the humble karabiner. Even the lightest rack has at least ten of these, so I would try and keep these as light as possible without compromising the size too much. There are some incredibly light models out there, but they achieve the weight by trimming the size. Small

Equipment

karabiners can be a fiddle to manipulate with cold hands or when wearing gloves, so I would suggest a mid-size is a good compromise between how easy they are to handle and weight.

Wire gate models are inherently lighter, the gates don't freeze when it gets cold and models with a clean nose are less prone to catching on things. Classic D shapes are great, but I also have two oval-shaped wire gates for my nuts to be carried on. The oval shape means the nuts don't bunch together so much and are easier to remove.

The karabiners I have on my cams are the same colour as the tape sling on the cam, this makes it easier to pick the correct cam off my rack every time.

  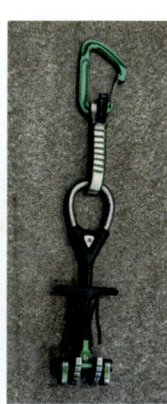

Left to right:
Wire gate, D-shaped karabiner.
Oval karabiners for racking wires on.
Cam with matching coloured krab.

Screwgates

It is easy to carry too many screwgate karabiners. However, they weigh more than a snapgate and every gram has to be carried a long way – think about what your screwgates will actually be doing and how important it is that they lock.

I will have one oval screwgate on my crevasse rescue kit attached to my Micro Traxion, and I will have four other screwgates with me. I usually have one HMS / Pear-shaped karabiner and two smaller screwgates. This allows me to have one karabiner at my waist to lock off my coils, an HMS for using an Italian hitch on for a direct belay, and a spare for tying into an anchor.

I would consider using a model that is shaped to avoid cross loading at the waist tie-in point where I lock off my coils.

I will have a further HMS with my belay device, and small screwgate to use with this when it is in guide mode.

This might not seem like many in total, but remember your partner will carry the same, so you can be sharing when swapping leads on a multi-pitch route.

Black Diamond Gridlock Karabiner

Screwgate and belay device

ALPINE CLIMBING

Belay devices designed for different thicknesses of rope.

Belay device being used in guide mode.

Belay devices

I will have a belay device on an HMS karabiner with me most of the time in the Alps, this allows me to belay another climber or abseil myself. It is very important that the diameter of the holes in your belay device match the diameter of your rope. If the holes are too large you will not be able to hold a fall or control an abseil.

My preference is for a device that has a 'guide mode' – this means a hole in the device that will allow you to direct belay from an anchor. The device is set up so it is easy to belay two seconding climbers at the same time, its design ensures that if someone does weight the rope it will lock while you are managing the other rope.

There is a rare exception to the rule. If my route only involves simple glacier travel, I may dispense with a belay device, knowing that I can use an HMS karabiner and an Italian hitch should I need to belay or abseil.

Passive protection

We are basically talking nuts; the only time I carry hexes in the Alps is when I'm climbing a Scottish style snowed-up rock route in winter. I usually carry a set of nuts 1-10. If I think the route only requires a very light rack, then I can trim that down by just carrying the odd numbers plus a number 6. I don't know why but a number 6 always seems to go in and I like having a number 1, hence the odd numbers plus number 6. On a technical climb without much fixed equipment, I may take a set and a half or even two sets.

The style of nuts that have a flare in them offer more variety of placements and work really well on granite. The DMM Wallnut is my favourite by a long way.

It is always worth having the second carry a nut tool too.

I always split the nuts between two karabiners. This way they are easier to find and if you drop one it is not a total disaster.

A set of DMM Wallnuts split across two karabiners, plus a nut tool.

Equipment

A Black Diamond Camalot Ultralight cam.

Active protection

These are cams, spring loaded devices that fit in a variety of crack shapes. They are very quick to place and, as long as they are placed sensibly, they are very quick to remove which will speed things along nicely. Like the nuts I am sure you will have a set already, but if you are upgrading, a lighter model will make the approach less painful. A double axle design will allow you to get the correct size off your harness more frequently due to the bigger range. This saves time.

I use Black Diamond Camalot Ultralight cams as I prioritise the weight saving. I will carry a 0.5, 1 and 2 as my standard rack on routes up to AD, if there is more rock then I will add in the 0.4 and 0.75. I would only take the 3 if I had a good idea that I would want it, as it's pretty bulky.

Quickdraws

A selection of lengths is the best idea, the number will depend on the route. I usually start with two short slings often referred to as alpine extenders, these have a circumference of 60cm (30cm long). You can triple them, so they are easier to carry then easily extend them if needed. I will then add in one 10cm extender and one 15cm extender. If I want more, then I would add one more of each smaller models, then build it up from there depending on the route requirements.

A selection of quickdraws: a 10cm, 15cm, and two 30cm.

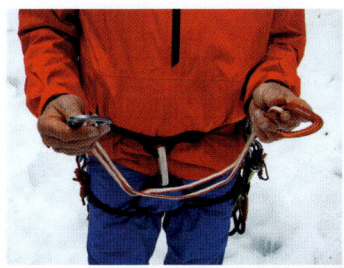

Tripling a 30cm sling.

ALPINE CLIMBING

A 120cm aramid sling on a snapgate.

Christmas tree style racking.

Slings

I carry two 120cm slings. I use aramid models as they are easier to untie once they have been loaded and they don't freeze as the fabric does not absorb water. I carry these with a snapgate on each.

Racking

This is quite a personal thing, but consistency is the key. No matter how you do it, as long as it is always the same way, you will be efficient. I use a Christmas tree approach. I have nuts on the right side of my harness on the front rack, then my belay plate, screwgates and one sling on the rear. On the left I have my cams at the front, then a sling on the rear, if I have an extra sling it will live there as well. I then have quickdraws on a bandolier. If you make sure the bandolier has a strength rating, then you could use it as abseil tat in extremis.

Equipment

Suggested rack

The rack you will take on a route can be tailored to the objective. This is the best way to keep the weight down. The following suggestions are a good starting place, I will begin with a glacier travel kit as this is the heart of any alpine rack. If I am not going to be on a glacier, then I simply remove the ice screws and mechanical pulley and take everything else with me. I will almost always carry a belay device.

Glacier travel kit / base rack

Glacier travel kit

The kit for glacier travel needs to allow you to climb out of a crevasse and pull / rescue your partner out of a crevasse. There should be two sets of this in the party. The glacier travel kit also forms my base rack as I will carry it with me all the time. If I am not on a glacier, I will simply remove the mechanical device but make sure I have 2 prussics with me, so I can climb a rope or make a haul system in a rescue situation.

- 2 x 120cm slings on snapgate karabiners, this way they are easily used as protection when on rocky terrain.
- 2 HMS screwgate karabiners.
- 1 D-shaped screwgate karabiner.
- 1 short Prusik made from 6mm cord.
- 1 mechanical device like a Petzl Nano Traxion, Petzl Micro Traxion or Edelrid Spoc. This can be replaced with a second short Prusik. I have my mechanical device on an oval-shaped screwgate karabiner.
- 1 karabiner with a small pulley like a Edelrid Axiom or DMM Revolver. The Axiom works better if using a Petzl Tibloc. There is no need for a screwgate on this pulley.
- 1 Petzl Tibloc, this grips the rope really well, especially a thin one, if you have to climb out of a crevasse over the lip then it is really useful for sliding up the rope ahead of you. A short Prusik can do most of the same tasks.
- 2 ice screws, I prefer a lightweight model; one longer, 22cm and one shorter, around 17cm.
- Ice screw threader.
- Small knife, I like to have a small knife with this kit, this can be used to remove old tat from abseil anchors but is also really useful in an emergency when you may need to cut the rope. A Trango Piranha at only 20g is perfect.
- Belay plate appropriate to the rope diameter on an HMS.

ALPINE CLIMBING

Facile
These routes are generally pretty straight forward, if a glacier is involved then standard glacier travel kit. If there are easy rock sections or steep snow, I would maybe add another 120cm sling and a quickdraw, in case I needed to clip in to piece of fixed protection like a peg or a bolt, or I decided to use an ice screw as a runner.

You should have two glacier travel kits in the team.

PD rack

Peu Dificile – PD
These are routes that have some technical difficulty, where you will place some protection; on classic routes there may be some fixed protection. Unless there is no glacier we will carry two glacier travel kits in the team. If there is no glacier, I will carry the same kit and remove the mechanical device but make sure I have 2 Prusiks with me.

- Base rack
- 4 quickdraws including 2 which are tripled 60cm slings – see p83.
- Half a set of nuts – my favourites are 1,3,5,6,7,9 on one snapgate karabiner. With a nut key.
- 2 cams size 1,2 (Black Diamond Camalot Ultralights).
- 5 metres of 6mm abseil tat. This just lives in the bottom of my rucksack all season in case it is needed.

Assez Dificile – AD
A route with more technical difficulty, maybe with some pitched climbing and sustained sections of moving together. If on a glacier then glacier travel kit.

- Base rack
- 6 quickdraws including 2 tripled 60cm slings.
- One set of wires split across 2 snapgate karabiners. With a nut key.
- 4 cams size 0.5,0.75,1,2 all Black Diamond Camalot Ultralights.
- 5 metres of 6mm abseil tat.

AD rack

Equipment

Difficile – D
A route with more technical difficulty, almost certainly involving pitched climbing. Depending on the style of protection, I will add more options. If the route has bolts, all I will add is up to 10 more quickdraws. If the route has more leader placed protection, then I will take more cams. With an experienced user these will be faster to place and remove than nuts. If the route is more mixed in nature, or has some sections of ice climbing, I will add a couple of extra ice screws of different lengths.

> **Personal preference**
> The suggested kit is a list that I have honed over 30+ seasons of alpine climbing. There are lots of other products out there that will do very similar jobs, I have found that these items work for me.

Ropes

What rope to choose for alpine climbing is always a difficult choice. To ensure speed on a long route you are unlikely to be climbing at your limit or in the situation where you will be taking falls. I would look to the lightest in class ropes in any situation. They will be thinner, so easier to pack and lighter to carry. I would always use a dry treated rope, as there is always a chance of getting caught out in a thunderstorm and a rope that is not treated will absorb water and become very heavy, very quickly. Bizarrely a rope that is wet loses a significant amount of strength – don't ask me the science, it just does.

Single rope in use on the south ridge of the Gletschhorn.

It is also very important to make sure that diameter of your rope matches your belay device. If the hole on the belay device is too large for your rope it will be difficult to hold a fall or control an abseil.

Rope systems

There are four rope systems in use:

Single rope – Where a rope can be used on its own. Currently the thinnest ropes are about 8.7mm. This system has the advantage of being extremely simple, and it is very easy to organise on a belay. The disadvantage is that if you want to abseil and pull the rope down after yourself, you can only abseil half the length of the rope you have with you.

Half rope – Two ropes are used in parallel. The lightest half ropes can be down to 7.7mm. They can be clipped on different runners but the two need to be used at the same time. With this system the weight of the rope is split between multiple people when

Half ropes being used on the direct route, Miroir d'Argentine.

walking in to the route. If you have to abseil, you can tie the ropes together and abseil their full length, pulling the rope down behind you. If one rope is damaged, you have another one. However, each individual rope is not as strong, and the change overs on belay are more complicated than a single rope system.

Twin rope – Two ropes are used effectively as one with both ropes being clipped into every runner. The system allows the use of two very light ropes and maintains the ability to tie them together and abseil the full length of the rope. These ropes are generally very thin so they tend to wear more quickly than a thicker rope and are therefore more suited to routes that are predominantly snow and ice.

Tag lines – This has become a popular option in certain circles. The idea is that you climb using a single weight rope. Then, if you need to abseil, you tie the thin rope to the thick rope and you can abseil the full length of the rope pulling it down behind you. To take a look at the technique, have a look at the chapter Going Down.

Group equipment / emergency kit

We have covered the array of kit that you will take for the actual climb, but what will you do if you have a problem? This can be something as simple as a broken crampon, to something as complex as a broken leg, in the dark, when you will have to wait for rescue.

Spares kit

It is inevitable that at some point something will break. Good maintenance and regular replacement of kit as it ages or wears out addresses most issues, however, things do just break. We need to have the ability to adapt. Sometimes you have no option but to turn around and go down. On other occasions it may be possible to adapt and carry on. A classic would be a broken crampon, either the metal itself or a binding issue, with some basic repair kit you can usually cobble something together.

- Leatherman / multitool
- Ski strap, these super-strong, stretchy straps are amazing for wrapping round a boot and crampon but can be used for loads of other issues.
- Cable ties, again really versatile, get the long strong ones.
- Tape, this doubles up with first aid, the physio type tape works best as duct tape doesn't stick well in the cold.

Group shelter

A group shelter is like a lightweight tent flysheet. Should you need to spend the night out unexpectedly, or have an injury and need to wait until assistance arrives, then this can keep you alive. It is amazing how much warmer it is inside one of these simple shelters; you just pull it over your head, loop the fabric under your bum and sit on your rucksack for insulation. They are generally made of waterproof and windproof fabric. They do not just help keep you warm; by keeping everyone close together, they do an amazing amount to improve morale. They come in

Spares kit

Group shelter

different sizes, 2,4,6 and even 8+ person models are available, and they pack down incredibly small. I treat these as a one-time use, emergency item and carry the lightest one I can, and always have one in my rucksack.

First aid kit

There are a few key first aid related things that you may have to deal with, and I would suggest that as a team you have the kit to deal with them. We split them into minor and major.

In the minor I would include, headaches, dehydration, the effects of altitude, blisters, small cuts, minor sprains.

In the major department I would include major bleeds, cuts and breaks. With these, there is only so much you can do until outside assistance arrives, but you will have to stabilise the casualty until this happens. Your first aid kit also needs to be of a size that you can automatically take it with you every time you go on the mountain, because if it is too big you will be tempted to leave it behind.

Suggested first aid kit:
- Israeli bandage – These are amazing. They can be used to put large amounts of pressure on a wound, or used as a crepe bandage to support an injured joint. I carry a 4- and 8-inch version. They come in vacuum sealed foil so are easy to look after.
- Tough cut scissors
- Paracetamol and Ibuprofen – In extreme cases, you can offset and layer these to get benefit from anti-inflammatory as well as pain relief effects.
- Surgical gloves – To protect the first aider from blood infections.
- Tape – Physio type tape seems to work best and can be used for everything from blisters to crampon repairs.
- Triangular bandage – These are very versatile.
- Tourniquet kit – It is possible to improvise one, but it is very difficult to do well and they are very light and effective in the event of a major bleed, such as may happen in a rockfall incident.

Simple alpine first aid kit

ALPINE CLIMBING

Garmin InReach® Mini

Navigation tools

Rescue beacon

While much of the Alps has great phone coverage, a secondary form of communication is a good idea. I use a Garmin InReach® as it works on the Iridium Satellite network, so it works globally. I can use it in SOS mode to call for help, and I can pre-program messages to a certain number e.g. "We are all ok just a bit late down". I can also bluetooth it to my phone so I can send email or text messages. You can also get a paid-for weather forecast which is really useful. The size is minimal, and the cost is not prohibitive.

Navigation tools

We will talk more about this in the navigation section, but I will always have a map, covering my route, and compass with me, and the ability to use them. This is a back-up, as the reality is that most of my navigation is done digitally on my phone. One thing I will consider, and I use a lot in winter on skis, is having a second phone that is dedicated to navigation. It has no SIM card and I have downloaded all the maps using WiFi. This way I have redundancy as, should my primary navigation tool run out of battery, I have a secondary unit and a map and compass. If your partner has the map on their phone as well, your chances of being electronically embarrassed are pretty slim.

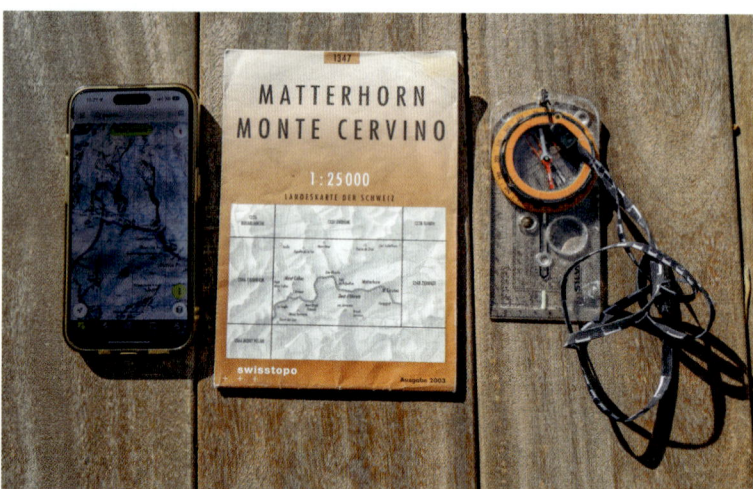

Climbing Up

Climbers on Piz Roseg, Bernina.

The glacier travel chapter should have got you to below your route, and if you are not on a glacier then the route description should have got you to within sight of the start. Either way, it is time to consider the different elements of how you are going to get established on the route, and how you are going to deal with the technical challenges that any route will present. We are going to look at route-finding, crossing a bergschrund, moving together, and some ideas to speed up pitched climbing. In the next chapter we will have a look at getting down.

Route finding

One of the most challenging things about making the transition from small to big mountains is the scale of the routes and the detail in a route description. How can 1,000m of climbing be condensed into few paragraphs of text in a guidebook, whereas a three pitch climb on a crag may get a whole page to itself? Alpine routes need the alpinist to look at the mountain and work out where the route may go. The route description should then just help you find the start and point out the key features to keep you on track.

The problem with a lot of guidebooks in any part of the world is they are written by people who know the area. This should be a good thing. However, they often forget that the reader does not have the same local knowledge.

ALPINE CLIMBING

Mike Austin enjoying the simple route-finding on the Aiguilles d'Entrèves traverse, Chamonix.

When approaching any route, I spend a lot of time with a map and the guidebook, building a mental map of the terrain I am about to approach and travel through. Once I have an outline, I will use 3D mapping tools to enhance this imagery, so that I have a three-dimensional image in my mind of what's to come and how to get down.

It is worth spending some time on the internet looking for as many images of the route as possible, to help build that mental picture. I will then break the route down into sections. These are usually defined by the difference in terrain or the technical difficulty of each particular section.

A simplistic way of breaking this down would be:
- The approach – Track to glacier, access to glacier, route on glacier, access to climb from glacier.
- Establishing yourself on the route – Getting off the glacier or approach track, finding the base of the route, organising equipment and starting the climbing.
- The route – The main body of the climbing to the summit (or high point).
- The descent – Leaving the summit and climbing down to reach the glacier or approach track. Then continuing to the hut or valley.

The beauty of having a phone with you is that you can have photographs of the guidebook and any other pieces of information at your fingertips when you are approaching and scoping out the day ahead. Just make sure you have enough battery life to sustain prolonged use – especially if your phone is your primary navigation and communication tool.

Many alpine days start in the dark. This investment in time early in the day builds us a buffer of safety at the end of the day when you are tired, and if you are going to be on snow at all it is much easier and safer to move around on if it is frozen. This requires the snow to crisp by a process of radiation cooling, and it is unlikely for the snow to crisp if the sky has not been clear the night before your ascent. Assuming it has frozen, then your day will be a race to get down before it starts to thaw. As the snow thaws, it becomes more and more difficult to walk on and your pace will get slower and slower, you will become more and more dehydrated, etc, etc.

Climbing Up

Scoping the route above the Monte Rosa hut the night before a climb.

Set yourself up for success right from the off by planning the approach and scoping out the first part of your day the night before your ascent. This makes for a smoother and more efficient start to your day.

Once I have arrived at the hut and checked in with the guardian, I will have a chat with them about conditions and whether there is anything unusual or specific that I need to know for the next day. When I have found my bed space and sorted my kit, I will head out and find the path I will use in the morning. I will then head some way up the path and work out where the route goes and my tactics for setting off.

This will make the departure in the dark much smoother and faster. If the terrain or the route is complicated, I may go quite far. I have often gone an hour above the hut to reduce the chance of getting lost in the morning.

The more preparation and the better your departure tactics and planning are, the more time you will buy yourself later in the day.

Think about:
- Will I need my harness on?
- Will I need to change layers when I put my harness on?
- When will I need my crampons, where are they in my rucksack?
- When will I need a helmet? Is it worth leaving the hut with it on and my headtorch already attached?
- How long will I need my headtorch for?
- When is sunrise, are my sunglasses better in my pocket or in my rucksack?

The more decisions I can make the night before, the more bandwidth I will have in the morning to react to unexpected conditions, other groups, or complicated navigation.

On complicated routes like the Matterhorn, I will often climb quite a bit of the route the afternoon before to make sure I know where I am going in the morning.

Having scoped the approach and the line to get yourself established on the route, you are ready to start climbing. How you actually climb will depend on the technical difficulty and your personal ability / comfort level moving over the terrain. If you are going to be doing pitched climbing, then you need to consider if you are going to swing leads or lead in blocks (see below). If you are going to move together you need to decide how much rope you are going to have between you, who is going first and so on.

When looking at the terrain ahead, remember what grade the route is supposed to be. If it's PD with the odd section of grade III and you find yourself on exposed overhanging terrain, I would suggest you are off route. Unlike a crag climb, where a route may seek out technical difficulty or climb a pure line for the sake of the line, most alpine routes climb obvious features like a ridge or a face by the easiest possible way. Most of these routes were first ascended by climbers wearing tweed clothing and hobnail boots, using hemp ropes; they were not seeking technical difficulty but trying to climb the mountain. Think: where would the first ascensionists go?

Keep looking ahead and looking for the easiest line. The thing that makes you quick in alpine climbing is not rushing but smooth, deliberate, efficient movement with slick ropework. You can aid this whole process by looking ahead as much as possible. Do not be static on the belay looking at the view – look ahead and see if you can see any signs of wear on the rock. Which way round a pinnacle looks easiest? Is there any fixed protection. When you are moving, keep looking ahead. If the route is a classic, it will be climbed many times a year, so there will be signs of wear, lichen will be worn off and there may be marks left by the rubber soles of a boot, or crampon scratches.

At the same time do not be intimidated by the scale and the fact that you cannot remember each section of the route description. This doesn't matter, just break it down into sections. Climb the first, check the description, then the next, then the next and so on to the top.

Kris McCoey on the Breithorn Traverse.

As you climb, try to keep track of where you are on the route in relation to the route description. Keeping track of where you are helps you get a handle on what's coming next and how far you still have to go. This can be really difficult on long complicated routes, so you need to pay attention.

If you do get lost, just stop, regroup, work out where you are, and if you have gone off route work out how to get back onto the correct line. While it may feel like you are wasting time, ultimately it will be faster than pushing on, on the wrong route.

If you feel you are being drawn onto the side or flanks of a ridge, you are almost certainly going off route. The best rock is almost always on the crest of a ridge and most routes will follow the best rock and the most natural line. There are occasions when you may drop onto the flank but this is usually highlighted in the guidebook.

If you are descending by the same route, make sure you look back **down** the route during your ascent. Take the time to spot key features on the route, such as any key changes in direction or abseil anchors. You will be amazed how different a route can look when travelling in the opposite direction.

When the descent is not by the route you came up, if you can see it while you are climbing up, it is worth trying to spot any key features that can help identify the route on the way down.

Climbing Up

Crossing a bergschrund

While the actual skills involved in crossing a bergschrund / rimaye seem simple, every year I observe multiple teams turning something that should be relatively manageable, into something really dangerous.

Let's think about the issues. A bergschrund is a crevasse that forms when the moving ice of a glacier pulls away from permanent snowfields. A randkluft is the gap between mountain or rock and ice at the top of the glacier. Although these names are correct, they are generally both referred to as a bergschrund or rimaye. These can be really big, deep, and impossible to cross, or they can be bridged by the winter snow. Sometimes you won't even notice they are there, and other times you will be climbing a steep overhanging wall of ice to become established on your route. Hopefully you will be dealing with something in between, a snow bridge or a steep pull over a short wall of snow and ice to get onto terrain that leads onto your route.

The thing to do is to treat it like any other climbing problem. The leader needs to be protected. So having positioned the team just below the bergschrund, the second places the leader on belay, then the leader climbs up and over the snow bridge or whatever else they have to deal with. Once clear of the bergschrund, the leader creates a belay and brings their partner across. When the leader is climbing, the belayer is anchored by gravity to the snow. If the snow bridge collapses while the leader is crossing, the edge of the bergschrund acts like a runner making it easy to hold a fall. The climber / leader can then climb out and work out what to do next. Once they have crossed the bergschrund, the leader needs to protect their second as they cross; otherwise, if the snow bridge collapses while the second is crossing, both climbers could be catapulted into the void.

It is essential that the leader creates an anchor and belays their second across. In my observations, people are lazy and think that because they have made it across their second will be fine as well. This is not always the

Crossing a bergschrund.

case. So, if you are the leader, take the time to create a belay – ice screw, buried ice axe or rock if you can reach it; that way everyone is protected. If this is your mindset every time you cross a bergschrund and you are unlucky and a snow bridge collapses, you are ready for it.

On occasion, it may even be possible to reach rock so why not uncoil all the rope and make a long pitch to the security of a solid rock anchor.

Moving together

To many, being able to move smoothly and efficiently over varied alpine terrain in some incredible places, is the essence of alpine climbing. We need to be clear that there is a big difference between moving together (as climbers of roughly equal ability), and short roping (which is a guiding technique honed over many years of training and practice). The focus of guided short roping is the guide looking after their guest and using the rope to protect the guest, preventing a slip from becoming a fall.

If you choose to move together, both climbers need to be comfortable with the terrain they are on; the rope then adds security should someone slip or fall. If either climber isn't comfortable operating in that style at that grade, I would suggest that they should start pitched climbing. The basic assumption is that no one will fall, though this is obviously a low probability, high consequence event, and that if they did the rope will stop a fall becoming any more serious.

The spare rope is split between the climbers in coils, so it is easy to drop the coils and move into pitched climbing. I will sometimes carry some of the extra rope in my rucksack as it is more comfortable to carry but only on routes where I will not need all of the rope.

Gareth Hughes placing a runner while moving together on the Dri Horlini ridge, Saas-Almagell.

Climbing Up

Moving together on snow

The terrain you are moving over will dictate the style you use. If you are moving together over steep snow, I would question why you have the rope between you – if one person falls, they will almost certainly pull off the other climber. This changes as soon as you are able to start placing protection or you are operating on a ridge crest.

You may choose to move together on steep snow in the anticipation of being able to place protection, for example if you have crossed a bergschrund (see below), then have some steep snow to climb to get onto a ridge. That way the rope is set up, ready to be used when you get to the ridge and you are effectively carrying it over comfortable ground. It is important that climbers are aware of the seriousness of this type of terrain. When you see guides short roping on this ground, they are using the rope to protect their client in the full knowledge that the guide must not slip, and that they are able to stop their client slipping.

As soon as you are able to place protection then everything becomes more secure. On steep snow this may be an ice screw, or if you are moving near some rock, you may be able to place a runner, or there may be some fixed protection, such as a bolt or a peg.

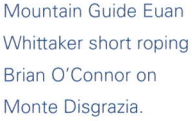

Mountain Guide Euan Whittaker short roping Brian O'Connor on Monte Disgrazia.

Moving together on a face

If you are moving together on a face, you are moving like you would in a pitched climbing situation, just not bothering to stop and belay. When the leader runs out of equipment, they make a belay and the second person, who by now will have most of the equipment, carry's on through. Alternatively, you could be climbing in blocks (see page 102), in which case the gear is passed back to the leader and they carry on.

Just like moving on snow and ice, in this scenario the worst thing that can happen is the second falls off, if the second falls off it is extremely unlikely the leader will be able to hold the fall and they may be catapulted off the mountain. Therefore, if the leader climbs a more difficult section that they think

ALPINE CLIMBING

Neil Stevenson on Pointe d'Amont, Ecrins.

would challenge the second, they must find a belay (dropping a few coils to let out a bit more rope if necessary), and safeguard the second over that section.

In the case of a leader fall the second climber is the belay, the leader should be caught by their protection and the system works much the same as in any lead climbing situation. The key element is that there is not too much slack in the system. It is inevitable that there is some, however the more there is the further the leader may fall and the greater the shock load will be on the runners you have placed. It is really important to maintain good communication between the climbers, so that this doesn't happen.

It is also important to make sure you do not have too much rope out between the climbers. With two people on the rope, I will have about ten arm spans of rope between each person, when moving on a face I will try and place more protection than on a ridge, as I do not have the option to counterbalance on either side of the ridge. With three climbers, I will have about six arm spans between each climber and try to have one piece of gear between each one. The further apart the climbers are the more difficult it is to communicate, if the rear climber is struggling and they can't communicate to the leader this can become very serious. If you have too much rope between you, you are also introducing a lot of rope drag. These are obviously ideals, and it is much easier to achieve if there is fixed protection, or on certain rock types like granite, where it is easier to place protection than on a compact rock like limestone.

Never be afraid to put extra protection or switch to pitching.

On a snow, ice or mixed face the techniques are the same, though you may consider having more rope between the climbers, as there is less friction in the system with the rope running over ice and snow rather than rock.

Moving together on a ridge

Moving together on a ridge whether it be snow, mixed or rock is much easier to protect than a face, simply by having one climber either side of the ridge – counterbalanced, you have made the team secure.

Climbers on a beautiful snow ridge on Castor.

Snow ridge

On a snow crest where it is not possible for the climbers to advance one on each side, the only defence you have is if one person falls one side of the ridge the other jumps the opposite way. Likewise, if a cornice collapses under one climber the other needs to jump onto the opposite side to protect the team. This sounds very dramatic, but it does work. While a track on the crest of a ridge (from which one climber can end up on each side) can feel airy and more exposed, it is actually much safer and easier to protect than a good track on the side of the ridge. A track on the side usually feels much more secure as you can place your ice axe into the snow beside you for security.

I would use about ten arm spans of rope between the climbers. They then carry this rope in coils in their hand, split between them. These should not be locked off so that in the event of a fall the climbers can easily let go of the rope giving them the reaction time to jump to the other side of the ridge.

Climbing Up

The author moving on a ridge with open hand coils.

Euan Whittaker and Brian O'Connor on the Biancograt.

The beauty of this system is that you can move closer together to communicate, then as the terrain changes you can spread the rope out accordingly. A great example would be a route like the Biancograt on the Piz Bernina where you are moving together on rock and mixed ground, then onto a snow crest. On the crest you move closer together until you reach a steepening that has become a bit too icy to move together on. You make a couple of short pitches up the ice or move together on the ice, spaced apart and using ice screws for protection. You then come together again, moving on a snow crest until you reach the final mixed / rock section.

Mixed or rock ridge

On a mixed or rock ridge you can really start to use the terrain and work the ridge to give you protection. By positioning the climbers on opposite sides of the ridge, or by using pinnacles, spikes, and rock features as natural runners, you save a lot of time.

Ben Wallace climbing on the Schijenstock.

Placing and removing protection

Nuts and cams take time, so if you can gain the security by using the terrain you start to move more quickly. Like so many things in alpine climbing the trick to doing this well is looking ahead. The more you can look ahead and plan what you are going to do as you move along, the faster and smoother you will be.

Traditionally this is one of the most difficult transitions to make in alpine climbing, as it feels alien and at times feels like you are soloing with a rope tied between you. With practice you will get used to it and it will become second nature.

To set yourself up for success, make sure you do not have too much rope between you. It is really tempting to think the extra rope will give you more security, as there will be more runners between you. In theory this is true, but what actually happens is that the extra rope introduces rope drag and the distance between you makes effective communication difficult. You need to be close enough that you can have a constant chatter between you. "I am just placing a runner" – means hang on a minute while I place this nut, cam, or sling. "I am just taking out a runner" – means hang on a minute while I take it out.

As you move along the ridge, if you come to a difficult section the leader can put some extra runners in and carry on as if leading; the body weight from their slowly moving partner acts as a belay. When they get to the top of the more difficult section, they can make a belay, bring their partner up, and then continue.

Taking coils while using a guide plate.

If the difficult section looks longer than the amount of rope you have out between you, bring your partner into the base of the difficult section. The leader can now drop their coils. The second puts the leader on belay and the leader sets off. When the leader reaches the top of the difficulties, they can bring the second up. If they need more rope the second can drop coils as the leader climbs.

Managing the rope in this way means you are usually only burning the time it takes to put on and take off one set of coils. It is worth counting the number of coils you take off so you can easily put that number back on before moving together again.

At the top of the pitch, if you are going to be moving together straight away, make an anchor and clip a guide plate into it, and then take in the slack rope and clip it into the guide plate. While your partner is getting ready to climb, put on the spare rope as coils, remembering to count them. As the second climbs, take in the guide plate adding coils as you have enough rope. It takes a fair bit of practice to ensure the rope is kept snug on your partner as you put the coils on and tie them off, but it does mean that as soon as your partner arrives you are ready to move off again. The downside to this technique is that you are standing on a ledge not tied in, rather than using the rope to secure yourself you are coiling it round your body. You may want to consider clipping with a sling or lanyard if doing this in an exposed place. I would argue that at this stage in your climbing career you are unlikely to jump or fall off a ledge and if you are moving together then the terrain is unlikely to be so severe that you can't stand and put coils on. If you are concerned you could use an adjustable cow's tail like a Petzl Connect Adjust to clip in with.

When placing protection while moving together, think about the direction the rope will be running through the karabiner. Is it likely to be lifted off or out of the placement? This is especially prevalent with slings, so if you can tuck them under a rough piece of rock this may help to hold it in place. Tape slings, when they are a little worn, are better at staying in place than aramid style slings. Cams are less likely to lift out than nuts.

In a perfect world, when using natural features, there will be a set of spikes running along a ridge crest and you can simply weave your way through them. Reality is seldom like this, and you will often be one side of the ridge or the other. Keep flicking the rope over spikes as you pass, your partner can then then flick them off as they come to them. Think about which direction you are travelling in, and if you did slip off, which direction you would fall and how that would affect the rope.

If you are a rope of three, then the middle person unflicks the rope from the runner or spike ahead of them as they arrive then connects or repositions the rope for the next climber. Many popular routes with moving together sections have fixed protection at the hardest or most awkward section which can aid progress significantly.

Henry Methold moving together with a bolt for protection.

A final word of warning on moving together: you will see all sorts of people moving together when they really do not have the climbing or technical ability to do so. You will also see guides short roping and climbers moving together in places you think are crazy. Do not be swayed by what you see. You have no idea how good those climbers are or how long the guide and guest have been climbing together. They may have climbed together every year for 20+ years and know each other's strengths and weaknesses. It is difficult but just because one team has adopted a certain technique doesn't mean it is right for you. Choose a technique that is appropriate for your technical expertise and experience, you can then build on what you have learnt.

ALPINE CLIMBING

Alternate leads or climbing in blocks

The author block leading near the Orny hut.

Climbers from a traditional background are used to alternate leads, where one climber leads a pitch, then their partner leads the next one. This works well as you get a rest every other pitch and you will have collected much of the kit while you were seconding, so it should be quick and simple to grab the rest of the kit and lead through.

An alternative system is to lead in blocks, where one climber leads multiple pitches in a row. This way the leader is completely focussed on the task in hand, and the second can be more relaxed for a while before taking their share of the leading. This is particularly useful if the climbing is technical, as the leader may climb with a lighter rucksack; then the second can climb with a tight rope above them with the heavier sack.

This system can allow each team member to play to their strengths. I can think of a route I climbed with a friend who is a much stronger rock climber but is less experienced at alpine climbing and moving together. We broke the route into sections where he led the most difficult pitches, and I managed all the moving together sections. This worked really well, we both contributed equally, and we climbed the route quickly.

Whatever system you choose, being slick with your belay changeover will save time on your route. This is something you can practice on smaller crags closer to home, so think about being as slick as possible on every change over. When these things become habit, you will be moving faster.

Rope tangles

A final thought before we look at some techniques for making change overs slicker: if your rope looks like it is in a tangle, stop and spend a minute sorting it out. Unless you are on a hanging stance try and stack the rope on a ledge or at your feet, it is much easier to pay out than if you have flaked it back and forth across the belay rope.

Direct belays

One technique that I use a lot in the Alps, and guiding elsewhere, is a direct belay. A direct belay is when a belay plate or friction hitch is clipped directly into the belay anchor and the second is brought up in this way. The advantages are that it is easier to position the leader for comfort and if a guide plate is used then there is a degree of flexibility to eat, change clothes, add sun cream, etc. A direct belay also makes changeovers much simpler as the belayer is not in the system.

The easiest direct belay to envisage is a sling over a spike. You then tie yourself into the sling, and clip in the guide plate / belay karabiner to the sling.

Climbing Up

Guide plate into direct anchor with belayer tied in.

Multiple anchors brought to a central point.

If you are using multiple anchors in a direct belay situation, you must bring these together to a central point, which is often referred to as the master point. This can be a loop you have tied in a sling or single screwgate karabiner that you clip others to. Once you get used to bringing your anchor to a central point your belay set up becomes much slicker.

An alternative to the above is to use the friction of the rope running around a spike, or running over a ridge, as a direct belay. It is amazing how much friction can be generated by the rope running over rock, though you need to be mindful of the potential to damage the rope. If you use a direct belay like this it is amazing how easy it is to hold a slip. The downside is that if that slip becomes anything more, it is very difficult to extract yourself from the situation as you will have someone hanging on the rope that you are tied onto.

Ben Wallace direct belaying round a spike.

ALPINE CLIMBING

A direct belay needs careful consideration as, in the event of a fall, all the load is placed on the anchor. In steep terrain the weight of the whole party may even be placed on the anchor. The anchor must not fail! If it is a spike or a block, make sure you test it. Kicking it, hitting it, and levering with an ice axe, are all good ways of making sure you have a solid anchor. You also need to make sure that the sling or rope round a spike won't lift off. This is aided by making sure you are always downhill of the anchor.

You may see people using a direct belay to belay a leader, while this does work in certain situations that can cope with an upward pull, like a bolt, or ice screw belay, this a very specialist technique that I wouldn't suggest unless you have tried it in other situations. Generally, it is best to use a direct belay for the second then switch to an indirect (belay plate on the harness or rope belay loop) when leading.

A direct belay with the belayer below a spike to keep the rope on it.

Direct belay using an Italian hitch.

Alternate leads, change overs

Wherever possible I will use a direct belay to belay a second when alpine climbing. With a direct system you can use either an Italian hitch or a belay plate in guide mode, if the climbing has any sideways element or there is a chance of needing to pay any rope out, then I would lean towards an Italian hitch, for everything else I would use a guide plate.

When the climber approaches the belay think about what direction they are going to leave, in that way you will position them in the correct place. Leave them on the guide plate, if you are worried about it slipping you can tie an overhand knot in the rope just below the plate on the dead side.

Sort out the rack then take the second's (now the new leader) belay device and set this up to protect them as they lead. When you are sorted, undo the guide plate, the new leader takes this with them and off they go.

Climbing Up

Slick belay change over, alternate leads.

Block lead changeover

The difference here is that the same climber is leading every pitch of their block.

Using the guide plate, bring the second onto the belay, think carefully before they arrive which direction you are going to set off in so you can position the belayer in the best place.

When they arrive tie them in.

The leader can sort out the rack, while the second back coils the rope, as mentioned above, the rope is generally less prone to tangles if it is back coiled onto the ground rather than flaked across the rope. The leader then sets off, making sure they take a belay plate with them.

Slick change over block leading.

The blend

The trick to fast, efficient movement is being able to blend what we have just looked at, mixing the right kind of movement to suit the terrain. It takes a lot of practice to feel like you are flowing up your route, choosing the right technique for the right part of the mountain. When you do, it feels great. You cover the ground, stand on the summit, then have a stress-free descent.

To achieve this skills blend, you need to have competence in all areas. Practising before coming to the Alps, then building your experience and confidence on routes at an appropriate level that will challenge but not over stretch you, is the best way to develop.

Approaching the summit of the Piz Palü.

Going Down

Matt Stygall abseiling on the traverse of the Perrons.

The summit of the mountain is only halfway. In fact, on some mountains it can take longer to climb down than go up. When guiding the Matterhorn, I would allow 4 to 4½ hours on the way up and 5 on the way down. It is also a sad fact that most accidents happen on the descent. We are tired, the conditions are generally getting worse, the snow will be getting softer, and we may be racing an afternoon storm; none of these things are a great recipe for safe travel in the mountains. You need to be on your guard and maintain your highest level of concentration until you are safely down on a path or other easy ground. Even then, I have had friends and colleagues who, when really tired, have sustained serious injuries on easy ground.

You need to plan the descent with the same care and attention that you planned the ascent. Spend time researching and studying the route. Are you going to reverse the line of ascent, or are you going to descend a different side of the mountain? Is there any abseiling involved? If so, how much rope do you need? Do you need two ropes, one rope, or even a tag line? We will look at all these questions.

ALPINE CLIMBING

Will Harris leading downhill, placing runners on the Dri Horlini ridge, Saas-Fee.

Climbing down

Accidents are more likely in descent. Make sure you have had some food and water before you set off down. This will help keep your concentration levels at their maximum.

Pitching

When climbing down it may be that one climber is stronger than the other so the weaker would go first with their partner belaying from above. As the leader descends, they place runners to protect the second as they down climb. While this works really well, it is pitching downhill and can be time consuming.

Moving together

As with pitching downhill, the weaker climber would go first. However, in this instance the climbers would be moving together with runners between each climber. If a section is particularly difficult, they are set up for pitching downhill whenever it is required.

Abseiling

When the terrain becomes too steep or difficult to climb down, abseiling is the next option. Route descriptions will usually inform you if an abseil or multiple abseils are involved in a descent. However, it is always worth having some abseil tat in your rucksack in case the in situ anchor is poor and needs replacing, or if you need to create an intermediate anchor.

How far you can abseil is a function of how much rope you have with you. With a single rope, you can abseil half the length then pull the rope down after you. With two ropes, you can tie them together and abseil a full rope length, pulling it down after yourself. You can also do this with a tagline (see p112).

Mark Dearnley abseiling off the Dent du Géant.

Going Down

One of the key things about abseiling is not dropping the ropes. Do not be afraid to tie them into something while you are arranging your anchor and getting yourself established on the rope.

Creating anchors on rock

On many routes the anchors are in situ, if this is the case then take the time to check them, some rotting tat that is so sun faded that it has turned white is not something I would want to trust my life to. If the tat looks new and well connected, that may be a good bet. If you are in any doubt, then replace it. This is why I always carry 10m of 7mm tat with me.

If you are creating the anchors don't let cost become an issue, spend the time to make sure an anchor is correctly equalised, you don't necessarily need to use karabiners when joining wires, pegs or cams together you can tie in directly. There shouldn't be any real movement that may damage the tat, but the key thing is to ensure that you are equalising solid pieces of protection before you abseil. Don't make the mistake of trying to save some money by placing only one piece – that may cost you your life.

Tying the ropes together

There are always lots of conversations around what is the best knot to use when tying two ropes together. In 30+ years of alpine climbing, I have always used an overhand knot with a 30cm long tail, if you use a longer tail there is always the chance of attaching your abseil device to the tails when really tired, this would obviously be a disaster. This knot is quick and easy to tie, easy to untie after being loaded, and when being pulled down under tension the knot assumes a flat position on the rock so is much less likely to snag. It is important when tying the knot to ensure it is really tight so there is very little chance of slippage. You can do this by pulling the individual strands. Having a 30cm tail also ensures that should there be any slippage in the knot it won't undo.

Tying two ropes together using an overhand knot.

ALPINE CLIMBING

Knots in the end of the rope

While sitting at home, it is inconceivable that you may abseil off the end of a rope, but it happens to someone every year. If I cannot see that the rope has reached the ground or a big ledge, then I will tie a thumb knot in the end of each rope. Don't tie them together as they will tangle. You need to be careful and remember to untie them when you are going to pull the rope down. The only time I would consider not tying them is if it is really windy and there is a risk the knots might get caught on something. As I get towards the end of the rope, I will usually pull the ends up and tie them then.

Protecting the abseil

When abseiling, it is a good idea to protect yourself using a French Prusik knot. This allows you the opportunity to let go with your brake hand to sort any issues with the rope, create the next anchor, etc. It also means that should you be knocked on the head by a rock and let go with your brake hand, you will stop.

There are lots of ways to set up an abseil, but the following has worked well for me for three decades of alpinism, so I know it works.

Take a 120cm sling and larks foot it through the abseil loop on your harness, then tie an overhand knot in the sling about 15cm away from your harness to create a loop. Clip your screwgate karabiner and belay device into this loop.

You can now use the rest of the sling as a 'cow's tail' to clip into the anchor, so protecting yourself while you are setting up the rope. Just make sure there is no risk of dropping onto this sling – it will take your weight, but not a fall. Some people prefer to use a lanyard, but a sling should suffice, so long as you are careful how you use it.

Abseil set up with sling.

Going Down

Climber clipped into an abseil anchor.

Take a karabiner and clip it into the belay loop on your harness. Clip in one end of your Prusik and wrap it round the two ropes and back into itself to create the French Prusik (aka autoblock). You can now pull up enough rope to thread the ropes through your belay device. The Prusik will hold the weight of the ropes while you do this. Once you are set up, slide the rope through the Prusik until everything is nice and tight and in alignment. Double check everything is ok, then unclip from the anchor. A great idea is to clip the karabiner you had attached to the anchor into the rope that you will pull down at the end of the abseil; this will remind you which rope to pull down.

When you reach the next anchor just unclip this karabiner from the rope, and clip into the new anchor.

Autoblock set up for abseiling.

Cow's tail clipped into the pull-down rope.

ALPINE CLIMBING

I will then undo the rope from my belay plate, sort out the ends, making sure they are not tangled, and then thread the rope we are going to pull down through the next anchor. I will pull some spare rope through my Prusik, so that there is enough slack to allow my partner to abseil, but I will usually leave the Prusik attached so I have control of it until my partner arrives, clips into the belay and detaches from the rope.

One person can then pull down the rope, while the other threads it through the new anchor, I would make sure you are clipped in to an anchor, even on easy ground or big ledges when pulling the rope; if the rope suddenly starts to run freely you could overbalance and fall off a ledge. Repeat until you get to the ground where you can move together again or walk off.

Tag lines

An alternative to having two half ropes is to use a single rope and a tag line. A tag line is a thin static rope, usually between 5-6mm. This is used in conjunction with a single rope. The climbing is done on a single rope which keeps the system really simple. The tag line, which is fairly light and easy to stow, is carried in a rucksack. It is then used for the abseil descent.

To set the system up thread your climbing rope through the anchor, then tie an overhand knot on a bight in the rope leaving about 60cm of tail. This knot blocks against the anchor, to ensure this is secure take a screwgate karabiner and clip the bight into the main rope. Apparently, this is called a Reepschnur Hitch. Then take the end of the tag line and tie it onto the tail of the main rope. I just use an overhand knot, as the knot isn't going to be heavily loaded (the climber's weight is only on the main line and the tag line is only used to retrieve the ropes), the difference in diameter doesn't matter.

Setting up a tag line.

I then set up the abseil as described. Although I will only weight the main rope, I still thread the tag line through my belay device and wrap the Prusik around both ropes. This helps prevent any twists and tangles. The lightness of a tagline does make it prone to being blown about, and it can catch on small flakes, etc. When you are at the next anchor, pull down on the tagline. These lines are thin and made of static rope, so I would suggest using gloves to pull them down.

Abseiling with a tag line.

The advantages of this system are that the system is light, and allows a simple single rope lead system, but maintains the ability to make full abseils should you want to. The disadvantages are that you need to reconstruct the system at each anchor, or pull the whole rope through the anchor, and the tag line is more prone to snagging than a full weight rope. The top of a ten pitch abseil descent is not the place to try this for the first time.

Abseiling on snow and ice

You won't always be abseiling on rock, and if you need to create an abseil anchor on snow your only real option is to dig out a snow bollard. This should be dug into the firmest layer of snow and be big enough for the top not to slice off when you weight the rope. It is particularly useful as an anchor to get down over a cornice at the top of a gully or face.

Abseiling on a snow bollard.

ALPINE CLIMBING

If you need to make an anchor on ice, then a V thread (also known as an 'Abalakov') anchor is your best option. This needs practise to get it right. Make a V-shaped hole in the ice by screwing an ice screw into the ice at an angle, then remove it and make another hole at an angle to intersect. Then use a tool to thread a piece of rope through the V thread. This can be a bent piece of coat hanger or a purpose made tool. Tie this into a loop and use as an anchor. It is worth using an ice screw as a backup for the first person down. If you are not sure about the strength you can use two anchors and join them together.

Some people advocate that you can thread the rope through the V thread and abseil without leaving anything behind, which is a nice clean method. However, I have had problems with the rope freezing in place and being difficult to pull down and would not recommend this practice, unless the ice is really dry.

Making a V thread.

The Alpine Progression

Kris McCoey climbing on the Dammazwillinge 3,274m, Furka Pass, Andermatt.

It is really easy to try and progress too quickly in the Alps. My first trip to the Alps was on the back of what we thought was great preparation; we had spent the winter climbing in Scotland then the spring climbing as much rock as possible. We could climb grade V and E2 and thought we were ready for anything. While we were repeatedly 'spanked' on routes that were too big or too difficult, friends, who on paper were not as good climbers as us, succeeded on route after route.

The difference was that they had nailed all the things we have been talking about in this book, and were choosing routes that were appropriate for their fitness, ability, experience, and the conditions. As their acclimatisation and fitness increased, they stepped up the length and difficulty of their routes while we kept throwing ourselves at inappropriate objectives.

The trick to progressing through the grades, or moving onto longer routes on the higher peaks, is to arrive prepared (more on this later). Pay attention to your nutrition and hydration, then choose something that will help you acclimatise, as well as hone your skills.

This is always a challenge when you have a two-week holiday, as you want it all at once – arrive, pack, get up high, and climb the route you have been dreaming about for the last six months. The reality is you will arrive and the weather and conditions won't be quite right, but you will try and make it work because this is what you want to do. You are then tired, in the wrong place, frustrated and disappointed ... not a great way to start a trip.

I would try and develop an open mindset. Arrive with lots of ideas to match different conditions, including routes at different altitudes. The perfect way to prepare for routes at 4,000m is to climb routes on peaks about 3,500m; you will enjoy them a lot more and probably be able to climb harder, as you won't be hypoxic. An alternative is to choose an easy route on a higher peak, knowing that it will hurt but the technical difficulty is easy. Personally, I find this really unsatisfying. I would rather climb something lower and technical, then move onto something longer and higher when my body feels ready for it.

One way of achieving this is to start in an area with lots of peaks around the acclimatisation altitude, for example the Andermatt area (see guidebook section). When those routes start to feel like you are climbing at sea level, you can consider moving onto the higher peaks.

When you are trying to judge your pace, comparing your speed to the guidebook times is a good metric. The guidebook times are set for an acclimatised party with the route in average conditions. If you can't match the guidebook time, ask yourself if you are using the best techniques. If you are pitching when the timing is for a team moving together, then the route is too difficult for your current level. If you feel you are moving smoothly but are still too slow, it is almost certainly because you are not acclimatised enough. You must also consider your hydration and nutrition.

There are no secret techniques. The key to progression is building on previous experience, and arriving in the Alps in the best physical and mental condition to take the next step.

Jon Holiday and team traversing the Läckihorn 3,068m, Furka Pass, Andermatt.

The Monte Rosa hut, Zermatt, during a resupply.

Spending the Night Out

The scale of alpine terrain is such that not many routes can be climbed in a single day from the valley floor, so you may have to spend the night out. The options are to stay in a mountain hut, camp or bivouac.

Huts

The hut network in the Alps is second to none, allowing you to move through the mountains with a relatively light pack and a credit card. Huts are not cheap, you need to allow €70-80 per night half board (2024 prices), and in the high huts you will need to pay for water as well. The huts are generally built close to the classic routes, and the guardians can be an amazing source of information on the routes in the area and the current conditions.

If you want to use a hut it is important that you make a reservation. This is best done by phone, so that you can also ask about conditions (all the numbers can easily be found on the internet). Some huts require a deposit if booking well ahead, but this is usually returned if you cannot arrive as a result of poor weather or conditions. When booking, make sure you inform the guardian of any dietary requirements. Please remember that they may be cooking for 70 plus people in a tiny kitchen at 3,000+ metres.

Winter rooms

When the huts are closed, it is a requirement that a room is left open for shelter. This is known as the winter room, and it will usually have blankets and often a stove and basic cooking utensils. These can make great bases out of the main season, and while you will need to carry your own food, they are often very quiet. It is always worth checking with the guardian (who will be based in the valley at that time of year), what equipment is in the winter room before heading up there.

In recent years these have become increasingly popular, so it is now necessary to book a place in a winter room. At the time of writing this was the case in France, Austria and Switzerland.

Jacchia hut on the Tronchey ridge, Grandes Jorasses.

Bivouac huts

In addition to huts with a guardian there are a number of bivouac huts around the Alps. These simple shelters give access to more remote routes. They generally have beds and blankets but not much else; though some huts have stoves and even gas. As above, you just need to check with the guardian. They generally do not have heating, so can be very cold.

Bivouacking

An alternative to staying in a hut is to bivouac or 'bivvy'; this can be a planned or unplanned. On big routes that are not possible to climb in a day, you will need to spend the night out under the stars. The level of discomfort you choose to endure is up to you. You just need to remember that every gram of comfort you add will be extra weight on your back, that you will need to carry it up every metre of your route. If the temperatures are warm and you don't mind some discomfort, then an extra layer of insulation and a group shelter that you can both hide inside will suffice for one night.

Spending the Night Out

Stoves

A stove is fantastic thing to have with you, as the positive effect of a warm drink is immeasurable. It may well be that you need to melt snow to gain water, so you will need a stove and a pan as a minimum anyhow. There is a choice between gas and liquid fuel stoves. I would suggest gas is the way to go in the Alps, as gas is easy and clean to carry, and while liquid stoves are much more efficient when melting water in the cold, you rarely need this capacity in the Alps in summer. There are a number of specialist stoves like the MSR Reactor and the Jetboil that have a heat exchanger to maximise their efficiency. They are amazing at boiling water but really difficult to cook on as they are difficult to run at a low temperature. When using one of these I will opt for a dehydrated meal where all I have to do is boil water. If you want to keep things really light, then opting for something like an MSR Jetboil and a titanium mug that you can melt water in is a good way to go.

MSR Jetboil and titanium pan

Keeping warm

The key to a vaguely comfortable night is to try and stay warm for as long as possible. As soon as you decide to stop, put on all your clothes, especially hats and gloves, then loosen boots to allow good blood circulation. Insulate yourself from the ground by sitting on rucksacks and having the rope under your legs. Pull your group shelter over the team and, if possible, lie close together to share body heat – anything to stop the heat escaping. Staying in the sitting position will make it easier to stay insulated but is less comfortable for sleep.

A step up from the group shelter is to use a waterproof, breathable bivvy bag you can zip yourself inside of and get more protection. The next stage is to add an insulated mat, then a sleeping bag. The warmth of the sleeping bag will be related to the temperature and time of year. You just need to remember that you have to carry everything with you.

Camping or bivvying near a hut

A bivvy or camp before climbing, instead of a hut, can be really good. It will avoid a busy hut and save some money. The disadvantage is that you will need to carry everything to your camp spot; but as long as you are returning the same way you can travel light on the route. On the plus side, you will be able to manage the timing of your day to be out of sync with those staying in the hut, and you will undoubtably get a better night's sleep.

There are some really light tents available. The breathable single skin ones, while expensive, are brilliant, having a small footprint, and providing increased warmth, and the camaraderie of being with your climbing partner. If you are going to carry a tent, carry a decent insulated mat with you to ensure a good night's sleep.

If you are camping close to, or passing, a hut on the way to your bivvy, it is worth considering buying water from the hut. This means you will not need to carry so much water or carry as much gas to melt snow.

Brian O'Connor camping at Upper Saddle on the Grand Teton before an ascent of The Exum Ridge.

When It All Goes Wrong

REGA Helicopter, after a rescue from the Piz Badile.

If we spend enough time in a hazardous environment, something will happen to either your party or another party around you. Having the skills to deal with these situations should be part of any alpinist's knowledge base.

A basic first aid course is an essential element of the preparation for any time in the mountains. First aid is a degradable skill that needs to be regularly updated, and this book is not the place to teach first aid; however, we will have a look at some key considerations.

When I was an aspirant guide, I had to deal with a serious incident where two clients were hit by rock fall, when one of them pulled a block that I had told them not to touch onto themselves. The result was a compound fracture in the arm and a crushed calf at 3,800m on the Weissmies in cloud – so no helicopter. Luckily, I was with another guide. First aid stabilised the situation, then one of us short roped the person with the arm injury, while the rest of the team manoeuvred the victim with the leg injury off the ridge onto snow. We then put him in a bivvy bag and lowered him a rope length at a time to lose height. A rescue team was dropped under the cloud base, and they came up and joined us with a stretcher and drugs. We then worked together to get under the cloud base, where a helicopter could get in and reach the casualties.

The priorities the whole time were classic first aid. ABC – Airway, Breathing, Circulation, and getting them to a spot where we could evacuate them.

ALPINE CLIMBING

Rescue helicopter at the Sasc Furä hut.

Rescue in different countries in the Alps

While a first aid course will educate you in the skills for basic life preservation, knowing who to call and how rescue works in the Alps is the next part of the puzzle.

France

Mountain rescue in France is organised by Le Peloton de Gendarmerie de Haute Montagne (PGHM) and the Compagnies Républicaines de Sécurité (CRS), depending on the area. These are both branches of the police and have a heavy reliance on helicopters, although they do also have on-foot teams. In some areas the cost of this rescue provision is borne by the local commune, e.g. Chamonix, so in this area rescue is free. If you happen to be on the Swiss or Italian side of a mountain, you probably pay.

Switzerland

Swiss rescue is a collaboration between the Swiss Alpine Club and Swiss Air Rescue (REGA). Commercial helicopter companies are often used to provide rescue services in areas not covered by REGA's own helicopters. They observe strict visual flying rules, so bad weather means no helicopter. The ground personnel are usually subcontracted local mountain guides. Rescue is charged for in Switzerland.

Italy

Responsibility for rescue lies with the Corpo Nazionale Soccorso Alpino e Speleologico (CNAS). This is a volunteer organisation which may charge depending on who's helicopter is used.

The message in all countries is: make sure you have rescue and medical insurance.

How to call for help

If you decide that you need a rescue and you have phone reception, the task is pretty simple. Call one of the numbers listed opposite and you will get through to the rescue services. The international help number from mobile phones is 112, so if you call this the operator will be able to put you through to an appropriate authority.

The app Echo SOS has the facility to send your position at the same time you call for rescue, though the call centre will not be specific to mountain rescue.

Echo SOS

When It All Goes Wrong

If you don't have a phone, or are not able to move to get reception, you will have to attract the attention of any climbers close by or any passing helicopters. The universal distress signal is six short blasts on a whistle followed by a minute's pause, then repeat. You can also use the same signal at night using a headtorch. If you attract the attention of a passing helicopter, you can then signal that you would like a rescue by holding your hands above your head in a Y. If you do not require a rescue, hold one arm up and one down to signal this – N.

Rescue Y symbol

Rescue N Symbol

Who to call

France: 15 or 112 (Chamonix direct line: +33 (0) 4 50 53 16 89)
Italy: 118
Switzerland: 144/1414

An alternative is to call the nearest hut; they can then coordinate any rescue effort. This is particularly useful in areas with poor phone reception as, once you have got the message through, the hut can deal with the details while you deal with the situation. Hut guardians know their local mountains and can often give a rescue team better directions to your location.

If you don't have phone reception, using a secondary form of communication like a Garmin InReach® is a great option as the signal is global. It may take some time for the receiving centre in the USA to work through the system and contact the best person to help you, but you should also know that some newer smartphones are also incorporating a satellite rescue system.

If you do not have this option and there is no phone signal, then you may need to leave the casualty and go for help. Make sure you mark the site so that you can find it easily on your return.

Information required

When you get through to the rescue services, they will ask you a pretty standard set of questions. Have as much of this information ready as you can; if possible, write it down in advance.
- Where did it happen?
- What is the grid reference (either the map sheet number, GPS coordinates or latitude and longitude). This should be accompanied by a description of the terrain around the scene, and any easily identifiable features.
- Your altitude will also be useful to the rescuers.
- How many patients and their injuries.
- What happened?
- When did it happen?
- What are the weather conditions at the scene (cloud base and visibility, wind speed and direction, temperature)?
- What obstacles or hazards are there near the scene (e.g. overhead cables, trees, cliffs, etc.)?
- Will a rescue hoist be needed or is there a landing site close to the patient?

Helicopters

If you have to call for a helicopter, it is useful to know what to do when it arrives. All rescue helicopter crews are used to dealing with incidents where the people on the ground are unfamiliar with standard procedures, so in effect they will manage the incident for you.

However, you can make things faster and safer for all by doing some simple things in preparation for the arrival of the helicopter.
- Pack away tents, bivvy gear, and any other loose items.
- If you are on steep ground, it is worthwhile having the casualty attached by a single point, which is easily released or may be cut.
- Warn any other people in the area to stay clear.
- Instruct anyone around to wear eye protection and provide the same for your patient (the downwash from the rotors can pick up a lot of grit and snow).
- On hearing or seeing the helicopter approaching, stand with your arms raised in a Y shape with the local wind at your back. If you are in an exposed situation, ensure that you are in a well-braced position so that the rotor wash will not blow you off the mountain!

It is most likely that the helicopter will drop off a crew member close to you or winch them down to you to assess the situation, before they come in to land or start any rescue. Only approach a helicopter if instructed to do so by a crew member, and always from the front. If you have open ground nearby, have a look for a good landing site. You are looking for reasonably flat and level ground, firm hard-standing (not boggy or deep vegetation) and an area ideally about 100m in diameter (60m is a workable minimum). Indicate the proposed landing site by standing at the upwind edge with your arms raised in a Y shape.

Managing an emergency

A cool and organised approach is required to ensure that an effective and efficient rescue is carried out with the best possible outcomes for everyone involved.

The first priority in any emergency situation is your own safety – don't become another casualty! Assess the immediate hazards, take stock, and start to form a plan to deal with the situation in front of you.

Actions

- Consider your safety and the safety of any others in the party.
- Ensure it is safe to approach injured persons. Only approach from the side or below on steep or loose ground, so that you don't knock anything onto the casualty.
- Secure injured persons to prevent further injury.
- Deal with any life-threatening issues (Airway, Breathing, Circulation).
- Gather the required what, where, who, when information report should external rescue assistance be required, and make the call or send for help.
- Continue with first aid care as required until the rescue services arrive.

Patient management

The following is only an aid memoire; if you are not comfortable or familiar with any of the following it's time to go and refresh your first aid training.

D – Danger Consider your own safety, what are the hazards around the patient.

R – Response Does the patient respond if you stabilise their head and speak or shout at them?

A – Airway Is the patients airway clear and open (you may need a torch to adequately check this).

B – Breathing Is the patient breathing? What is the rate? Is it rhythmical? Is it quiet or noisy?

C – Circulation Are there any signs of bleeding? Outdoor waterproofs are equally good at keeping fluids in, so check inside clothing. After blunt trauma we can bleed internally as well as externally, so we need to be vigilant for signs of shock developing.

D – Deformity / Deterioration Are there any large fractures? A femur fracture can cause so much blood loss that a patient may die, and therefore needs urgent attention.

Continue to assess the patient's level of consciousness as this may change over time, indicating a deterioration in their condition.

Gary Veitch on the Portjengrat.

Robin Clothier climbing on the Wichelplanggstock.

GUIDEBOOK

Introduction

The following guidebook is a collection of my favourite routes across the Alps. It is unashamedly personal as they are all routes I have climbed and loved, some of them many times, with guests or with friends. The common thing about all the routes is the quality of the climbing and the beauty of their situation. An important part of the routes' selection has been their appropriateness in this time of rapid climate change. You will see that there are no north faces. Although they are referenced, it has been many years since the classic north faces were climbable in the summer months. I decided to focus on routes that were climbable in most alpine seasons, given the conditions we have had in recent years.

When flicking through the list you will see there are some routes that rely on snow and ice, or are much safer when frozen together earlier in the season. Where this is the case, it has been indicated in the route information. Some routes are better in the season when the route is clear of snow, again this will be mentioned in the text.

The book covers routes from Monte Viso in the south-west round to mountains and climbs in the Bernina and Bregaglia in eastern Switzerland. There are many more amazing routes and mountains in the Alps; this is just a selection.

Kate Scott on the Traverse of the Aiguille de la Vanoise.

How to use the guidebook

The days of taking guidebooks on the mountain are long since gone, so I expect you to photograph or photocopy the pages you need.

Each route covered in the book has enough information to get you to the base of the route with the right equipment, and guide you to the summit and back. Where other guidebooks exist, I have referenced them.

Routes have been grouped geographically with a map introducing each area. The map is not designed for navigation but to orientate you. I have made a conscious decision not to include GPS references as this is an essential part of the planning phase.

Each section has an area overview to help guide you to the most appropriate routes, then specifics about grade, length, timings, conditions, and equipment. The information given is for average summer conditions; so, if a route that is usually climbed as dry rock is covered in snow, it will obviously be more difficult. Conversely, some routes, like the Cosmiques Arête in Chamonix, are significantly easier with lots of snow on them, as found in the early part of the season.

Suggested timings are always a bit difficult as they assume you are acclimatised, the route is in average condition, and you are used to the style of climbing. If you find you are taking significantly longer than the book suggests, I would consider the conditions, your fitness, acclimatisation and your matrix of ambition and ability, before sending me an email.

You will notice that we have used a variety of grading systems. Each route has an overall alpine grade, and if the nature of the climbing is generally alpine in style, we used the UIAA grading system for individual pitches. If the route is purely rock climbing, we have used the French grading system. While this may appear confusing, it means our gradings will match up with those in other guidebooks to each individual area.

Even with an up-to-date guidebook, the minute it is sent to the printers it becomes out of date, so the user still has the responsibility to check on local conditions. This can be done by talking to hut guardians, local guide offices and researching on the internet.

While alpine climbing is hard work it is also meant to be fun. So, start easy and build things up and you will have a lot more fun, and ultimately be more successful. Enjoy.

Mark Chadwick climbing one of the steep walls on the East Ridge of Monte Viso.

Monte Viso, seen from the summit of Punta Udine.

Monte Viso

When you stand on any of the peaks on the southern side of the Western Alps and look south, one big peak sticks up way to the south. It is a beautiful pyramid standing above all the peaks around it. This is Monte Viso, standing 500m above all the surrounding mountains. It is a fantastic mountain with no easy route on it, and sitting south of the main alpine chain it often gets good weather.

While Monte Viso is the main event, there are lots of other great routes in the area, and combining a route on Monte Viso with the East Ridge of Punta Udine makes for a fantastic 3- or 4-day trip. You can drive to Pian del Re, walk to the Giacoletti hut, climb the East Ridge of Punta Udine, stay the night in the Giacoletti hut, and then walk over to the Sella hut ready for a route on the Viso the next day.

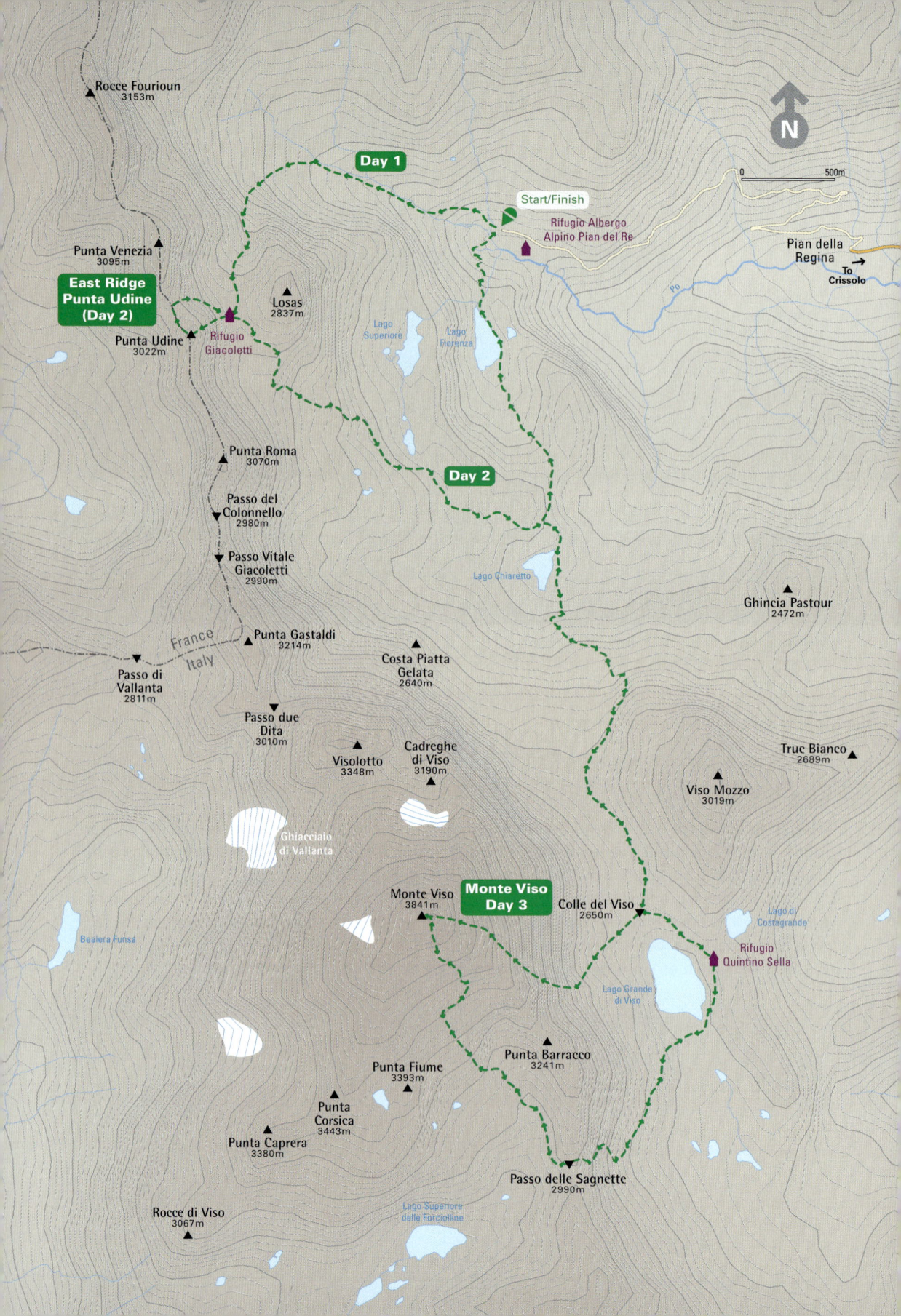

Monte Viso

Punta Udine 3,022m

A fantastic 12 pitch rock climb that starts just behind the Giacoletti hut. There are a number of other rock climbs on the east face but the East Ridge is more mountaineering in character and can easily be climbed in mountaineering boots. This makes it easy to combine with a route on Monte Viso without having to bring rock shoes.

East Ridge

Grade	AD+ 4c	Length	400m
Exposure	East	Rock type	Gabbro but not like Skye
Protection	Fully bolted	Conditions	Dry
Time	4hrs		
Descent	Scramble down the north west ridge to the Couloir del Porco Col 2,920m, then descend the east side.		

Map
1:25,000 Fraternali Editore 10 Valle Po Monviso

Alternative guidebook
Pays du Viso – Escalade en Queyras entre France et Italie by Sylvain Pusnel and Guillaume Vallot

Equipment
50m rope, 12 quickdraws

Mark Chadwick leading pitch 3 of the East Ridge.

133

ALPINE CLIMBING

ABOVE: Punta Udine, seen from the valley approach. The route follows the skyline and the descent follows the terrain to the right of the loose gully.
LEFT: Punta Udine, seen from the Giacoletti hut, route marked in red.

Hut
Rifugio Giacoletti, www.giacoletti.it tel. +39 0175 940104

Hut approach
From Pian del Re follow the good path (marks GTA, V16) to Colle delle Traversette, rising NW and reaching the height of 2,280m. From here leave the main path and turn left on another good path (marked V19) rising below Rocce Alte del Losas. The path climbs more steeply into a valley and the peak ahead of you is the Punta Udine with the East ridge in profile. Follow the path to the col and the Giacoletti hut, 2,741m (2hrs from Pian del Re).

Route approach
The route starts two minutes' walk behind the hut. You can gear up on the terrace, then follow a small path that starts immediately behind the hut and leads up into a corner.

Route description
Pitch 1 – 30m 4c	Climb the chimney, and at the top move right to a belay.
Pitch 2 – 20m 3c	Step right and climb a slab over some grassy steps to belay below an obvious crack.
Pitch 3 – 40m 4c	Climb the crack, the first move to establish yourself is quite tricky. Follow a ramp that trends left, then easy ground to a belay. You may want to split this to avoid rope drag.
Pitch 4 – 20m 4c	Climb up and right via a short chimney to a grassy ledge.
Pitch 5 – 30m 3a	Climb up over easy steps on the right side of the ridge to belay on a ledge.
Pitch 6 – 30m 3a	Follow the ledge up and left to a ridge. There aren't many runners on this pitch but it's easy.
Pitch 7 – 25m 3b	Follow the ridge.
Pitch 8 – 25m	Walk up easy ground to belay on a sloping gravel ledge below a slab.

Pitch 9 – 30m 4a Climb the slab on your right. Reach the ridge and follow it for 5m to a belay.
Pitch 10 – 40m 4c Follow the ridge then climb an obvious corner to the top of the East Ridge.
Pitch 11 – 40m 3b Follow the ridge left, just below the crest, to reach the summit block.
Pitch 12 – 20m 4a Follow the ridge for 3m then climb the slab to reach the summit and belay on boulder just below the summit.

Descent
Leaving the summit, head north-west down broken ground with the odd flash of yellow paint, this leads to a col above the Couloir del Porco, 2920m. You will find a via ferrata that leads down the side of the couloir. When you reach easy ground cross the couloir and a path leads back to the hut.

Monte Viso 3,841m

The East Ridge of Monte Viso is a long alpine route, right up there with the great ridges of the Valais. At 1,200m in length it requires good technique in moving together, with short pitches on the steeper sections. It has the beauty of a short approach from the hut and mainly solid rock. If you don't fancy the East Ridge, the South face is a great climb in its own right. It is far from a 'normal' route and should not be underestimated.

East Ridge or Voie Normal South Face

Grade	East Ridge – AD with steep sections of grade III, there is a pitch of 4c if you climb over the Tour St Robert.
	South Face – PD+ with short sections of III
Length	East Ridge – 1200m
	South Face – 600m of climbing but a much longer approach.
Exposure	East
Rock type	Metamorphic - schist
Protection	There is very little in situ equipment on the route, so you need to be able to place your own protection
Descent	South face – PD+
Conditions	Dry is best. There is often snow in the approach gully and some snow on the descent can make things easier on the knees.
Time	East Ridge – 5-6hrs for the ascent, 3-4hrs for the descent.
	South Face – 4hrs.

Map
1:25,000 Fraternali Editore 10 Valle Po Monviso

Alternative guidebook
Pays du Viso – Escalade en Queyras entre France et Italie by Sylvain Pusnel and Guillaume Vallot

Hut
Rifugio Quintino Sella, www.rifugiosella.it tel. +39 0125 366113
Albergo Ristorante Pian del Re, www.rifugiopiandelre.it tel. +39 0175 94967

ALPINE CLIMBING

The East Face of Monte Viso and the Sella Hut.

Equipment

There is usually a snow gully to climb to get onto the start of the East Ridge so you will need a pair of crampons and a light ice axe. There can be some steep snow sections to turn the Tour St Robert early in the season so, at the least, the leader would feel more comfortable with a second axe. Ask the hut guardian about this when you call to reserve. Even if the snow has melted out high up, you may still need crampons with a single axe for the approach. If you decide you don't need them, you can always leave them at the hut.

There is no glacier and no need for ice screws, but you will need an AD rack and a 40m rope.

Hut approach

To get from the hut, start at the big car park at Pian del Re (it is possible to stay in the Albergo Ristorante Pian del Re which is right in the car park). This is a popular walking spot as it is the source of the River Po, and you need to pay for the parking in the main summer season. Leave the car park and follow signposts for the V13 past the Lago Fiorenza, over a small col, then past the Lago Chiaretto and over the Colle del Viso to the hut, which sits above the Lago Grande di Viso. Look out for the small path leaving the Colle del Viso heading west towards the obvious couloir between the Pta Sella 3,449 and Monte Viso. The route to the East Ridge starts just to the right of the base of the couloir.

If you are coming from the Giacoletti hut, follow V14 south to join V13 that leads to the Sella hut, this should take about two hours.

Route description – East Ridge

You will have spotted the approach from the Colle del Viso on the walk in, so retrace your steps and follow this faint path with the odd cairn to the base of the couloir, between Pta Sella 3,449 and Monte

Monte Viso

ABOVE: Monte Viso East Ridge, approach, and route. **RIGHT**: The Tour St Robert, this can be avoided by a leftwards traverse just after the white rock above the climbers, signposted by yellow paint splashes.

Viso. As you approach you will see yellow paint splashes on the rock. You will probably need crampons to reach the rock early in the season. Follow the paint splashes up left then back right on grassy ledges leading to the crest of the ridge. The route now follows the crest of the ridge, turning most of the difficulties on the climbers left. There is the odd cairn and old orange paint dots to keep you right in the lower section of the route.

When no obvious way round an obstacle presents itself, the route is straight up. Quite a few of these short pitches are quite steep and intimidating, but the holds are big and positive.

As you move higher on the ridge the tower of the Tour St Robert looms ahead. This is turned by climbing a series of grooves trending left, then a traverse along a ledge leads to the edge of a couloir and a large ring peg. Here we put crampons back on and climb three pitches on excellent névé to regain the crest of the ridge. Later in the season this melts out and may be a bit loose. It's not horrendous and is easier than climbing the Tour St Robert. If you prefer the solid rock on the tour, climb it directly at 4c with a short abseil down the summit side.

Having skirted the Tour or climbed it directly, regain the ridge crest. This is followed with moving together and short pitches, and there is the odd peg to speed things along. Not long after the tower there is an escape ledge which runs left to the Voie Normal, marked with yellow paint. This never looks that appealing but may be a consideration if caught in a thunderstorm. There is one small section of poor rock between here and the summit, but it isn't very long, and you will soon join the South Face route on the final summit ridge.

The top has a fantastic feeling of space, being so much bigger than all the peaks around it. The view is superb, taking in the whole of the main alpine chain from Monte Rosa to the glaciers of the Vanoise.

Route description – Voie Normal South Face
PD short sections of III, 600m, 4hrs

Monte Viso is a steep mountain on all sides, so although this is the 'normal' route of ascent, it is a steep and exposed undertaking. Leaving the hut, head south round the lake looking for a smaller path that cuts off the main track to the west, the U24. It is worth spotting this the night before. The path climbs steeply to the Passo delle Sagnette 2,990m (there are a number of chains on the approach to the col). On the other side descend for about 100m, keeping an eye out for a path heading to the right (NNW) marked with yellow paint splashes. This leads to a big cairn on the moraine at the end of the small Glacier de Viso. This is more like a permanent snow field than a glacier these days.

Leaving the cairn, keep heading in the same direction looking for a ramp that cuts up to the right, about 150m above the cairn. The start of the ramp is identified by the small green and yellow Bivouac Andreotti. This is a small six-man emergency shelter equipped with blankets. From the bivouac, continue up the ramp passing a big cairn looking for yellow paint marks on the rock on your left. Follow these up a series of ramps and ledges (yellow paint), which lead up the face until you join the East Ridge just below the summit.

Descent
Leaving the summit, the descent is the reverse of the description for the South Face. Retrace your steps down the ridge for the first 150m, then follow the paint splashes down and right. The route is easy to follow but the ascent over the Passo delle Sagnette to get back to the hut feels like hard work at the end of the day. You will soon be enjoying well-earned beer and pasta outside the hut in the sun.

Rifugio Pontese with the Becco Meridionale della Tribolazione behind.

Valle dell'Orco

Situated on the south side of the Gran Paradiso national park, the Valle dell'Orco is famous for its granite rock climbs. It is sometimes described as the Yosemite of the Alps; I would argue that the rock is as good and the coffee is significantly better. The valley-based rock climbing attracts most climbers – *Valle dell'Orco* by Maurizio Oviglia (in English) available from www.versantesud.it. The alpine climbing on the mountains around the Pontese hut shares the same quality of rock but in a higher mountain setting, perfect for the warmer summer temperatures. The situation south of the Gran Paradiso also means that this area often gets good weather when the Mont Blanc Massif or the Valais is getting rained on.

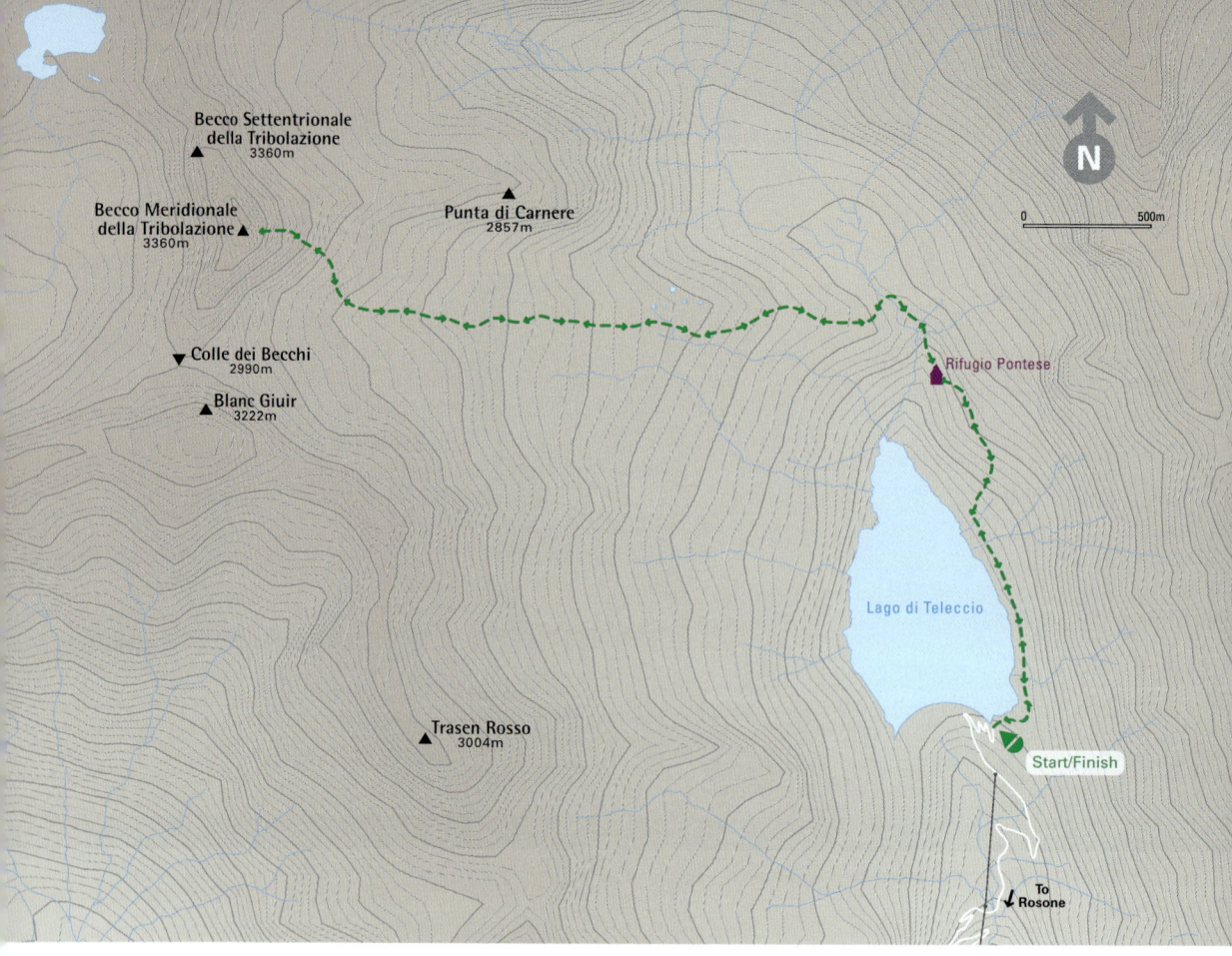

Becco Meridionale della Tribolazione 3,360m

There are lots of routes that get described as the best route of its grade in the Alps and, while many of them are good routes, not many of them quite stand up to that lofty title. However, I think the Malvassora definitely does deserve that accolade. The route is accessed from the Pontese hut, one of the friendliest huts you will find, with great food and a stunning position.

Malvassora

The Malvassora is a mountaineering undertaking requiring movement on snow early season, then exposed scrambling to get onto the route itself with a multi-pitch abseil descent.

Grade	D 4c – The pitch grades below have been left as per the local guidebook, but I felt that they were actually a full grade harder in reality. The route is very sustained at the grade with no easy pitches and steep climbing on big holds.		
Length	280m	Exposure	SSE
Rock type	Granite	Protection	Bolt belays and trad runners
Descent	Abseil	Conditions	Dry
Time	2hrs for the approach, 4hrs for the route.		

Valle dell'Orco

Malvassora line in red, the abseil descent in the lower section follows the slanting gully line to the right of the route.

Map
Carte dei Sentieri 1:25,000. Sheet 14 Valle dell'Orco, Gran Paradiso, www.escursionista.it also available as a digital download.

Alternative guidebook
Arrampicare in Piantonetto Valsoera Forzo (in Italian) by Gianni Predan and Rinaldo Sartore

Hut
Rifugio Pontese, www.rifugiopontese.it

Equipment
Depending on the time of year, you may want boots, ice axe and crampons to approach the base. These can be left at the foot of the technical climbing, as you abseil back to the same point.

The belays are all equipped with 2 bolts, some of them joined together as possible abseil anchors. You will then need a rack to protect each pitch; a set of wires (1-10), then 5 Camalot cams (0.4-2), 10 quickdraws and a few slings will do the job. 2 x 50m ropes required for the descent.

Hut approach
To reach the Pontese hut, you turn north out of the Valle dell'Orco at Rosone and drive to the dam at the Lago di Teleccio. This road could be described as sporting, or for the more expressive 'mental', so if you don't like switchbacks and drops this isn't for you. It is spectacular though, and takes you to 1,900m where there is a large car park at the east end of the dam. Leaving the parking area, a short walk of 45mins – 1hr up the east side of the lake, followed by a short climb, takes you to the hut.

On the approach to the hut, you can see the mountain really clearly. It is the beautifully shaped one with an obvious buttress running up the centre of the face, blending into the face near the top. This is the line of our route.

ALPINE CLIMBING

Mike Austin climbing on the Malvassora.

The author leading pitch 6.

Route approach

Leaving the hut, follow the path heading north until it is possible to cross the stream, Rio di Piantonetto, at a bridge. Follow the path until a junction, and take the right fork (with a sign to the Colle dei Becchi). At about 2,800m leave the path and cross rough ground heading for the south face. If there is no snow then you will find rough tracks and cairns. If there is snow, there will almost certainly be some tracks heading for the route, as it is one of the most frequented routes in the area.

Aim for the bottom right of the spur. Here, it is worth putting on a harness and helmet before scrambling up the broad buttress to the base of the steeper upper wall. Where the terrain moves from scrambling to climbing, you are looking for an open chimney at the right-hand side of the spur that splits the south-east face. There is a cairn at the base and a double bolt belay marks the start. You can leave boots / approach shoes here.

Route description

There are two starts marked in the guidebook but I couldn't find the right hand one and the pitch straight above the belay is excellent anyway.

The climbing is generally steep and exposed for the grade, but on big holds and fantastic rock, so you can enjoy the feeling of exposure.

The route above is really obvious. You pretty much go straight up with a few old pegs to help mark the way.

Pitch 1 – 4c 50m Climb the chimney corner straight above the belay, stance on the left.
Pitch 2 – 4b 40m Follow the superb corner cracks, belay on a comfortable terrace.
Pitch 3 – 4b 25m Climb the steep wall above then cross a grassy terrace to belay at the bottom of a steep corner.
Pitch 4 – 4b 40m Climb the steep sustained corner above, exiting on the right onto another comfortable stance.

Pitch 5 – 4c 40m		Start up the crest of the pillar before moving to the left-hand side of the pillar, climb the corner to a small belay ledge on the left-hand side of the pillar.
Pitch 6 – 4c 35m		Steep moves up the wall past two pitons, then move right into another steep corner, pull out of the top of this to the right to a belay.
Pitch 7 – 4c 40m		Climb the wall above, then easier moves left lead to a big ledge with an amazing smooth wall to your right. If you look above, you should be able to see the abseil chain at the top of the descent.
Pitch 8 – 4b 50m		Pull off the ledge with a few physical moves to gain a ramp that leads up and left to the summit.

From the summit you are looking across to the south side of the Gran Paradiso with stunning mountains all round.

Descent

Once you have had a drink and enjoyed the view, scramble along the ridge to the north; you are looking for a good ledge with a bolt and chain belay that hangs from an overhang. This is the top of the more difficult route 'Gran Finale' which is abseiled to the base of the spur you have been climbing. You can do this in a series of long abseils, but it may be worth making a few shorter ones high up, where there is more chance of catching your rope, then making some longer ones where the terrain is steeper. There are plenty of bolt anchors to make either option possible.

When you reach the base of the pillar you can change back into approach shoes / boots, then either scramble back down the way you came up or head a bit north (left, looking out) and scramble down to find an abseil anchor. A series of abseil anchors approx. 48m apart (there is the odd little walk between anchors) now lead down the side of the gully. The left trending nature means that anything knocked by parties above would miss you. Then walk back to the hut. If you are tired, or the rock / grass ledge you scrambled up is a bit slippery, it is definingly worth considering the abseil option rather than an exposed scramble.

The author climbing above the notch on the initial section of the Aiguille de la Vanoise.

Kate Scott on the Aiguille de la Vanoise with the Grande Casse behind.

La Vanoise

The Vanoise is not an area that's on many alpinists radar. It is most famous for large ski resorts, however the Vanoise National Park has an amazing wild feel to it, and though not famed for the quality of its rock it does have some hidden gems.

Aiguille de la Vanoise 2,796m

We are going to look at the traverse of the Aiguille de la Vanoise, an amazing ridge traverse that clears quickly after bad weather.

Traverse of the Aiguille de la Vanoise E-W

Grade	AD 3c	Length	250m vertical
Exposure	Mainly on the south side of the ridge	Rock type	Limestone
Protection	Mainly bolts	Descent	West ridge
Conditions	Dry	Time	3-4hrs for the route.

Map
IGN 1:25,000 Les Trois Vallées Modane 3534OT

Alternative guidebook
Le Topo de la Vanoise, Philippe Deslandes and James Merel

La Vanoise

Approach to the traverse of the Aiguille de la Vanoise.

Equipment
50m rope, AD rack with 8 quickdraws. The route is most fun in light mountaineering boots, but you could climb in rock shoes. Early in the season, if there is still snow, you may need boots and a light ice axe for the approach to the start of the route, check with the hut guardian.

Hut
Refuge du Col de la Vanoise, also known as the Felix Faure hut. There are some amazing camping and bivvy spots in the area but this isn't allowed in the Vanoise National Park.
www.refugecoldelavanoise.ffcam.fr   tel. +33 (0)4 79 08 25 23

Hut approach
Park at the bottom of the ski lifts at Fontanettes, just outside of Pralognan-la-Vanoise. The approach takes the path of the GR55. Head north-west initially, under the ski lifts and past the Refuge Les Barmettes, following a beautiful valley. Crossing the Lacs des Vaches on the stepping stones is brilliant, then the path steepens to the hut. It is also possible to approach via the south side of the Aiguille de la Vanoise. A nice loop is to ascend one way and descend the other.

Route approach
Leave the hut and head north-west towards a grassy ramp that leads up onto the ridge. As you approach you will find faint tracks in the scree slope which will lead you up the ramp. Turn some steep rocks on the left to reach a brèche (gap). At the time of our ascent there were two wooden poles jammed into the ground which marked the start of the route proper.

ALPINE CLIMBING

Kate Scott crossing the Lac des Vaches.

Route description

With a route like this a description is almost superfluous as you just keep on the crest until you reach the top then carry on along the ridge to easy ground.

I will of course be of more help than that. Above the brèche with the sticks, climb the ridge and trend round onto the north side. Regain the crest and follow it with excursions onto the south side. You are generally following the line of least resistance on the best rock. There are a few bolts to help you on your way.

After a few hundred metres the ridge eases in angle and becomes broader, here you can relax and walk for a little bit to reach the east summit of the Vanoise. Apparently, it is possible to escape on the south side from here, but it looked pretty loose to me.

Leave the east summit and follow a track on the south side. When it reaches an area of smooth slabs, climb up to the ridge crest. The next section is a spectacular knife edge of limestone in a spectacular position. Stay on the south side of the ridge to reach the west summit.

Descent

Carry on along the ridge, this feels quite exposed in places. There are bolts roughly every 10m, and some of the downclimbing is quite steep but never more difficult than 3c. When the ridge becomes steep and the rock quality deteriorates, descend on the south side with bolts for protection. Continue along the ridge and where it becomes horizontal, make a 20m abseil on the south side to reach a path which leads back towards the hut. Do not be tempted to cut the corner on the descent or you will end up amongst a series of rocky bluffs.

Mont Blanc at dawn, seen from the Dent du Géant.

Mont Blanc Massif (Chamonix)

The Mont Blanc Massif encompasses some of the most famous peaks in the Alps. Mont Blanc is obviously the crown, and a route to the highest point in Western Europe is on most alpinists tick list. While an ascent of Mont Blanc is a great thing there are lots of other amazing routes that can be climbed that offer an experience with less problematic hut bookings.

The speed of access via cable car from the alpine centres of Chamonix and Courmayeur make it possible to ascend routes in a day that would normally require a day's approach to a hut. This has the obvious advantage that quick, easy access can maximise your climbing time, but it also has the disadvantage that some of the routes can be unpleasantly busy. So, I would suggest that you don't climb in the massif in August when most of Europe seems to descend on the area.

The other consideration with the Mont Blanc Massif is that it has been particularly affected by global warming. Many of the approaches and routes are in the middle of deglaciation, so are more prone to rockfall.

I find the best time to climb in the massif is late June through to mid-July, or when the snow starts to melt and the rock is exposed for the first time that year. Rockfall can become so serious in some years that the local Maire (town hall), has closed the huts on the Gouter route on Mont Blanc to encourage

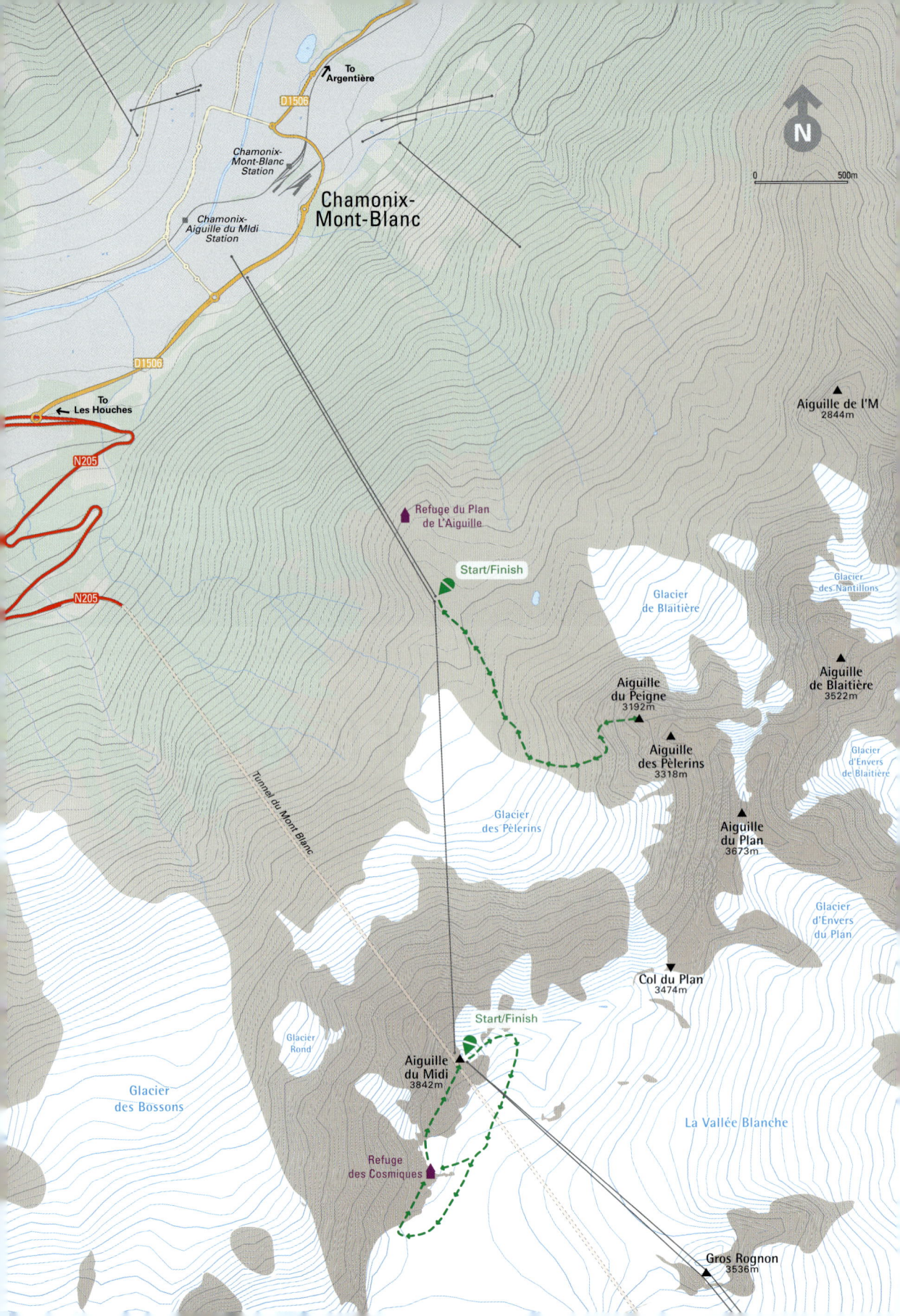

climbers not to climb the mountain, exposing themselves and potential rescuers to the high risk of rockfall. September can also be a good month, as things cool down the hazard reduces, though the mountains will not miraculously stick themselves back together again.

There are a number of other guidebooks to the Mont Blanc Massif that cover all the classic routes, so I have just included a number of personal favourites to get you started. Then, if you enjoy climbing here, you can branch out.

In selecting the routes, I have chosen routes that are a mix of accessibility and quality to give you the best introduction to the range.

Aiguille du Midi 3,842m

The Cosmiques Arête on the Aiguille du Midi is possibly the most famous day route in the Alps, and rightly so – great positions, fun climbing and amazing views. Easy access from the Aiguille du Midi cable car means that you can snatch a day between the weather or other plans.

Cosmiques Arête

The ease of access does mean that the route can be busy. I would make sure you get an early cable car or consider staying in the Cosmiques hut the night before to avoid the crowds. There have been a number of rockfalls on the route in recent years, mainly on the south side as the glacier which supported the ridge has retreated, I would only consider an ascent before mid-July when the route is well frozen together.

The route can also be combined with an ascent of the Arête Laurence which is the rock / mixed ridge that descends west from the Cosmiques hut.

Grade	AD 4c	**Length**	300m of altitude gain but there is plenty of climbing in that 300m.
Exposure	South	**Rock type**	Granite
Protection	Mixed	**Descent**	Cable car
Conditions	The route can be climbed in pretty much any conditions.	**Time**	Anywhere from 2½ - 5hrs depending on traffic.

Map
1:25,000 IGN Mini Carte de Randonnee M3531ET

Alternative guidebook
Rockfax Chamonix by Charlie Boscoe and Luke Davies

Equipment
AD rack and glacier travel kit

Hut
Cosmiques hut

ALPINE CLIMBING

Aiguille du Midi, red line indicates approach and traverse of Arête Laurence, then green for the route.

Hut approach
Take the cable car to the Aiguille du Midi then descend the exposed east ridge. Where the angle eases, spread out the rope in glacier travel mode and walk under the south face of the Aiguille du Midi to reach the hut. You will see all sorts of rope techniques being used in this area and people wandering about un-roped. Don't be influenced by them as there are some big, hidden crevasses in the area.

Route approach
Arête Laurence – Do not ascend to the Cosmiques hut, continue under it and keep heading west until it is possible to scramble up onto the rock ridge above you.
Cosmiques Arête – Follow the well-worn track towards the Cosmiques hut then trend right to a ledge next to the Abri Simond hut, which is on the col just east of the Cosmiques hut. This basic bivouac hut is open when the Cosmiques hut is closed.

Route description
Arête Laurence – Follow the ridge towards the Cosmiques hut with some great views and positions, the rock is generally good, the only awkward section is where you have to downclimb across a slab not long before the hut. You arrive on the hut terrace where you have to take your boots off to walk through the hut. It is always nice to stop for a coffee before carrying on to the Cosmiques Arête.
Cosmiques Arête – Starting at the ledge on the east side of the Abri Simond hut, ascend a groove / chimney for a couple of hundred metres, you can mix moving together and short pitches. Where the terrain steepens, trend right to the ridge then traverse right on some ledges to a flat, exposed section of ridge. Here, you can either climb straight up to a small summit or trend right then back left to the same point.

This is the first abseil / downclimb and can be a bit of a bottleneck. There is a big ring bolt and a sling in situ so you can make a 25m abseil, which is a little awkward as you need to descend for 5m, then climb / step awkwardly over a ridge and then descend to a big ledge. Alternatively, you can just climb down. Do not be tempted to abseil straight down as it is very awkward to regain the ridge.

When you are on the ledge you can see the second abseil anchor just ahead of you. Scramble down to the anchor and make a 20m abseil down a chimney line to a ledge on the right. You can change back into climbing mode now.

Move along the ledge in the direction of the Midi for a few metres, then climb a chimney exiting right onto a ledge with a peg belay. Step down off the ledge and make a few moves down and right before climbing a groove in a long pitch to a col.

Mont Blanc Massif (Chamonix)

Mark Senior on the Cosmiques Arête.

Above the col, climb up a short distance and then take a ramp that leads up and right. The ramp is underneath an overhang, when it runs out make a few steep moves and climb up to the ridge. Follow the ridge to a big tower. Turn this on the right by climbing down a few metres and then walk round the tower on a big ledge, before climbing back to the ridge. Follow the ridge to the next steep wall.

Make steep moves up a wall, this is the crux of the route (there are drilled holes for crampon points to slot into). You can either belay on the ledge above the wall (bolts) or clip the bolts and move right into a tight chimney. Climb the chimney then exit left onto a ledge.

At the left end of the ledge, step down onto the north side of the ridge and follow some ledges to the base of an open chimney. Climb the chimney. Where it stops you can either move left and make a few steep moves to regain the ridge or do something similar on the right.

Follow the ridge to a ladder, climb the ladder to the viewing platform at the Aiguille du Midi.

You are now in everyone's holiday snaps.

Soos Donaldson climbing on the Cosmiques Arête.

ALPINE CLIMBING

Aiguille du Peigne at sunset, seen from the Plan de l'Aiguille.

Aiguille du Peigne 3,192m

The Peigne is a fantastic rock peak in the Chamonix Aiguilles. The rock is excellent, and the summit is spectacular. The peak clears quickly after bad weather and the access is straightforward.

Voie Normal

There are many great rock routes on the Peigne and the route we have included is the classic Voie Normal, this is far from 'Normal' with lots of moving together and exposed pitches of 4b leading to a spectacular summit. The route is a great place to hone the skills of moving quickly and reading the terrain, as the route finding is complicated.

Grade	AD 4b	Length	600m
Exposure	SW	Rock type	Granite
Protection	Mixed	Descent	Abseil and downclimbing
Conditions	Dry	Time	4-5hrs up, 2-3hrs down.

Map
1:25,000 IGN Mini Carte de Randonnee M3531ET Mont Blanc

Alternative guidebook
Rockfax Chamonix by Charlie Boscoe and Luke Davies

Mont Blanc Massif (Chamonix)

Equipment
You may need an ice axe and crampons for the approach. AD rack, 50m rope. Rock shoes make the upper pitches more enjoyable.

Hut
It is possible to climb the route in a day from the first lift. The time varies through the summer, so I would only suggest doing this when the early lift is operational. Alternatively, bivouacking between dusk and dawn is tolerated and a really nice way to spend an evening.
There is also a really comfortable hut below the mid station of the lift.
Refuge du Plan de l'Aiguille, www.refuge-plan-aiguille.com

Hut approach
If you are staying at the Refuge du Plan de l'Aiguille, come out of the lift station at the Plan de l'Aiguille then follow the path north-west that runs almost under the lift line to the hut.

Route approach
Leave the lift station and follow the path that heads SSE. The path parallels what is left of the Glacier des Pélerins. At a fork in the path, carry on in the same direction (the right fork leads onto the glacier and in the direction of the Grands Mulets hut). The path follows the crest of a moraine until you reach a flattening just above point 2,468m on the map. There is an area of glacier marked on the map in a bowl, this is now a semi-permanent snow patch that disappears in a hot summer. You can gear up here.

Route description
If the snow patch is there, climb it by the easiest line to reach the rock above, there are usually some good steps in place. This snow is in the shade and is often hard, requiring an ice axe and crampons. When you reach the rock continue up until you reach an obvious horizontal path, the rock is usually clear of snow before you reach the path. If the snow patch has melted out, the easiest way to climb the rock is on the right side of the bay, there are a few moves of grade III.

Approach to the Peigne, Voie Normal route.

Will Harris on the upper section of the Papillons Arête which is common with the Voie Normal route.

Tim Connolly climbing above the notch on the Voie Normal route.

When you reach the path, follow it heading left (north-west), the path climbs round a couple of buttresses with two obvious notches in the ridge. This is easy to follow and after 100m you arrive in a wide gully, bounded on the left side by the Papillons Arête. This gully is often referred to as the South West Gully or the Papillons Gully.

The route follows the gully to start with. Climb a series of ledges (with height, the rock gets better). Climb initially on the left, then the right, following the easiest climbing, the difficulty is nowhere more than III. As the gully begins to narrow you are faced with a corner crack. Climb this (4b), and about 15m above this look out for an obvious thread belay on your left. This is at the start of a rising ramp that leads out left to join the top section of the Papillons Arête.

Follow the arête in some superb positions. When the route is blocked by a difficult step, turn this by slabs on the left then make a steep, athletic move back to the ridge. Follow the ridge more easily on a ledge that runs above the Peigne slabs. Be very careful with any loose rock as there are usually climbers on the slabs below.

Follow the ledges for 100m and, at a cairn, turn right and climb blocks and slabs to a ridge. Descend slightly, then climb a gully with some loose rock to a notch. Climb loose ground above to a col with a big pinnacle on your right. Move together on a rising traverse on a ledge to another notch and ledge. Above you is the South West Ridge; this also leads to the summit but is more difficult (V). This is a good place to change from mountaineering boots to rock shoes, you can leave your boots here as you will pass here on the way down.

The way ahead has lots of possible variations, having climbed most of these over the years I would suggest the following is the best option.

Leave the ledge and climb down a few moves until you reach a bolt, clip this and move up and right into a crack system. Climb this either in one very long pitch or split it to arrive in an overhung corner belay; this almost feels like a cave with a fixed anchor. The route now traverses right and there are some pegs to keep you on the right track. If you pass a big ledge with quartz on it you are on the right route. Keep heading up and right, the ledge morphs into a groove then steepens into a chimney which leads to the ESE ridge. Belay at the base of the open chimney.

Climb the chimney past some pegs (4c), the climbing is on positive holds. Where the chimney becomes steep, move out onto the right arête in a superb position, belay when you reach the ridge. Follow the crest of the ridge, sometimes easier on the left or right, to reach a notch.

Make a 5m abseil diagonally onto a ledge, then climb through a slot to reach the summit.

Descent

Make a 25m abseil onto a ledge (make sure you have a 50m rope as 25m is only just enough), then scramble down to another abseil anchor. Make 3 x 20m abseils to reach the quartz ledge you climbed past earlier. Reverse the traverse to the cave belay then make two abseils to get back to the ledge where you changed your boots.

Ian Hope on the crenellated upper ridge of the Peigne.

Reverse your route of ascent until you reach the top of the Papillons Arête, then make a 25m abseil back into the SW gully. Climb down this, although, depending on how comfortable you are with downclimbing, you may want to make a couple of abseils to reach the approach traverse. Reverse this and climb down onto the snow.

When you reach the start of the traverse path it is really tempting to follow the paths that lead down and right, it is possible to follow these paths then make a series of abseils onto easy ground. However, these paths are well worn from climbers going down them not liking the look of the terrain and coming back up again. Retracing your steps from the morning is faster and easier.

Mark Dearnley on the Perrons traverse.

Matt Spencley on the final section of the Perrons traverse.

Les Perrons de Vallorcine

The Perrons lies at the north-east end of the Aiguilles Rouges just inside Switzerland.

Les Perrons 2,673m

The mountain offers some amazing bolted rock climbing on its south side, but we are going to focus on the incredible mountaineering journey offered by the traverse of the ridge from the summit of the Aiguille du Van to the Pointe de l'Ifala.

Traverse of the Perrons East - West

The route can be traversed in either direction but is easiest in this direction. Going east to west also means you are climbing with the incredible backdrop of the whole Mont Blanc Massif in front of you.

Grade	AD 4a	**Length**	800m
Exposure	NE and SW	**Rock type**	Microgranite
Protection	Leader placed, except for the abseil anchors.	**Descent**	Scramble and walk from the Brèche du Perron.
Conditions	Dry on the route, snow on the approach is not an issue.	**Time**	6-8hrs for the round trip.

Les Perrons de Vallorcine

Perrons approach.

Map
1:25,000 IGN Chamonix 3630 OT

Alternative guidebook
The Aiguille Rouges 2 by Michel Piola

Equipment
AD rack. A 50m rope will suffice but no shorter; in fact, a 60m does make one of the abseils more comfortable. You may need an ice axe and crampons for the approach, but you can see if this is necessary from the car.

Hut
N/A (day route)

Route approach
Park at the Emosson dam. Walk across the dam then take the track heading south, signposted to the Refuge de Loriaz. After about 400m, turn right at a cairn and follow a small path which trends up and right (west). You are aiming for the rock barrier that guards the entrance to the snowfield (this may melt out later in the summer and become a scree slope) on the north-east side of the Aiguille du Van.

Route description
There are good ledges to gear up on under the rock barrier. Look for the rock that has been most travelled and the odd bolt. Climb the rocks straight up, then right and back left past some bolts to easier ground. Either climb the snow or, once it has gone, small tracks on the left side of the scree until a

traverse right can be made into a gully. Climb this to an obvious notch in the ridge between the North and South summits of the Van.

Descend from the notch on the north side then take a rising traverse back to the crest of the ridge (this avoids going over the South summit of the Van.) Follow the ridge, turning obstacles as they present themselves to reach the summit of the Grand Perron. Scramble past the summit to reach an abseil anchor. Make an abseil down onto a sloping green slab, walk across this to an anchor on the edge. The take-off for the next abseil is quite awkward.

Abseil steeply down the line of a chimney crack to a ledge. Go back to moving together mode and scramble down to a third abseil anchor and make a 20m abseil into a notch. Sort the rope here and either make a short pitch which leads up a groove onto a platform and belay below a steep wall, or run that and the next section into one long pitch. If you do that, climb to the platform then make steep moves up the wall (III+) above on positive holds. As the angle eases, trend slightly left and climb to a ledge and chain belay (abseil anchor for those going in the opposite direction).

The next section of ridge can be turned by a rising series of ledges on the right (north) side. Carry on along the crest until it narrows and downclimb the ridge in an airy position to a ledge and bolt abseil anchors. Abseil 23m down a steep wall to a good ledge and bolt anchors. Make a second, 25m abseil to small ledges and a bolt, this is where having the ability to abseil 30m using a 60m rope might feel nice.

Scramble along ledges in the line of the ridge and down into another brèche.

Climb a really nice series of grooves heading up and right, then up a corner past a peg leading to a ledge below a big, jammed block (cams 0.5, 1 and 2).

Climb round the block and up to the ridge crest. Follow the crest in some great positions until the angle eases and you reach the summit of Pointe de l'Ifala.

Descent

Continue along the ridge in the direction of the Brèche du Perron, turning various gendarmes on their right (north) side. Do not be tempted to cut the corner early before the Brèche as this will lead into steep, loose ground.

Pick up a faint path that leads down on the north side of the Brèche, past some lakes and down to a good path that leads to the dinosaur footprints. Follow the path back to the Emosson dam.

The author on the traverse of the Entrèves with the Dent du Géant and Grandes Jorasses in the background.

Mont Blanc Massif (Courmayeur) Routes from the Torino Hut

The Torino hut is a large (200 beds) hut on the Italian side of the Vallée Blanche. Its ease of access via the Skyway cable car from Courmayeur makes it a justifiably popular venue. It is possible to bring up a change of clothing for the evenings and bring kit for multiple activities.

In this guide we have included four routes: the Aiguilles d'Entrèves and Aiguilles Marbrées, which can both easily be climbed from the first lift, and the Dent du Géant and Rochefort Arête, which are longer undertakings.

The Torino is also the starting point for an ascent of the Kuffner Arête on Mont Maudit and the excellent rock climbs on the satellite peaks of Mont Blanc. The Tour Ronde is also regularly climbed from here but, as a result of large amounts of rockfall on the normal route in recent seasons, I have not included it.

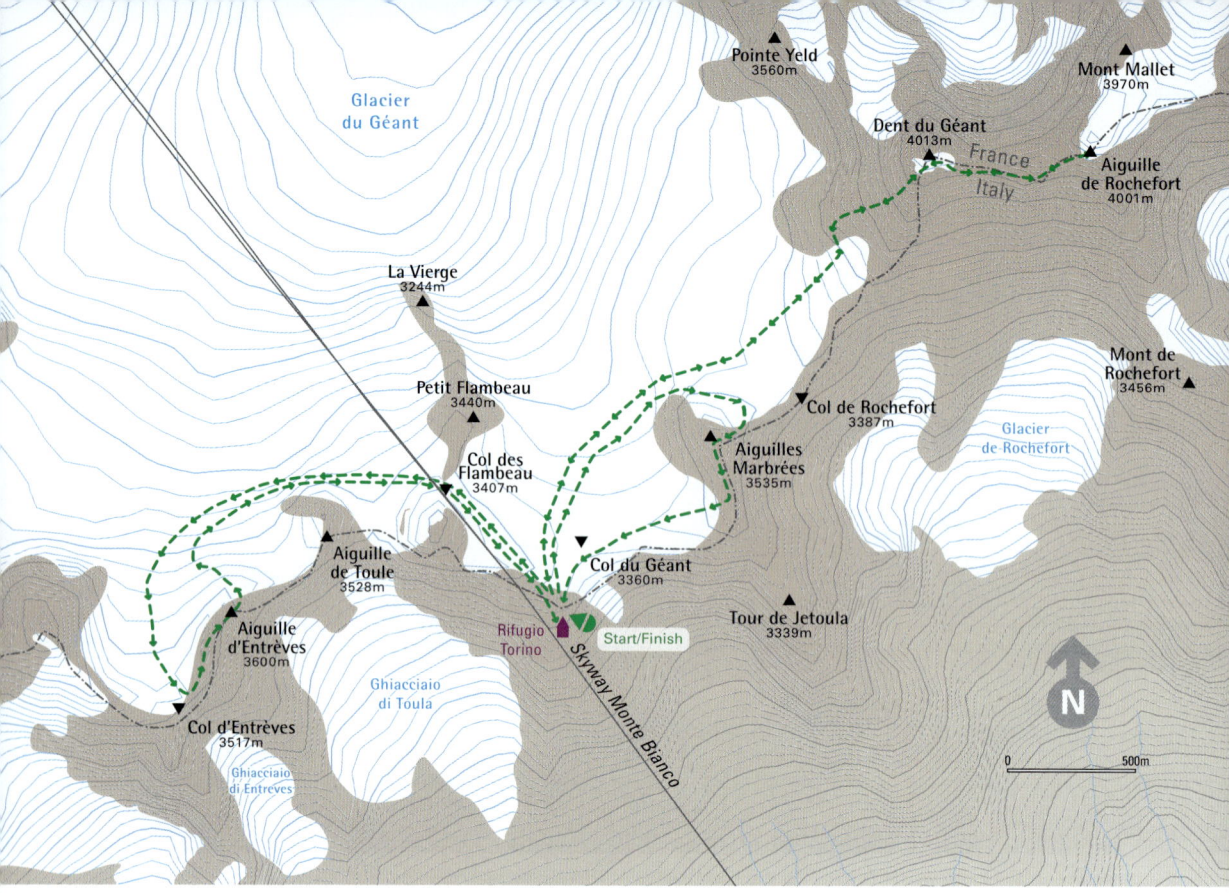

Aiguilles Marbrées 3,535m

Aiguilles Marbrées Traverse NW to SE

To many this would be considered a training or acclimatisation route, a role it serves incredibly well, offering a variety of techniques: glacier travel, pitching, moving together and an abseil in descent. This however is not the whole story, as the route actually offers some great climbing in superb positions and offers a day out that is much more than just a training climb.

You can climb the route from either direction. The direction described has the advantage of making the longer walk on the glacier in the morning when the snow is more frozen and the return to the hut / lift is much shorter.

Grade	PD IV	**Length**	200m
Exposure	North then SE	**Rock type**	Granite
Protection	Leader placed	**Descent**	South-east ridge / abseil
Conditions	The route can be climbed in any conditions but is better when there is still some snow.	**Time**	4hr round trip

Map
1:25,000 IGN Mini Carte de Randonnee M3531ET Mont Blanc

Mont Blanc Massif (Courmayeur)

Alternative guidebook
Rockfax Chamonix by Charlie Boscoe and Luke Davies

Equipment
Glacier travel and PD rack.

Hut
Torino Hut, www.rifugiotorino.com/
tel. +39 0165 844034

Hut approach
Skyway from Courmayeur or from Chamonix via Aiguille du Midi and via the Panoramique gondola, or a walk across the Vallée Blanche.

Mark and Elisabeth Senior on the traverse of the Marbrées.

Route approach
Leave the Torino / Skyway and get onto the glacier. Go past the Col du Géant, then climb up the glacier past the north end of the peak itself. Head east towards the Col de Rochefort. You want to climb up onto the ridge that descends from the Aiguille Marbrées Nord towards the Col. The exact access will depend on the snow.

Route description
When you reach the ridge, you can decide if you want to continue with crampons or not. If the rock is dry, it is much more fun without.

Follow the ridge crest until the rock becomes steeper and more compact, then climb cracks on the crest of the ridge to a belay under an awkward perched block.

Make awkward moves onto this block (more like a slab you have to climb over). Then step down and across a gap to belay on good spikes.

The approach to the Aiguilles Marbrées.

Step left then climb up a series of ledges to below the summit block. You can climb the summit block directly at 4b, or more easily if you traverse slightly right then climb up the ridge, just right of the summit and onto the top. Reverse this route back to below the summit block.

The ridge now turns south and you follow the crest. The route weaves through some pinnacles, the first is turned on the south-west side, the second on the north-east. When back on the crest the ridge dips down to a col. It is possible to descend from here by abseiling down a gully; there will either be one or two abseils from fixed bolts. A 50m rope will suffice and the exact length will depend on the snow level. Later in the season when the snow in this gully melts out this area can be very prone to rockfall. However, you can continue along the ridge climbing a steep wall to a pinnacle, then following the ridge with one abseil to easier ground and then south-west onto the glacier.

Mark and Elisabeth Senior on the traverse of the Marbrées.

Descent
See route description.

Aiguilles d'Entrèves 3,600m

Aiguilles d'Entrèves Traverse SW to NE

This is one of the best short alpine routes you will find anywhere. It has everything: a glacial approach and descent, exposed climbing on excellent granite with a high mountain ambiance and incredible views in every direction. It can be climbed in a day from a lift, or you can stay in the Torino hut and combine it with other objectives.

Grade	AD 4	**Length**	200m
Exposure	Ascend the SW ridge and descend the NE.	**Rock type**	Granite
Protection	The route lends itself to using spikes and terrain features to wrap the rope round. There are a few bolts and some opportunities for trad gear.	**Descent**	Scramble, with a couple of possible abseils.
Conditions	Climbable in most conditions but more fun if the ridge crest is dry.	**Time**	6hr round trip from the lift.

Map
1:25,000 IGN Mini Carte de Randonnee M3531ET Mont Blanc

Mont Blanc Massif (Courmayeur)

Alternative guidebook
Rockfax Chamonix by Charlie Boscoe and Luke Davies

Hut
Torino hut, www.rifugiotorino.com/
tel. +39 0165 844034

Equipment
50m rope, glacier travel kit and AD rack

Hut approach
As for Aiguille d'Entrèves.

Mike Austin on the traverse of the Aiguilles d'Entrèves.

Route approach
Rope up for glacier travel then head through the Col des Flambeau. (Le Petit Flambeau is a nice little scramble when it still has snow on it and is an incredible viewpoint. I had my wedding pictures taken there). Head north-west following the blue dotted ski line on the map until a flattening under the Aiguille de Toule. Head west then start a rising traverse towards the Tour Ronde, you need to take quite a big loop to avoid some pretty big crevasses as you come into the valley that leads to the Col d'Entrèves. You can see the route in profile on your left as you head up the glacier to the Col d'Entrèves, it should take about an hour from the hut / lift station to the col.

Route description
You can take off crampons and shorten the rope at the col. This is a good place to put your ice screws away, so they don't get scratched and damaged on the rock and get out your rock gear.

Scramble along the ridge. There are loads of spikes to flick the rope over, making it really easy to move together, and the climbing is generally on the right side of the ridge. When the ridge drops steeply, you can now downclimb awkwardly into a deep notch (this is sometimes abseiled). Alternatively, backtrack

Aiguille d'Entrèves Traverse, approach and route.

Mike Austin on the traverse of the Aiguille d'Entrèves.

The author on the crux moves.

about 20m then climb easily down a ramp on the right (a little loose in places) to below the notch, where a few steep moves lead you into the notch.

The section climbing out of the notch on the north side is quite athletic, but when you commit there are some good holds that lead onto the crest. The next section of the ridge is spectacular, with a few bolts for protection leading to a ledge and bolt belay.

The next couple of moves are the crux of the route. In a crack just to the right of the belay there is often a jammed sling, and with a high left foot and pull on the sling you can reach up for a good hold on the right (4b and A0 or probably about 5b without the sling). Follow the ridge above to a bolt belay at the summit.

Most people don't actually stand on the summit as the belay is just under it. Head right from here, across an exposed stretch of ridge into a notch with a groove leading down the north side and a bolt belay at its top. Either climb or abseil down about 5m to a ledge and bolt belay on the right. From here you can either downclimb or abseil 25m to a ledge. If there is any snow or ice about, I would suggest abseiling. There is a good spike on the ledge for a belay. You now need to downclimb on the left side of the crest and around a corner to reach another bolt anchor. You can abseil 25m or downclimb again depending on conditions. You are now on a big ledge so time for some fuel and a rope sort out.

Head along the ridge on pretty easy ground, where there is often snow when the rest of the ridge can be dry. When the ridge starts to ascend, avoid a block on the right that leads into a notch. You can turn the next section on the right or the left. I always go left as I think the rock is better and I witnessed a nasty accident when someone pulled off a block on the right and broke their leg.

Step down through the notch, then traverse a few metres before being able to climb back to the ridge, where easy moving together leads to the final summit. There are two options to get off the ridge, depending on conditions:

1. Carry on along the ridge towards the Aiguille de Toule – heading north-east. A bit of route finding is required to find the best way down onto the glacier, head left a little until an obvious ramp leads back right. Scramble down this to a ledge on the right then follow the road most travelled (crampon scratches) down a few moves on the left to where you can climb down to the snow / glacier. Put crampons on here, then traverse under the ridge to a blunt snow crest that leads down onto the glacier.
2. If the traverse mentioned above is icy, as it often is later in the season, instead of taking the rightward ramp carry on north-west. Where the terrain steepens you will find an abseil anchor (usually a collection of slings and tat). Make a short abseil (15m) onto the blunt snow ridge mentioned above.

Mont Blanc Massif (Courmayeur)

Descent
Head down the blunt snow rib and head north-west to regain the track you walked in on. If you are tempted to cut the corner from the end of the blunt rib towards the Aiguille de Toule, consider the conditions very carefully as there are some very big crevasses that will almost certainly be hidden.

Dent du Géant 4,013m

When you look above the town of Courmayeur your eyes can't do anything but be drawn to the shard of granite reaching into the sky. This incredible needle of rock is the Dent du Géant.

South West Face

When you look at the Géant it is hard to imagine that it can be climbed at anything approaching a reasonable grade, but the addition of fixed ropes by the Courmayeur guides has made this possible. However you feel about fixed ropes or other artificial aids on a mountain, these ropes have been in place for so long that they have become part of the history and story of the mountain. It is still possible to be a purist and climb the route entirely free, this takes the grade up to 5c.

It is worth considering tactics on the Géant. The route faces south-west and being a rock climb is best enjoyed in the sun, so there is little need for an early start. However, the approach to the route is loose and dangerous once it dries out later in the season.

When the weather is good with no afternoon storms (the Géant is a perfect lightning conductor), I have climbed the route in a day, coming up from Courmayeur on the first lift then getting back for the last lift in the afternoon. This required the approach to have plenty of snow on it to allow for swift, easy movement throughout the approach. If you are staying at the hut, it is difficult not to get swept away

Dent du Géant seen from the Rochefort Arête.

ALPINE CLIMBING

with the general enthusiasm for an early start, and if the weather dictates that you need to be down early, you will have no option but to climb in the cold and the shade. One alternative is to climb the Rochefort Arête then climb the Géant on the way back when it is in the sun. This link up has to be one of the finest in the Alps, delivering two of the Mont Blanc Massifs finest summits.

A final consideration is whether to climb in mountaineering or rock boots. I prefer baggy rock boots as this allows me to move more quickly over the rock. If it's cold I will use some thin leather gloves to make it easier to grip the fixed ropes.

Grade	AD+ IV if you use the fixed ropes.	**Length**	350m
Exposure	SW	**Rock type**	Granite
Protection	Mainly in situ with a fixed rope.	**Descent**	Abseil, then reverse of approach.
Conditions	Dry rock with snow on the approach.	**Time**	5hrs up, 3hrs the return.

Map
1:25,000 IGN Mini Carte de Randonnee M3531ET Mont Blanc

Alternative guidebook
Rockfax Chamonix by Charlie Boscoe and Luke Davies

Equipment
You don't need much kit because of the fixed ropes: eight quickdraws including some 4ft slings (which can be wrapped round the fixed rope as runners), a half set of nuts and cams 1 and 2 will plug any gaps in the fixed equipment. Glacier travel kit for the approach. You will need either a 60m rope or two half ropes.

Hut
Torino hut, www.rifugiotorino.com/
tel. +39 0165 844034

Hut approach
As for Aiguilles d'Entrèves

Mark Dearnley on the upper section of the Dent du Géant.

Route approach
The hut and lift are situated right next to the glacier so you can come outside, put on your crampons and set the rope up for glacier travel. Walk past the Col du Géant then pass to the north of the Aiguilles Marbrées. Walk up the steepening glacier heading north-east into a bowl, you are aiming for a couloir that drops from a col on the ridge below the Géant. Climb this couloir, if it has melted out the rocks to the left are pretty straightforward. At the top of the couloir turn right and follow the ridge, where it blends into the face trend up and left. When you get to a big triangular rock head right, cairns show the way. This leads to a ridge that leads back left to the 'Salle à Manger' – a big flat area close to the base of the Géant.

This is the point where you can leave ice axes and crampons and get your head into rock climbing mode.

Mont Blanc Massif (Courmayeur)

The approach to the Dent du Géant.

Kate Scott approaching the summit of the Dent du Géant.

Route description
There was a rockfall at the base of the route a number of years ago, so if a rock on the first pitch looks out of keeping with the rest of the route, this is why.

Standing at the Salle à Manger looking up at the Géant, head left. The route starts by climbing down and left to reach a belay. Head up and left passing plenty of bolts, there is usually a fixed rope here and the climbing is about 5a free. This leads, in about 15m, to the original route. There is a big metal ring and some bolts for a belay.

Climb the gully above the belay to a ledge at 30m (4b/4c), the ledge is at the foot of the Burgener Slabs where the fixed rope begins. The route finding now is somewhat easy, follow the fixed rope for 100m. You can use a sling round the rope for a quick runner, and its anchor points for belays. If you choose to free climb, the climbing is actually really good and it seems a shame the rope is there.

Where the route traverses right, I think it is easier to climb the rock on some really good flakes rather than pull awkwardly on the rope.

The traverse leads to a steep corner (4c), then a chimney (4b), that leads via an exposed traverse to the top of Pointe Sella 4,009m, the lower of the two summits. Climb down into the notch between the two summits via a chimney (III), before more fixed rope leads to the summit of Pointe Graham 4,013m.

Descent
It is possible to retrace your steps then abseil down the line of ascent, but this seems ridiculous as you will be descending through any parties behind you and ruining their day.

It is much better to retrace your steps to the bottom of the chimney that descends from the summit of Pointe Sella and then abseil down the south face in 4 x 30m abseils. This will land you back on the snow of the Salle à Manger. Be very careful not to abseil too far between anchors as the wall is very steep, and if you go too far you may end up spinning in space. It would also be very difficult to retrieve a stuck rope so if you are using two 50m ropes I would avoid the temptation to make long abseils.

Retrace your steps from the route approach back to the hut.

The Rochefort Arête, seen from the summit of the Dent du Géant.

Aiguille de Rochefort 4,001m

Rochefort Arête Traverse

The Rochefort Arête is one of the classic snow crests of the Alps. Like all great snow crests, if you get the conditions right you will have an amazing day, get them wrong (ice, not snow) and you are in for a scary and dangerous time. The arête is the border between France and Italy, and threads an incredible line through some of the best high mountain scenery in the Alps, with incredible views in every direction and an amazing sense of space.

Grade	AD II	Length	200m vertical from the base of the Dent du Géant.
Exposure	East and west	Rock type	Granite
Protection	Mixed	Descent	Reverse the route of ascent.
Conditions	Snow, especially important on the approach.	Time	5hrs up and 3-4hrs down.

Map
1:25,000 IGN Mini Carte de Randonnee M3531ET Mont Blanc

Alternative guidebook
Rockfax Chamonix by Charlie Boscoe and Luke Davies

Mont Blanc Massif (Courmayeur)

Rochefort Arête seen from the summit.

Equipment
Glacier travel kit plus AD rack. A 60m rope will make the abseils much easier.

Hut
Torino hut, www.rifugiotorino.com/
tel. +39 0165 844034

Hut approach
As for Aiguilles d'Entrèves

Approaching the summit of the Aiguille de Rochefort.

Route approach
Follow the route description for the Dent du Géant to the Salle à Manger.

Route description
Leaving the Salle à Manger follow the snow crest, where there will almost certainly be a track. Keep a wary eye out for cornices, especially around the area of the big serac where the ground is usually easier angled and less exposed.

Continue along the crest to point 3,933m where you make a 30m abseil or a steep downclimb on 50-degree snow.

Carry on along the ridge on mixed / rock until you reach the summit buttress.

Climb the buttress, steep at first, then trend right to reach a ramp that leads back left (4a). This leads to steep, loose gully that leads back to the ridge and then the summit.

173

ALPINE CLIMBING

Climbers setting off from the Salle à Manger, at the start of the ridge.

Descent
Reverse the line of ascent. The summit buttress is pretty loose. Some people abseil the buttress, some downclimb, so you need to make a personal decision on the quality of the anchors.

Cabane d'Orny

Cabane d'Orny

Situated above the village of Champex, the Orny hut is almost perfectly positioned with a cable car taking up some of the heavy lifting of the approach, followed by a stunning walk. The hut sits above a glacier giving an alpine ambiance, but much of the year it and the climbs below, can be accessed using approach shoes.

The granite is as good you will find in the Alps and the routes are a short walk from the hut with relatively easy descents. We have three routes to choose from and it is easily possible to climb all three over three days. The hut walk is easily accomplished in the late afternoon. You could then climb the Aiguille d'Orny the next day (day 1), the Aiguille de la Cabane the day after that (day 2) and, if you were quick, you could walk out that afternoon. Alternatively, you could climb the Aiguilles d'Arpette that afternoon, or do it the next morning (day 3) and walk out that afternoon.

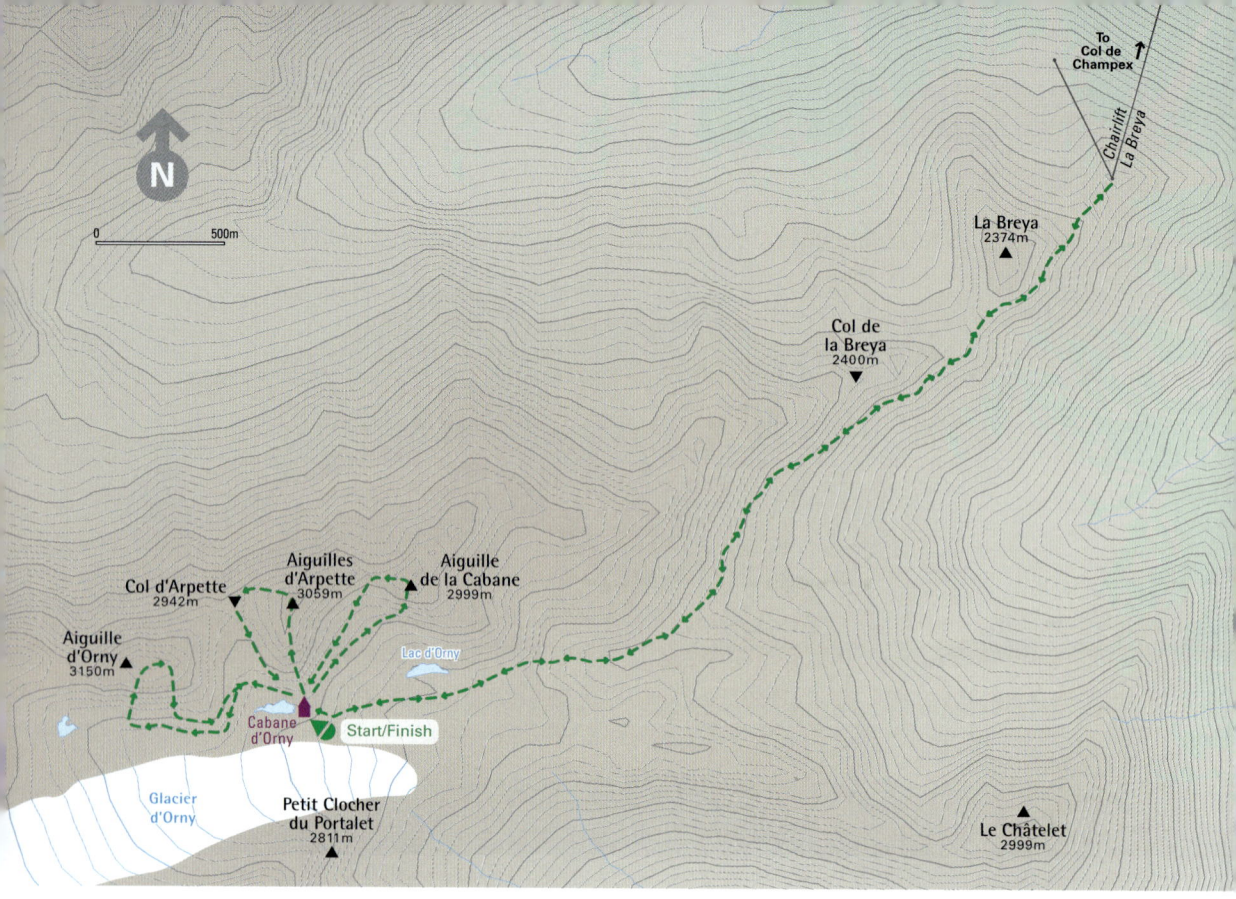

Aiguille d'Orny 3,150m

South Ridge Direct

A fantastic route on great granite with an incredible back drop. The positions and view make this feel like you are in the heart of the mountains, with the Aiguille d'Orny behind and the higher peaks of the Aiguilles Dorées on the horizon. All belays are in situ.

Grade	D 5a	**Length**	350m
Exposure	South, though most of the climbing is on the west side of the ridge so if you want it cool, climb in the morning, if you want more sun, climb in the afternoon.	**Rock type**	Granite
Protection	A mix of bolts and trad gear. All belays are in situ.	**Descent**	25m abseil then walking.
Conditions	Dry	**Time**	An hour approach from the hut then 3½hrs for the route.

Map
1:25,000 Swiss Topo Orsiere 1345

Cabane d'Orny

ABOVE: The author climbing on the South Ridge of the Aiguille d'Orny.
RIGHT: Mike Austin on the Orny South Ridge with the Aiguilles Dorées behind.

Alternative guidebook
Schweiz Plaisir West Band II, edition Filidor (English, French and German)

Hut
Cabane d'Orny, www.cas-diablerets.ch/cabanes/cabane-orny
tel. +41 27 783 1887 online reservation through the Swiss Alpine Club website.

Equipment
50m rope, half set of nuts, cams (0.5 – 2,) 8 quickdraws. Early in the season there may be snow on the approach so mountain boots, crampons, and a light axe. Later in the season approach shoes may be sufficient.

Hut approach
The hut is approached by catching the Breya lift from the west side of Champex-Lac (open 08 June -22 September in 2024) www.champex.ch. At the top of the lift the path is well signposted. Head south-west then follow a stunning traverse round the hillside for about an hour, before coming into a fantastic hanging valley that makes the perfect spot for a break.

The path now climbs more steeply, past the site of the old hut which was destroyed by avalanche some years ago. From point 2,692m the path follows the crest of a moraine with great views of the Petit Clocher du Portalet to the south and the Aiguille d'Orny, before a final short climb takes you to the hut.

Start of the South Ridge.

Route approach
Leave the Orny hut and follow the path that goes to the Trient hut. This goes past the lake and round a shoulder, parallel with the Glacier d'Orny. From here you will see the obvious summit of the Aiguille d'Orny. The route starts just to the right of the gully that bounds the left side of the south ridge. A small path leads up through the scree from the main Trient path.

There are some good flat spots to gear up at the base of the climb. Scramble up an easy ramp to find a bolt belay at the start of the climbing (there is a faint paint arrow and the name painted next to it).

ALPINE CLIMBING

The author climbing on the South Ridge of Aiguille d'Orny.   South Ridge of Aiguille d'Orny route.

Route description
Pitch 1 – 3c 30m Climb easy rock above the belay, heading for the obvious corner.
Pitch 2 – 4b 40m Climb the superb corner above the belay, exiting right at the top. Continue across easy ground to the base of a steep slab.
Pitch 3 – 4a 40m Climb the slab by its left side, belay on the right.
Pitch 4 – 4a 30m Climb the superb steep slab on excellent holds.
Pitch 5 – 4a 40m Climb the continuation slab on the right to the top of a tower. This is an amazing position with incredible views back across the Glacier d'Orny and onto the Trient plateau.
Pitch 6 – 3 50m Follow the ridge crest easily to the base of the steep final tower; you may want to move together a little to save making an intermediate belay. Belay at the base of an obvious corner with a grey slab on the right.
Pitch 7 – 3c 30m Climb the blunt rib on the left of the corner. Belay on the left where the grey slab on the right becomes more defined.
Pitch 8 – 4c 30m Step right across the base of the corner, then follow cracks back left into an overhung corner.
Pitch 9 – 5a 40m Step up and left out of the corner, then follow cracks in the wall above to belay just below the summit.

A short scramble now leads to the top.

Aiguille d'Orny descent.

Descent
Leaving the summit, scramble down the east side to find an abseil anchor. Make a 25m abseil to a bolt on an easy ledge. Scramble along the ledge to easy ground where you will pick up some cairns. Head down and right following cairns. Where the ground steepens, keep traversing right on a small ledge, which eventually leads to an easy gully that you scramble down onto easier ground and the approach path.

Aiguille de la Cabane 2,999m

Bon Accueil

Another amazing route on great granite with great positions. The top two pitches are two of the finest I have climbed on mountain granite. All the belays are in situ. There are two possible starts to the route: the original, which is more in keeping with the grades on the rest of the route, or a lower start that takes the striking corner seen on the approach but is quite a bit more difficult. It is the corner start that you will find in most other guidebooks to the area.

Grade	D 5b (4c with the original start)	Length	180m
Exposure	SE	Rock type	Granite
Protection	Mixed natural and in situ rock protection.	Descent	Abseil and scramble
Conditions	Dry rock	Time	4hrs for the climb.

Map
1:25,000 Swiss Topo Orsiere 1345

Alternative guidebook
Schweiz Plaisir West Band II, edition Filidor (English, French and German)

Hut
Cabane d'Orny, www.cas-diablerets.ch/cabanes/cabane-orny
tel. +41 27 783 1887 Online reservation through the Swiss Alpine Club website.

ALPINE CLIMBING

Bon Accueil route.

Mike Austin climbing high, Aiguille de la Cabane.

Equipment
50m rope, half set of nuts, cams (0.3 – 1), 10 quickdraws. Early in the season there may be snow on the approach, so mountain boots, crampons, and a light axe. Later in the season approach shoes may be sufficient.

Hut approach
As for Aiguille d'Orny.

Route approach
The route approach is easily seen from the hut. Leave the hut heading north-east. The path is pretty faint, but you are heading for the impressive buttress with a cracked slab and an obvious corner at the top right of the slab. The route starts by a short wall, just up from the toe of the buttress.

Route description
Starting just up from the toe of the buttress makes for some steep moves.

Pitch 1 – 40m 5b Make steep moves up the wall onto the cracked slab. Climb up and right towards the obvious sharp corner. You can either belay at the bottom of the corner or continue, if you have managed to avoid rope drag. The moves up the corner are steep and positive; don't linger as they are as steep as they look. If 5b is your max grade you will find this pitch is pretty difficult, but the difficulties are short.

Original Start Scramble further up the gully and start in a shallow corner with a crack that leads up and right.

Pitch 1a – 4a 25m Climb up and right, following the top edge of the slab to a bolt and chain belay.

Pitch 1b – 4b 30m Traverse up and right to join pitch 2 of the alternative start on the crest of the ridge, belay on 2 bolts.

Cabane d'Orny

The author at the start of Bon Accueil.   Mike Austin high on Bon Accueil.

Pitch 2 – 4c 40m Leave the belay, heading diagonally left towards the edge of the buttress, then follow cracks and flakes just right of the buttress edge to belay on a ledge.

Pitch 3 – 4b 35m Follow the edge of the buttress. Where it narrows follow the crest of the buttress, turning difficulties generally on the right side to belay below a steep wall.

Pitch 4 – 4b 30m Climb the buttress, then trend right to easy ground.

Scramble up, then trend right to a big ledge. Have a good look around as the col you are now on is crossed on the descent. It's worth checking this out as this will speed your descent, especially if the weather comes in. From the col head down and right along a ledge. On the upper buttress there are three routes and the start of each one is not that obvious, so look for the three separate lines of bolts. Your route takes the central line.

Pitch 5 – 40m 4b Trend up and slightly right, heading for the obvious corner. There are many amazing pitches of climbing in the Alps but seldom one that will put as big a smile on your face as this one. Climb the corner, bridging, pulling on big holds, the full gamut of climbing techniques. Exit the corner onto a ledge on the left.

Pitch 6 – 4c 35m If you thought the last pitch was good, you are in for a treat. Follow the cracks above the belay, where stunning climbing in a great position leads to the summit.

Descent

Just below the west side of the summit, find an in situ abseil anchor. Make a short abseil – 15m, then scramble down on the west side. Follow some small cairns until you can cross onto the south side of the ridge, which will lead to the col mentioned above. Scramble down the steep gully, it's a bit loose but not that bad, paint marks will lead you back to the start of the route and then back to the hut.

Aiguilles d'Arpette 3,059m

South Ridge

The Aiguilles d'Arpette is a lovely short climb immediately to the north of the hut. The South Ridge is well worth climbing.

Grade	AD	**Length**	240m
Exposure	South	**Rock type**	Granite
Protection	Leader placed with the odd bolt and peg.	**Descent**	Scramble down the north side, then 2 abseils.
Conditions	Dry	**Time**	3hrs up, 1½hrs down.

Map
1:25,000 Swiss Topo Orsiere 1345

Alternative guidebook
Schweiz Plaisir West Band II, edition Filidor (English, French and German)

Hut
Cabane d'Orny, www.cas-diablerets.ch/cabanes/cabane-orny
tel. +41 27 783 1887 online reservation through the Swiss Alpine Club website.

Route description
Scramble up the right side of 'Ecole d'Escalade' above the hut, via a chimney. Follow the crest of the ridge via some short pitches and moving together. There are a few bolts but you will need an AD rack.

Descent
To get down, head north from the summit, then make a 25m abseil and scramble down a loose gully and a path that leads down the Trient approach path. The round trip should take no more than 3 hours.

Mike Austin climbing on the Aiguilles d'Arpette with the hut behind.

Mark Dearnley on the Arête du Doigt, Pointe Percée, the highest point in the Aravis.

The Aravis

The Aravis is a range of limestone mountains to the west of the Mont Blanc Massif. There is great climbing in the Aravis, both multi-pitch and Alpine in style. The range has a maximum height of 2,750m, is non-glacial, clears quickly after bad weather, and has a longer season. Pointe Percée is the highest peak in the range, its north ridge – the Arête du Doigt, is a fantastic outing. The Arête Marion is another fantastic route that sits above the Col des Aravis. A great combination is to climb the Arête Marion then walk up to the Gramusset hut, spend the night and climb a route on Pointe Percée the next day. You could even spend a second night and climb another great rock route from the hut, L'Été Indien on the Pointe de Chombas (5c), and The Voie de Trou on Pointe Percée are both excellent.

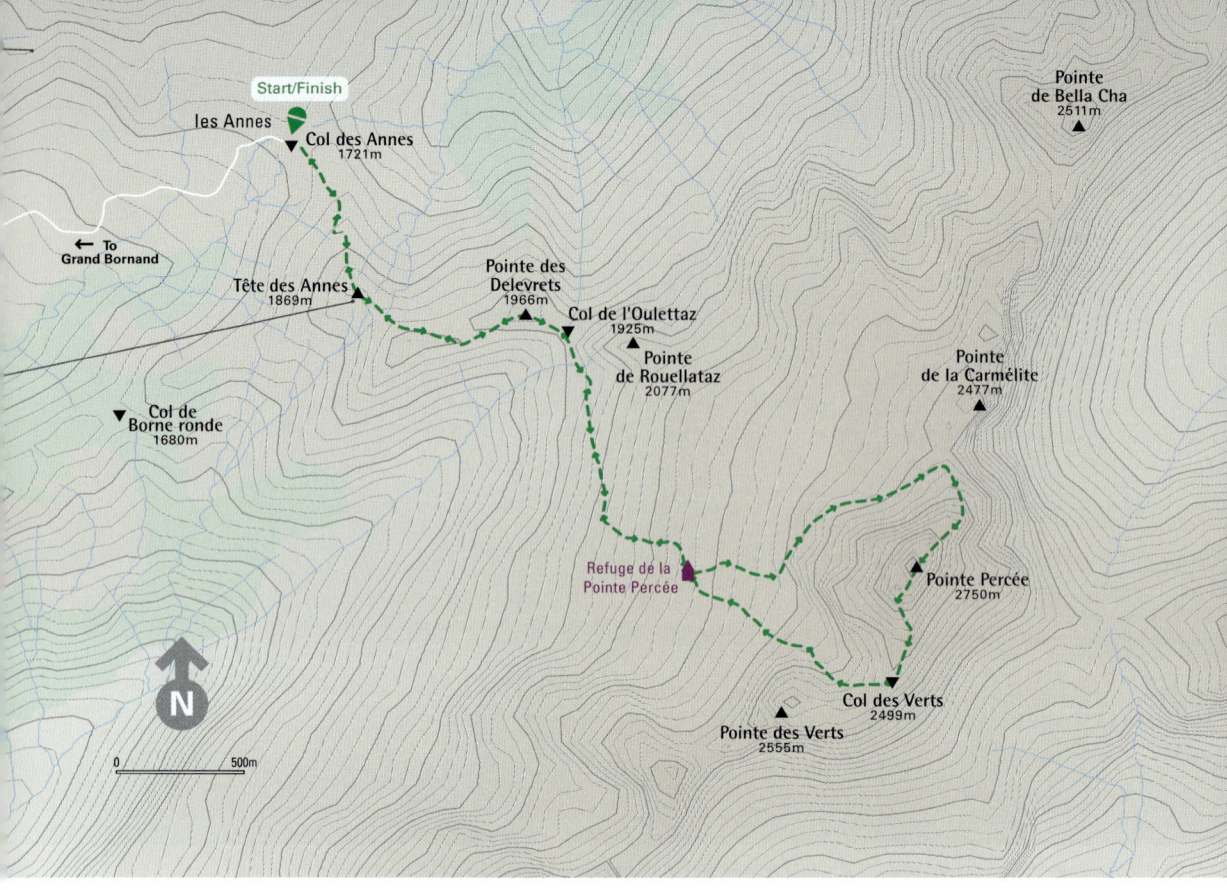

Pointe Percée 2,750m

The highest peak in the range is Pointe Percée. As you look at it from the motorway, you will notice a natural traverse ascending the right skyline and descending the left. As a mountaineer there can be few finer things than a skyline traverse, and we will focus on this, but it is also worth looking at the other guidebooks for the area as there are a few other superb routes. This route is an excellent option in hot weather as it is in the shade for much of the day.

Arête du Doigt

This route is the skyline, and it follows the crest of the north east ridge (Arête du Doigt), over the Doigt (finger), to a superb, exposed finale.

Grade	D 5c+ A0	Length	400m
Exposure	North-east	Rock type	Limestone
Protection	Bolted but a small rack would be useful.	Descent	Scramble with a couple of possible abseils.
Conditions	Dry, the route is north facing so good when the weather is really hot.	Time	Approach from the hut 1hr, then 4hrs to the summit and 1½hrs for the descent.

The Aravis

Mark Charlton and Mike Austin approaching Le Rasoir on the Arête du Doigt.

Mike Austin climbing on the Arête du Doigt.

Map
IGN La Clusaz Grand-Bornand 3430ET 1:25,000

Alternative guidebook
Schweiz Plaisir West Band II, edition Filidor (English, French and German)
Bornes Aravis Tome I by Gilles Brunot, (French)

Hut
Refuge de la Pointe Percée – Gramusset www.refugelapointepercee.ffcam.fr

Equipment
50m rope, half set of wires (1,3,5,6,7,9), 4 cams – Camalot .5,.75,1. 10 quickdraws. You should be able to approach and descend in approach shoes, early season you may want to consider a light ice axe to cross hard snow patches. Ask the hut guardian for information.

Hut approach
The route can be climbed in a day. If you are starting from the Chamonix area you will need an early start as the drive to the parking takes about an hour and a half. Alternatively, stay at the hut.

Start at the Col des Annes 1,721m, which is reached via Grand Bornand. Parking is next to a collection of summer dairy farms which sell a selection of local cheese, butter and refreshments. They are working farms so please park considerately.

ALPINE CLIMBING

Pointe Percée, routes and descent.

Leave the parking heading south on a footpath that takes you to the summit of the Tête des Annes (winter chairlift). From here, follow the well-signposted path to the Col de l'Oulettaz. There is a chain on a short descent from the col then a rising traverse followed by some switchbacks which take you to the hut. About 1¼ hrs.

Route approach

The hut sits at the base of an amazing limestone pavement. If you look up at Pointe Percée from the hut, the Arête du Doigt takes the crest of the ridge on the left skyline. The peak has two normal routes that can be used as descents. One is marked with orange paint and we can use this as the start to our approach.

Starting behind the hut, follow the orange paint marks heading north-east. You should pick up a number of cairns along the way as the path starts to climb uphill into a big gully. Keep following the cairns out left, until the limestone you are scrambling over gives way to loose scree with a path. Follow the path along the base of the cliff and round to the base of the ridge

To reach the start of the Arête du Doigt follow the path all the way to its base where a flat ledge makes a good gearing up spot.

Route description – Arête du Doigt

There are two bolted lines that lead up the crest of the ridge; take the right hand one. The climbing is pretty straightforward but the bolts are spaced, so can be difficult to spot (though the climbing is only 3c for the first two pitches). There are double bolt belays. The difficulty increases with height, with the climbing generally on the north side of the ridge. Four pitches of 4a-c lead you to the summit of the 'Le Doigt' (*the finger*). You can miss this out by traversing a ledge on the east side, but to do that would miss the point of the route.

After savouring the position on the Le Doigt, make a 20m abseil into a notch. The pitches leaving the ledge are on the left (east side), and you can either climb a crack at 5c or an easier pitch, in a groove in the crest of the ridge. The rock on the crest looks a bit poor but it is actually ok and both pitches are ok. The next pitch of 4b takes you to a belay on top of the Trou (another superb route). You are now well-established on the ridge proper with 'Le Rasoir' (*the razor*) ahead of you. It looks significantly more impressive than it is difficult, and two pitches lead you across this to a belay looking onto a steep wall.

You now have three possibilities:

1. After a short downclimb, you can take a long detour (four pitches plus scrambling and downclimbing) that takes you eventually to the normal route (orange paint marks) which can be followed to the hut. This is really an escape route should a thunderstorm be approaching.
2. Start as per 1. After two pitches you reach the base of a chimney, climb this in three pitches to the summit. The climbing is easy, if a bit loose, and you will need to place a few pieces of protection, although there is the odd bolt. There is a more difficult line of bolts just to the right of the chimney on better rock at 5c. The chimney is known as the Cheminée Guttinger, and I would only really suggest this (option 2) if there is a traffic jam ahead.
3. In my opinion this is the best and most fun finish.

   After the short downclimb, belay then climb the steep wall above (5c+). The first few moves are the most difficult and there is often a rope on one of the bolts to make things a bit easier. The climbing is steep but on excellent holds and is well-protected. When a narrow ledge leads to the right, follow this then climb a short wall to a belay on a ledge. The next pitch climbs a wall then follows the ridge crest at 5a, in superb positions, to below an imposing wall with a line of closely spaced bolts up it.

   You can free climb this at 6c or A0, or more in keeping with the rest of the route climb a groove on the right, there are a couple of green painted bolts at the start. The groove leads right then back left to the end of the climbing.

   Now scramble along to the summit cross and enjoy some incredible views of the Mont Blanc Massif.

Descents

Leaving the summit, head south until you pick up orange and red paint splashes. Scramble down polished rock until a level section in the ridge, here you will notice the orange paint splashes head off down on the right. This is one of the classic routes of ascent. You can go down this way, but I find it a bit loose and not that much fun.

I prefer to go down the Cheminée Sallanches. Carry on along the ridge until a pinnacle with a large metal ring is reached, with an arrow and Cheminée Sallanches painted on it. Scramble down following green and yellow paint splashes. There are three steep sections where metal rings allow for an easy abseil if you are not confident downclimbing these sections. The descent takes you down through some improbable ground trending left, (keep an eye out for the paint splashes) until a final steep downclimb (which can be abseiled in 2 x 20m abseils) takes you to a path that leads to the head of the Combes des Verts. From here, a path, a bit steep and loose at first, leads you back to the hut.

Mark Dearnley on the hanging slab pitch.

Pointes de la Blonnière 2,369m

L'Arête à Marion

An excellent limestone ridge with three steeper introductory pitches, some moving together, and a technical finish.

Grade	AD 5a	Length	300m
Exposure	North-east	Rock type	Limestone
Protection	Fully bolted	Descent	Scramble and one or two short abseils
Conditions	Dry	Time	5hrs up, 2hrs down.

Map
IGN Megeve - Col des Aravis 3531 OT

Equipment
12 quickdraws, 4 x 8ft slings, 50m rope. You can climb the whole route in light mountaineering boots. These are more comfortable than rock shoes when placing your foot in the waterworn grooves at the start of the route. There can be snow on the approach and steep snow on the descent, this can be assessed from the car park. If there is snow, a light pair of crampons and an ice axe is a good idea.

The Aravis

Route approach
This may feel like the crux of the route as it is pretty steep, and the best path is not initially obvious. Be ready for a sweaty hour if you don't start early enough.

Park at the Col des Aravis, next to a collection of cafés, and follow the farm road south to the farm at La Grande Montagne. After the farm a rough track heads south-west. This turns into a small track that leads across fields towards the start of the Combe à Marion. This is a working farm so please be sensitive to livestock and electric fences that may be in your way. Follow the track up the Comb à Marion, you are heading for an obvious steep yellow buttress. Turn this on the right, then continue up for 100m before a path leads back left to a ledge with belay bolts at the bottom of some 'cannelures' (water worn grooves). It may be worth putting your harness and helmet on before the final section as you are exposed to stone fall from the descent gully and there are quite a lot of Chamois and Ibex about that may knock something off. If you have your harness on, you can quickly clip into the belay.

Route description
The route starts with three great pitches of limestone climbing.

Pitch 1 – 4c 40m Leave the belay and climb the superb cannelure. The best technique is to torque your foot into the grooves, this is much more comfortable in mountain boots that have torsional stiffness.

Pitch 2 – 4b 35m Leave the belay, step up and right to follow a series of grooves and cannelures to a bolt belay in a small hole.

Pitch 3 – 4c / 5a 40m Move up the easy ground above heading for an open chimney, there is a bolt on the way. Climb the chimney; the climbing is steep but there are lots of bolts for protection or assistance. Belay where the angle eases.

Change mode to moving together and follow the ground above to a grassy col where the ridge narrows. Follow the crest of the ridge for 200m, there are bolts for protection or belays. It is possible to pitch but this would be very time consuming.

You will reach a steep wall with a hanging slab above; belay here on bolts.

Upper Pitch 1 – 4b 45m Change back to pitching and make a pull up onto the slab, then follow cracks to the ridge crest. Belay where the ground ahead becomes steeper (bolts).

Approach and descent from the Arête à Marion.

Hazel Allen climbing on the upper part of the Arête à Marion, with the route above marked.

ALPINE CLIMBING

The author on the Arête à Marion.

Upper Pitch 2 – 5a 45m Make delicate moves up the ridge to reach a narrow crest. Step over this and descend one move, then make a rising traverse left following bolts. Some of the rock feels a little suspect here, so take care. Keep moving up and left, then climb a short wall to the ridge and a bolt belay.

Upper Pitch 3 – III 20m Move easily along the ridge to the summit.

Descent

Head west and descend steep grass, via a track and cairns, cut right into a sort of rock crevasse that leads to a wide chimney, you can downclimb into this or make an abseil from bolts.

Descend the chimney, a bit loose. Where it steepens, exit down and right (facing out) across a slab – bolt to easy ground. Follow a track down to a col at the head of the Combe à Marion.

Follow tracks in the scree, it is worth keeping a helmet on for this. These will lead you back to the base of the route and the track you approached on.

Mike Austin climbing on the west ridge of the Dent de Tsalion.

Val d'Hérens

The Val d'Hérens is one of the main valleys that lead north / south in the Swiss canton of Valais. It is known to many as a great place for an introduction to Alpine mountaineering, and in fact featured three routes in my previous book *Alpine Mountaineering*. The area is not just home to some great mountains to cut your teeth on, but it is also home to some fantastic climbing on more challenging routes.

The two routes we are going to cover in this chapter, The Dent de Tsalion, and Mont Blanc de Cheilon are fantastic, and very different routes, both approached from excellent mountain huts.

Dent de Tsalion 3,589m and Aiguille de la Tsa 3,668m

As you will have noticed from reading the rest of the book, the Valais is not known for its excellent rock, so if you have got used to working around loose rock you are in for a treat – solid granite. If you look west from the village of Arolla your eye is drawn to the beautiful, pointed needle of the Aiguille de la Tsa. The Tsa is a stunning summit, but it is a long walk for about 80m of actual climbing. It's not an unpleasant walk to get there, but a much better way of getting to its base is via the West Ridge of the Dent de Tsalion. The Tsalion is a completely separate mountain but makes a very logical enchainment with the Tsa.

West Ridge

Grade	AD 4b with lots of II/III	**Length**	600m
Exposure	West	**Rock type**	Granite
Protection	Trad with a few bolts and pegs.	**Descent**	Glacier over the Col de la Tsa, or via the Bertol hut and the Col de Bertol.
Conditions	Dry on the route, but the descent is easier if it still has snow on it.		
Time	Approach from the hut 1hr, 5hrs for the route, and another hour if you include the Tsa. Allow 3hrs for the descent.		

Map
Swiss Topo 1:25,000 Matterhorn, Monte Cervino 1347, 1:50,000 Arolla 283

Alternative guidebook
Valais Alps West, Switzerland: Alpine Club Selected Climbs by Lindsay Griffin
Swiss Alpine Club Guide du Valais by Hermann Biner (French or German)

Hut
Cabane de la Tza, www.cabtza.com

Equipment
50m rope, half set of wires (1,3,5,6,7,9), 4 cams – Camalot (.5,.75,1,2), 6 quickdraws. On the descent you will need an ice axe and crampons, standard glacier travel kit and a headtorch.

Mike Austin high on the Dent de Tsalion.

Hut approach
The route is approached from the Cabane de la Tza, a small hut owned by the local guides bureau situated about 2 hours (600m) above the road. There is a car park on the outside of the last big hairpin in the road before you reach Arolla (1,986m). Leave your car here and walk south along the road for about half a kilometre until it is possible to cross a stream, La Borgne d'Arolla. Then follow the signposts to

the hut, initially traversing through larch forests, then more steeply to the hut which sits on a ridge crest with superb views over the valley.

The hut is a small low-lying building with beds for 30 in two dormitories; but it is seldom busy and often pleasantly quiet. It has plenty of space inside and a tap with drinking water round the back.

Route approach

The route from the hut to the base of the route is over a boulder field and a moraine, so it is worth checking out the night before as you will want to set off in the dark to get the glacier descent in the best possible condition. Leaving the hut, head initially east following cairns and a plastic water pipe. While not very aesthetic, the pipe is heading in the general direction you want to be heading in. Small cairns and bits of path take you up onto a moraine and then cairns and boulder hopping take you south-east to the base of the West Ridge. This should take about an hour.

Route description

The route starts with an obvious crack on the left of the toe of the ridge. Now, it seems a bit of a cop out as a guidebook writer to say "now follow the ridge for 600m", but that is pretty much what you do. As with most alpine ridges the best rock is on the crest, and it is also where the best climbing is to be found. The climbing is a mix of short pitches and moving together with most things being climbed direct at about grade III. At about half height the ridge steepens, where a crack on the right of a steep wall is protected by two bolts. This pitch is about 5a but pulling on the well-positioned bolts will make this section A0 and keep you moving. As you move higher the position becomes airier, and a superb section of climbing on the poorly protected crest now has a welcome bolt to steady the nerves.

As the ridge comes to its conclusion you are faced with the only pitch of suspect rock to reach the summit. Traverse a ledge to the right then cut back left to the summit. There are some suspect rocks but nothing too bad (5-7 hours to the summit from the hut).

The approach to the Tsalion, seen from the Tza hut.

Climbers at the start of the West Ridge.

Mike Austin on the Tsalion West Ridge.

You now have a couple of decisions to make. If you have the time and inclination, you could climb the Aiguille de la Tsa (description below), you could descend back to the Tza hut or descend via the Col de la Tsa, or the Bertol hut and the Col de Bertol.

Descents
See end of next route.

Aiguille de la Tsa – East Face

From its base, the Aiguille de la Tsa is reached either by a 20-minute climb from just below the summit of the Dent de Tsalion or by an ascent of the Glacier de l'Aiguille from the Bertol hut.

Pitch 1 – III+ 25m From the base of the east face, take a rising rightwards traverse to a ledge.
Pitch 2 – III+ 35m Climb more-or-less straight up on good rock. Belay on an abseil anchor, bolts and chain.
Pitch 3 – III Take a rising traverse left to the ridge bolts for protection, then follow the ridge before climbing right, following a ledge to a bolt belay.
Pitch 4 – 4a Move slightly left and climb a corner to a wobbly chockstone which, if you use it, makes the pitch about 4a (if you don't it's a bit harder). The corner then leads easily to the top.

The Tsa is descended by abseil. If you are climbing on one 50m rope this is possible; you just need to be careful as you will be operating near the ends (a knot in the end would be a good idea), and make sure you don't pass any abseil stations. This will take you back to the base in three abseils. Then choose one of the descents below.

The round trip on the Tsa should take about 2 hours.

Val d'Hérens

East Face of Aiguille de la Tsa.

Descents

Back to the Cabane de la Tza
Head north past the Dent de Tsalion, then along a ridge to the Pointe de Tsalion (grade II). Pick up some red paint markers and cairns that lead down a ramp. Keep an eye out for a turn to the right (facing out) about a quarter of the way down. Head towards the Pointe des Genevois, crossing a number of gullies on the way. I have not been down this way very often, but I have never enjoyed it, it being loose and rubbly. In good snow it is a quick and easy descent, but in anything else I would not recommend it.

Col de la Tsa
Head south traversing the top of the Glacier de l'Aiguille. Be aware that you will be travelling parallel with the crevasses, so you need to pay attention. Descend towards the col. You will almost certainly want to make an abseil from the col, as the slope is steep and the bergschrund gaping. There is an abseil anchor on the rock on the north side of the col that should take you over the bergschrund in 25m. The more snow there is, the easier it will be. Take care as there is quite a lot of loose rock, and I would not want other parties abseiling above me while I climbed down the steep last few metres once you have pulled down your rope. It is worth asking the guardian of the hut about conditions here and the length of rope required. As glaciers retreat this may require a longer rope, or loose rock may make this unfeasible.

Once down, descend the Glacier de Bertol until it is possible to head south-east and join the path to the Bertol hut just above the Plan de Bertol. You can now follow the never-ending path back to the valley.

Col de Bertol and Bertol Hut
If you do not fancy the Col de la Tsa or it is not in condition, carry on round the glacier aiming for a notch in the ridge that drops east from the Point de Bertol, just east of point 3,373m. Here a chain leads down, then a scree or snow slope leads onto the upper Mont Miné glacier, traverse to the Col de Bertol. If your legs are finished the Bertol hut is a great and spectacular place to spend the night, but it is more likely that you will want to get down. So, follow the well-marked approach path down what's left of the southern branch of the Glacier de Bertol and the path as described on the descent via the Col de la Tsa.

Mont Blanc de Cheilon 3,870m

Mont Blanc de Cheilon is a fantastic mountain; so much so that having included the normal route in *Alpine Mountaineering* we will revisit it again, this time by climbing the more difficult East Ridge and descending the normal route.

Traverse East to South West

The route can be climbed either from the Vignettes or the Dix hut. My favourite is to go to the Vignettes hut, then traverse the Pigne d'Arolla to the Col de la Serpentine, then onto the East Ridge of the Cheilon. The same point can be reached from the Dix hut via the Glacier de Tsena Réfien. The route itself is primarily on rock, but the approach and the descent are on snow and glaciated terrain.

The descent is via the Dix hut, where you can spend the night and climb the excellent ridge that sits between the Pas de Chèvres and the Col de Riedmatten. You can of course just cross the pass and descend to Arolla. If you do this, the descent to Arolla can feel like a long way.

Grade	AD III	**Length**	1,000m
Exposure	East ascent, SW descent.	**Rock type**	Schist
Protection	Leader placed	**Descent**	South west ridge
Conditions	Snow on the approach then dry rock on the ridge traverse.	**Time**	4½hrs from Cabane des Dix, or 5½hrs from Vignettes to summit.

Map
Swiss Topo 1:50,000 Arolla 283 1:50,000 Chanrion 1346 and Matterhorn 1347

Alternative guidebook
Valais Alps West, Switzerland: Alpine Club Selected Climbs by Lindsay Griffin

Equipment
Glacier travel kit, AD rack, 50m rope, ice axe and crampons

Hut
Vignettes hut, www.cabane-des-vignettes.ch
Dix hut, www.cabanedesdix.com

The north face of Mont Blanc de Cheilon.

Hut approach

Vignettes Hut
Park at the highest point in Arolla, the best parking is in shade, under the trees by the Hotel Kurhaus. Walk past the north side of the hotel and pick up a track, signposts for Dix hut (maybe Vignettes as well). Cross the stream and continue past a small lake, then head south-west then south on good tracks; you can either carry on to the chalet / buvette at Les Tsijiores Nouves 2,165m, or cut south earlier. This leads across the hillside (the tracks join) to a bridge at point 2,133m, at the base of a moraine ridge.

The same point can be reached from the valley floor directly from the ski area car park.

Follow the moraine to a small lake. At point 2,494m the track skirts the edge of a little plateau before climbing through some rocks to the glacial outwash plain in front of the Glacier de Pièce. Follow a track, then the east side of the glacier to the Col des Vignettes. You can see the helicopter landing pad from a long way off, and the hut sits on the south side of the ridge.

Dix Hut
Take the same approach to Les Tsijiores Nouves 2,165m, then follow a path that parallels the ski lift cables. Where these turn north, carry on up the track, signs and paint splashes point you to the Pas de Chèvres. However, in recent years the moraine below the ladders on the Pas de Chèvres has dropped away leaving steep, unstable rubble. At the time of writing (2024), most people are crossing the Col de Riedmatten which is situated just to the north. You follow the same path to point 2,741m where the path splits, the right hand one going to the Col de Riedmatten and the left to the Pas de Chèvres.

The approach to the Cheilon traverse.

Route approach

Vignettes approach
Leave the hut and head south across a flat area until you can climb steeply through some rocks, past a cairn, to gain the glacier on the east side of the Pigne d'Arolla. Glacial recession has meant that this is more challenging than it used to be. The exact line of ascent of the Pigne will depend on the condition of the glacier, but navigation is usually easy, and the summit is an incredible viewpoint. Leave the summit and head south-west to the Col du Brenay then north-west passing a steep area, often referred to as the Serpentine, then head west to the Col de la Serpentine.

Dix approach
Leave the hut and descend on to the Glacier de Cheilon; this is usually dry from early summer. Head south-east to the bottom of the Glacier de Tsena Réfien. Head up the glacier, keeping to your left in an arc to avoid crevasses and stay on the easiest angled ground. When the ground angle eases, head slightly south-west to reach the Col de la Serpentine.

ALPINE CLIMBING

Route description

Starting at the Col de la Serpentine, follow the broad snow ridge to point 3,821m. This used to be a continuous snow slope but in recent years, with warmer summers, there is often a band of rock to negotiate. As height is gained the ridge narrows, and large cornices can form above the north face, so be aware of these.

Beyond point 3,821m the terrain drops away to a col. Some people abseil this steepening, but personally I have never been convinced by the anchor. If you back track a few metres from the abseil anchor, it is relatively easy to downclimb on the south side, down and round to the same point you would abseil to. This also saves a changeover in rope system.

The next section of the ridge is usually all rock so, if you haven't already, I would take your crampons off.

Cross two small pinnacles and follow the ridge to a brèche below the final steepening. Climb this directly on good rock with excellent holds to the summit ridge, and then the summit.

Descent

Leave the summit heading south-west; this involves some downclimbing to reach the ridge proper. Follow the ridge, exposed in places. You may need to put your crampons back on depending on conditions. The ridge leads to a col that separates point 3,877m from the main summit. You now have three options:

1. Head north from the col then west under some crevasses, and then north-west to the top of the rock ridge that leads to the Col de Cheilon. Descend the rock ridge. The easiest way off the end is usually to drop off the south side before the col, this is the descent marked on the map in the book.
2. South of the ridge mentioned above is a snow gully; in good snow conditions you can descend this gully to the Glacier du Giétroz, then return to the Col de Cheilon. In good snow this can be very fast so check with the guardian about conditions.
3. When you re-join the snow at the col, contour around point 3,827m and head SSW to carry on down the glacier. Keep on the left-hand side to avoid the big crevasses that are down there. Check with the guardian what the conditions are like.

Climbers on the Cheilon traverse.

The author climbing on the Cheilon East Ridge.

Tanya Noakes on the Traverse of the Miroir d'Argentine.

Le Miroir d'Argentine – Alpes Vaudoises

The Miroir d'Argentine is a huge limestone slab situated above Solalex, near Villars in the Swiss canton of Vaud. Vaud is the French speaking canton of Switzerland east of Lake Geneva and north of the Rhone valley. It is an area of limestone mountains which don't attract the same attention as the snow-capped peaks which surround it. The mountains are a bit lower, and not being surrounded by 4,000m peaks often avoid some of the bad weather that the bigger peaks can attract.

If the weather is coming from the south or the east, then the rain shadow from the Valais or the Oberland can really shelter this part of the Alps.

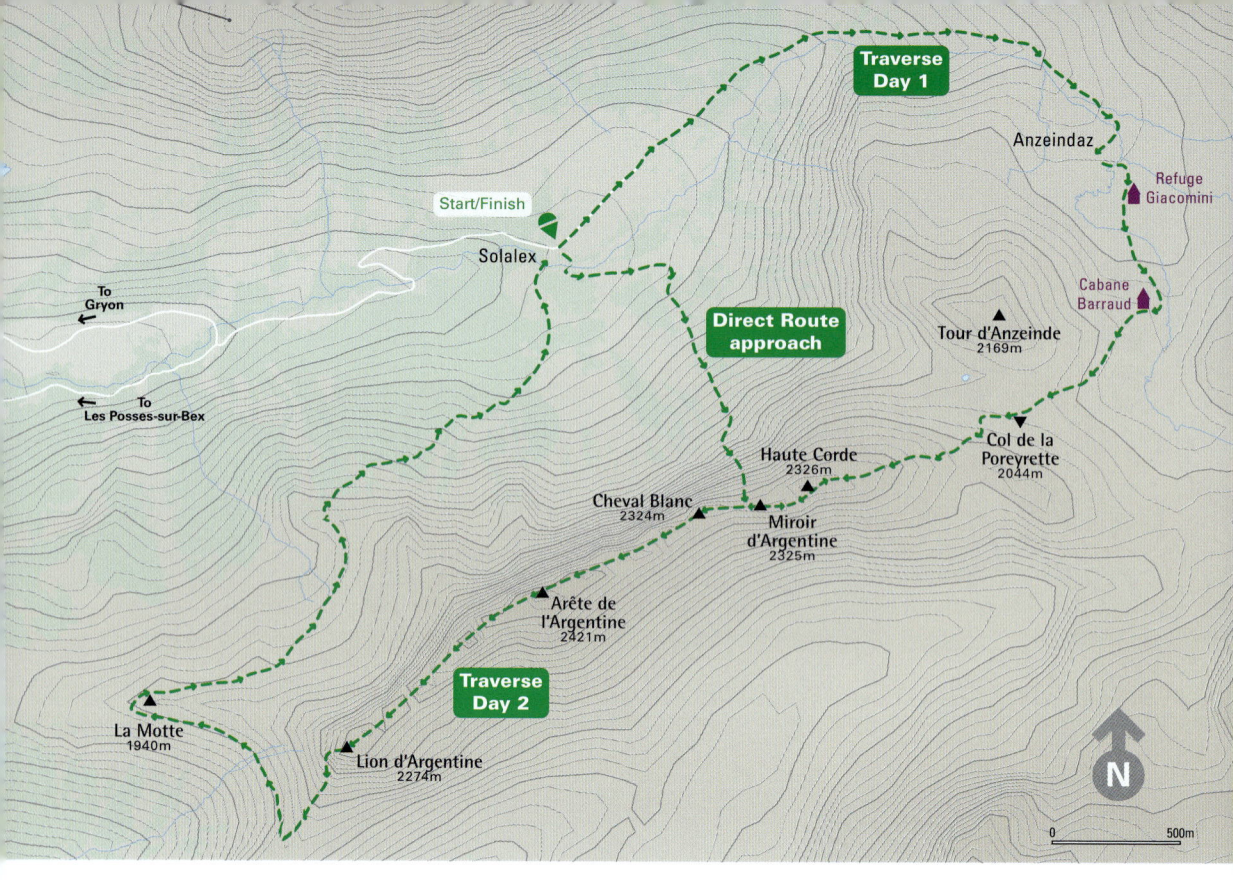

Le Miroir d'Argentine (Haute Corde 2,326m)

The Miroir is famous for its face climbs. It is a vast area of slab, seamed with cracks and grooves, offering loads of routes. The climbs are big, with many of them being 15 pitches in length. The classics are the Y, which is mainly 4 and 5, with one hard move through an overlap, which can be aided to make for a more homogeneous route, and the direct route (5a), which is my favourite.

We will start with the traverse of the ridge. This is a big undertaking and should not be underestimated, as many parties have spent the night out here, having not started early enough, or maintained a sense of urgency throughout the day. We will then look at the direct.

Traverse of Miroir d'Argentine

Grade	D	Length	2km of ridge
Exposure	NE and SW	Rock type	Limestone
Protection	A mix of in situ bolts and leader placed protection.	Descent	Scramble and abseil.
Conditions	Dry rock	Time	8-10hrs for the traverse from Refuge Giacomini.

Map
The best map is the Chablais Vaudois 1:25000 from the Topo Rando series which you can buy locally.
Swiss Topo 1:50,000 St Maurice Map 272
Swiss Topo 1:25,000, you will need the Le Diablerets 1285 and a tiny piece of the Dent de Morcles 1305.

Le Miroir d'Argentine – Alpes Vaudoises

Alternative guidebook
Escalades Vaud, Chablais, Bas-Valais, Sanetsch by Claude and Yves Remy
Schweiz Plaisir West, Edition Filidor

Hut
It is possible to climb the traverse from the car park at Solalex. However, it is much more pleasant to start from the Refuge Giacomini. This allows for a more relaxed approach and a guaranteed early start. www.anzeindaz.com

Equipment
Standard AD rack, 50m rope. You can climb the route in mountaineering boots, with the length of the route you might like the support. Approach shoes also work well.

Hut approach
Park at Solalex, van camping and overnight bivvying seems to be tolerated and there are public toilets. The car park is 500m before the hotel and restaurant at the end of the road. Leave the road and follow the 4x4 track that heads north-east then climbs steadily over 400m to the hamlet of Anzeindaz and the Giacomini hut.

Paul Warnock on the Miroir traverse.

Route approach
Leave the hut and follow the track south passing the Cabane Barraud, then south-west passing point 2,130m and onto the Haute Corde at 2,326m. This is the place to gear up and look at the ridge ahead.

Route description
The route finding is easy, you just follow your nose most of the time. The description can be difficult to keep track of as it doesn't mention most of the easy sections and the route is so long, so don't worry if you can't place yourself.

There are lots of moves of III and one pitch of 5a. The 5a pitch is only 25m and is well protected, and if you pulled on a bolt it would take a grade off.

Leaving the summit of the Haute Corde, backtrack a short distance east then descend a couloir SE for 50m. Traverse a short distance and head west on ledges then a ridge crest; follow this to a summit, then make a 25m abseil onto an arête. Follow the arête for 300m, then downclimb to a gendarme. Abseil 20m down the arête, then pass two gendarmes. Abseil 10m or downclimb (III). Climb a fourth gendarme on its NW side, then follow the crest to central summit.

Descend the far side on the grassy slopes of the SE shoulder to the base of a big V notch. Climb out of the notch on the slabby face (plenty of bolts), 25m (5a). Follow the crest to a summit, then descend to a small V notch.

Climb the next gendarme via a narrow chimney (bolts) on its left side; it would be easy to miss this by carrying on along a ledge on the left, but this blanks out. From the summit, abseil 15m down a slab then climb a ramp on the SE side of the arête to the summit of the Lion d'Argentine.

That is a lot of climbing for not much description so keep your foot down and follow your nose.

Descent

To descend from the Lion, follow cairns west then north down some steep grass to an abseil station, then make a 15m, followed by two 25m abseils to easy ground. Head south down rough ground until you pick up a track. Follow the track north then west, passing under La Motte, 1,940m, to a ridge crest at a path junction. Head north-east making a slight ascent over the Roc du Chatelet, then keep heading north-east back to Solalex.

Miroir d'Argentine Direct Route

There are lots of great routes all over the north face of the Miroir. My favourite is the Direct Route, which offers great varied climbing in some superb positions. The lower section is steep climbing on great holds, then higher up the route follows a series of excellent cracks on a beautiful slab.

Grade	D	**Length**	400m
Exposure	N and NW	**Rock type**	Limestone
Protection	A mix of in situ bolts and leader placed protection.	**Descent**	Walk off
Conditions	Dry rock	**Time**	6-8hrs for the round trip.

Map

The best map is the Chablais Vaudois 1:25000 from the Topo Rando series which you can buy locally.
Swiss Topo 1:50,000 St Maurice Map 272
Swiss Topo 1:25,000 you will need the Le Diablerets 1285 and a tiny piece of the Dent de Morcles 1305.

Hut

Climb from the car park at Solalex.

Equipment

It is worth having twin ropes for any of the routes on the face, in case you need to retreat in bad weather (there are abseil anchors on many of the routes). The slabby nature of the upper section makes abseiling awkward, but the rock becomes incredibly slippery if it rains, and abseiling is the only real option if you are caught out.
10 quickdraws, set of nuts and cams (0.5, 0.75, 1 and 2).

Approach and Direct Route on the Miroir.

Route approach

Leave the lower car park and cross the river via a bridge. Find a steep footpath that climbs directly towards the face; it roughly follows the line of a stream which is in a steep-sided riverbed. The path can be difficult to find lower down so don't become disheartened; keep forging upwards, as the trees thin the path is easier to find. As you approach the cliff, the route starts right-of-centre at the base of a steep corner chimney. There is a plaque at the base with the name and a bolt belay. All the belays are big door-knocker style rings.

Route description

Pitch 1 – 5c Climb the steep corner. The holds are all there and the bolts are where you need them. Belay on a good ledge.

Pitch 2 – 5a Follow the corner; avoid the temptation to follow the bolts on the left. Belay in the chimney.

Pitch 3 – 5c+ This pitch is difficult to grade as years of climbers thrashing in the bomb bay chimney have polished it to a fine sheen. Where the chimney narrows it is worth either hanging your rucksack from your harness or leading on one rope and not clipping any runners on the other; you can then use that rope to pull up your rucksacks. Climb into the back of the chimney and then climb up and right to exit the chimney, where there are plenty of bolts if you need them.

Pitch 4 Climb the easy chimney above, then a corner, to land on a big ledge. Belay on the ledge.
Move 10 metres left, don't be tempted to run pitch 4 and this together as the rope drag will be horrendous, and there is some loose rock on the ledge that could be brushed off by the rope.

Pitch 5 – 5b Step left from the belay and climb steeply, following bolts that lead to the upper slab where the terrain lies back.

Pitch 6 – 4b Climb up and right in a crack.

Pitch 7 – 4c Climb up and right, following the crack line.

Pitch 8 – 4b Follow the crack above. Cross a ledge and keep climbing to another ledge.

Pitch 9 – 5b Make thin moves in a small crack that heads diagonally left.

Pitch 10 – 5b Climb over a small overlap, then climb parallel cracks trending left.

Mike Austin climbing on the lower chimneys on the Direct Route.

Mike Austin climbing on the superb slabs of the Direct Route.

ALPINE CLIMBING

Mike Austin on the exposed descent after climbing the Direct Route.

Pitch 11 – 4b Trend up and left climbing cracks and slabs; you are heading for a notch in the skyline. There are a number of routes coming together at this point on the slab so don't be put off if the lines are confusing, as they are all about the same grade.

Pitch 12 – 4c Keep trending up and left to reach a steep wall with the notch above you. Move slightly left to avoid the steepest climbing and climb a shallow corner / groove to easy ground and the top.

Descent

If you are tired or anyone is wobbly in exposed places, I would leave the rope on for the first section. Follow a track that heads towards the Haute Corde; the ridge narrows and is quite exposed but there are a few bolts. When you reach the steep wall of the Haute Corde, follow a track and ledges that lead round the right side (these go up and down and have a big drop on their right side so watch your step). The track descends, and then seems to vanish. At this point start heading up and right (easy scrambling) to reach a path that leads down to Anzeindaz and then Solalex. It is possible to cut the corner and descend beside the Poreyrette ravine; this is steep and, unless it is really dry, is incredibly slippery and serious but it probably saves an hour of walking.

Zermatt dawn, seen from high on the Dufourspitze.

Zermatt

Zermatt is to Switzerland what Chamonix is to France: majestic, glaciated mountains with one of the highest concentrations of 4,000m peaks anywhere in the Alps, 38 in total. If you asked a child to draw a mountain, they would almost certainly draw the Matterhorn and there is no greater symbol of alpinism. I'm sure you can sense the however coming ...

However, when the Matterhorn is in condition, it is busy, incredibly and unpleasantly so. The hut is expensive and it is not an experience that I would suggest to a budding alpinist until they have a few seasons under their belt. When you have a handle on alpine climbing, you can take a perverse pleasure in the ridiculousness of the hierarchy of departure from the hut in the morning and all it entails.

Zermatt does offer some other incredible mountaineering objectives that are quieter and offer climbing that, I would argue, is better in quality than anything on the Matterhorn. The half traverse of the Breithorn is one of the best routes of its type in the Alps, and Dufourspitze is the second highest mountain in the Alps. The classic route on Dufourspitze is a much greater achievement than the classic route on Mont Blanc. There are, of course, many other amazing mountains and routes in the area but climbing this pair should whet your appetite for future adventures.

Jean Pavillard and client Monica high on the West Ridge of the Dufourspitze.

Dufourspitze 4,634m

At a mighty 4,634m, Dufourspitze is the second highest mountain in the Alps and is the crown of the Monte Rosa Massif. It sits in a remote and lofty position looking over the stunning peaks of Zermatt and the Central Valais.

When talking with other climbers about Dufourspitze, it seems that its summit is not as prized as that of Mont Blanc. This, to my mind, is a shame, as it is a far better outing, requiring focussed and sustained cramponing and mixed climbing techniques at 4,500m, with no simple way down. In addition, you have the whole of the Alps stretched out before you, from Piz Bernina in the East to Mont Blanc in the West, then all the way south to Monte Viso.

The distinguishing feature of Dufourspitze is its size, rather than its actual height. Its size and remoteness make it a much longer day than Mont Blanc, with over 1800m of ascent and a significant horizontal distance. This means that you need to be well acclimatised and moving efficiently for the day not to turn into something much longer than you had planned. The classic route is the West Ridge, from the modern and extremely comfortable Monte Rosa hut.

West Ridge

Grade	PD+ / AD-	**Length**	1,800m vertical from the hut.
Exposure	West	**Rock type**	Metamorphic
Protection	There is a short section of fixed rope below the summit and a possible abseil descent; other protection must be placed by the climbers.		
Descent	In good snow conditions, descent can be made by retracing the line of ascent. If this is at all icy, it is advisable to continue east along the ridge from the summit to join a series of abseil anchors that lead to the Silbersattel (as shown on the map).		
Conditions	Snow on the glacier and the lower part of the ridge. The upper ridge is best with snow or mixed conditions.		
Time	6hrs up and 4-5hrs down.		

Map
Swiss Topo 1:25,000 Zermatt-Gornergrat

Alternative guidebook
The 4000m Peaks of the Alps by Ben Tibbets Volume 2 East
The 4000m Peaks of the Alps Selected climbs by Martin Moran

Hut
Monte Rosa Hütte, www.monterosahuette.ch tel. + 41 27 967 21 15
Book online through www.alpsonline.org

Equipment
Ice axe, crampons, standard glacier travel kit plus a small rack – nuts (1,3,5,7,9), 3 quickdraws. A 50m rope makes the abseils more comfortable, though it is just possible with a 40m.

Hut approach
The Monte Rosa hut, where our adventure begins, is one of the newest and most modern huts in the Alps. Some may even say it's an architectural masterpiece. This is perhaps a bit of an overstatement, but it is a very nice place to stay. Like all things in Zermatt, it is expensive but, when you are sitting on the terrace absorbing the incredible view with a post climb beer, the cost is easily forgotten.

The approach to the hut is a great day. (The local guides bureau actually offer a night in the hut as an excursion, which is really popular.) The day starts by getting the Gornergrat railway (next to the main train station in Zermatt) to Rotenboden. This station is also the starting point for climbs on the Riffelhorn, which has a pleasant east ridge and some excellent multi-pitch rock climbs on the south side, overlooking the Gornergletscher. The route called Egg is particularly good, and the backdrop is amazing.

The approach to the hut starts with a gentle downhill, following a good path with blue and white paint splashes; this leads to the edge of the Gornergletscher. Put your crampons on and then follow the marker posts climbing eastwards. In the summer the glacier is usually dry, so you can see all the crevasses and can probably dispense with a rope. If it is snow covered, I would always advise a rope. You keep climbing the glacier until you are above the altitude of a series of crevasses at about 2,900m; here, you can turn south to reach the edge of the glacier and a moraine. You are on a marked path now (blue paint) that leads you across moraine and rock slabs to the hut. This section is much longer than it looks, and the approach takes about four hours.

Route approach
The route starts at the door of the hut on the Monte Rosa side. It's worth making sure you have time to scope out the route for the next morning as the terrain above the hut can be really confusing in the dark. There are cairns, marker posts and paint splashes, but they don't all lead the correct way.

Route description
Leave the hut and head south-east, crossing large areas of slab and moraine following paint splashes, cairns and marker posts. There is a split in the path after about an hour and you take the left fork (the right leads to the Grenzgletscher); it is worth going at least this far the night before. The path follows slabs and moraines crossing the Plattje Obere (as it is marked on the map), until it climbs more steeply to reach an easing in angle at about 3100m; this is usually the edge of the snow, so it's a good place to rope up and put the crampons on. You are on a glacier for the next few hours and the initial section through a crevassed area can be quite confusing in the dark. A worthwhile technique is to download the

West Ridge of Dufourspitze route, seen at dawn above the Monte Rosa hut.

map onto your phone using the App *'SwitzerlandMobility'* or *'Swisstopo'*; the ski line on the map will help keep you on track. The route heads generally south-east, and by the time you pass the rock rognon at 3,827m, it should start to get light, so you can see where you are going. Skirt left round some ice cliffs before the steep final climb to the Sattel at 4,359m.

The terrain changes completely here, from classic glacial travel to more exposed mountaineering. The way ahead is up a snow / ice ridge, and how these next sections will feel depends entirely on conditions. In good snow you will move easily over the terrain, whereas in hard ice conditions I have climbed three or four pitches using ice screw belays. Follow the ridge in front of you over a few steps, where the ridge drops in altitude

Below the summit block, turn a tower on the right then a series of ramps that lead up the left side of the ridge to a final chimney. This is easier than it looks and there is often a fixed rope in place (6-7 hours from the hut).

The view from the summit is incredible and gives a real impression of space. Soak up the view, but don't linger too long as the descent is long.

Descent

There are two options: either go back the way you came which is fine in good snow conditions, or, if things are at all icy, I would suggest the second option of descending by abseil to the Silbersattel, between the Dufourspitze and Nordend.

If you are going to abseil, continue east along the ridge turning a small tower on the left. Where it feels as if you are about to start climbing again, look out for a metal stanchion which is the first abseil anchor.

Make six abseils onto the snow at the Silbersattel, if you still have the legs, you can carry on and climb Nordend, 4,609m, from here (about a two hour round trip). Once back on the glacier, spread the rope out and head north-west to find your way steeply through a band of large crevasses, and then head west to join your line of ascent from this morning.

Mike Abrahamsson (Swedish Mike) and client approaching the summit of the Dufourspitze.

If you are not fast and the snow starts to soften, the descent can feel really long, so leave as early as the guardian will give you breakfast (2am usually) and keep moving. You should get back to the hut with enough time to have a drink, and make for the last train to Zermatt, however … I would suggest that you don't. It seems like a great idea when you are having a cold drink at the hut. The reality is that, unless you are really fit, the climb from the glacier back to the train station at Rotenboden will spoil the whole experience. Have a drink, rehydrate, have an afternoon nap, rehydrate some more, then leave the hut at 0700 the following morning, and you may actually enjoy the walk out.

Breithorn 4,164m

When you arrive in Zermatt, and finally drag your eyes away from the Matterhorn, the wall of snow and ice that greets you is the Breithorn 4,164m. For many this is the easiest, and perhaps their first, 4,000m peak. The classic route is only 370m from the Klein Matterhorn lift to the summit, but the mountain is much more than just the classic route. The traverse, either full or half, is one of the finest outings at its grade in the Alps; the climbing is superb, and positions and views are unrivalled.

In my opinion the half traverse is actually a better climb than the full traverse, as all the difficulties are in ascent, on good rock, and there are no awkward downclimbs or abseils like there are on the full traverse.

The route can either be climbed from the first lift or after a night in the Cervinia guides hut, or the Ayas hut. A great combination is to climb the South West Ridge on Pollux (see *Alpine Mountaineering*) on the way to the Ayas, and then make the half traverse of the Breithorn on the way back.

I will describe the half traverse from the Klein Matterhorn lift, which is the way you would also approach from the Cervinia guides hut. If you come from the Ayas hut, you retrace your steps from the day before until you are under the rock pinnacles on the ridge, as described on the next pages.

ALPINE CLIMBING

Kris McCoey approaching the rock pinnacles on the Breithorn traverse.

East Ridge half traverse

Grade	AD	**Length**	500m
Exposure	East	**Rock type**	Metamorphic - Gneiss
Protection	Leader placed. There a few in situ pieces of gear but not that much considering how popular the route is.	**Descent**	Descend the normal route down the south-west flank to the Klein Matterhorn lift.
Conditions	Snow on the approach then dry rock / mixed conditions on the ridge.	**Time**	4-5hrs up, 1½hrs down.

Map
Swiss Topo 1:25,000 Zermatt-Gornergrat

Alternative guidebook
The 4000m peaks of the Alps by Ben Tibbets Volume 2 East
The 4000m Peaks of the Alps – Selected Climbs by Martin Moran

Hut
You can start from either the Ayas hut or the Cervinia guides hut at the Testa Grigia. If these are full, the Teodulo hut also works and adds about a 30 minute walk in the morning.
www.rifugioguidedelcervino.com
www.caitorino.it/rifugi/teodulo
www.rifugio-lambronecca.com

Equipment

The approach to the route from any direction requires travel on serious glaciated terrain, so you will need glacier travel kit. On the ridge all the difficulties are on rock, so a standard AD rack with a 50m rope is required.

Hut approach

Cervinia Guides hut

This is situated in part of the Testa Grigia lift building. The hut can be approached using the cable car from Cervinia which takes you right to the door, or from the Klein Matterhorn lift (a 30 minute walk down the piste), or down the new lift that connects the two. It takes about an hour to reascend to the Klein Matterhorn lift the following morning but gives you the advantage of being able to start earlier and be ahead of anyone coming from the first lift.

Ayas hut

On leaving the Klein Matterhorn, traverse under the south side of the Breithorn, heading for the base of the south west ridge on Pollux. Keep heading south-east past the base of the ridge to a flattening, then head west down the glacier; this avoids an area of seracs. The hut sits on a rocky promontory on the south side of the glacier at an altitude of 3420m. You could climb Pollux in the morning from the first lift, and then descend to the hut.

Route approach

The starting point for our excursion is the top of the Klein Matterhorn lift. If you are not staying at a hut, make the effort and be on the first lift; this way you will enjoy the best snow conditions when traversing under the south side of the Breithorn. Leave the lift station and follow the ski piste for a short distance, cross the rope marking the edge of the ski area and rope up for glacier travel. You will see all sorts of people wandering about in town shoes, with dogs, completely oblivious to the crevasses under their feet. Cross the Breithorn Pass then traverse under the south side of the Breithorn; there will almost certainly be a good track. Pay attention to the rope as the track runs parallel with the direction of the crevasses.

The route for the half traverse of the Breithorn.

As you pass under the south side of the Breithorn keep looking up to your left. You are aiming for the col just to the east of the rock pinnacles, marked as spot height 4,020m on the map. Branch off from the main track, which will be heading for Pollux and the Ayas hut, and work your way up onto a flat section of the glacier below the col.

Route description

Climb up onto the ridge joining it just before the rock pinnacles. In a thin snow year this slope can become very icy and may require a couple of pitches with ice screw belays. Once on the ridge, the rock is generally excellent and can be climbed in crampons when snowy, or in boots when dry.

The ridge rises in three towers. The first tower can be climbed directly at an exposed IV with bolt runners, or it can be turned on the left by crossing a snow gully and then climbing a series of ribs back to the crest (III). The second tower is climbed by a crack that splits a slab of excellent Gneiss. The third tower is climbed on the crest in superb positions. You keep mainly on the crest of the ridge until you reach a final steep step which can be climbed directly via a steep pull, or a delicate traverse to the left; there is a piton in place to protect the first steep move.

The route now changes back to snow, so if you have been climbing without crampons now is the time to put them back on. Follow an exposed ridge over the Breithorn central summit to a col, and then continue up another snow crest to the west and highest summit.

Climbers on the traverse with the Dufourspitze behind.

Descent

You can now descend easily via the SW flank to the cable car, and the bright lights of Zermatt.

The skyline above Saas-Fee, seen from the Almageller hut.

Saas-Fee

The area around Saas-Grund and Saas-Fee has one of the highest concentrations of 4,000m peaks in the Alps, and it is a justifiably popular area with those taking their first steps onto the larger peaks. The Allalinhorn is one the most accessible 4,000m peaks with a train that takes you to within 500m of the summit. There are also mountains that shun the use of mechanical uplift; making this a great area for all types of alpinism.

While the Valais is not known for the quality of its rock there is some brilliant climbing to be found on the Jegigrat and at the head of the valley on the Joderhorn. In this section I have included pure rock routes on both those peaks. I have also included the North Ridge and traverse of the Weissmies, which links perfectly into an ascent of the Dri Horlini ridge above the Almageller hut. The final route in the area is the traverse of the Lenzspitze and Nadelhorn one of the finest high-altitude routes at its grade in the Alps.

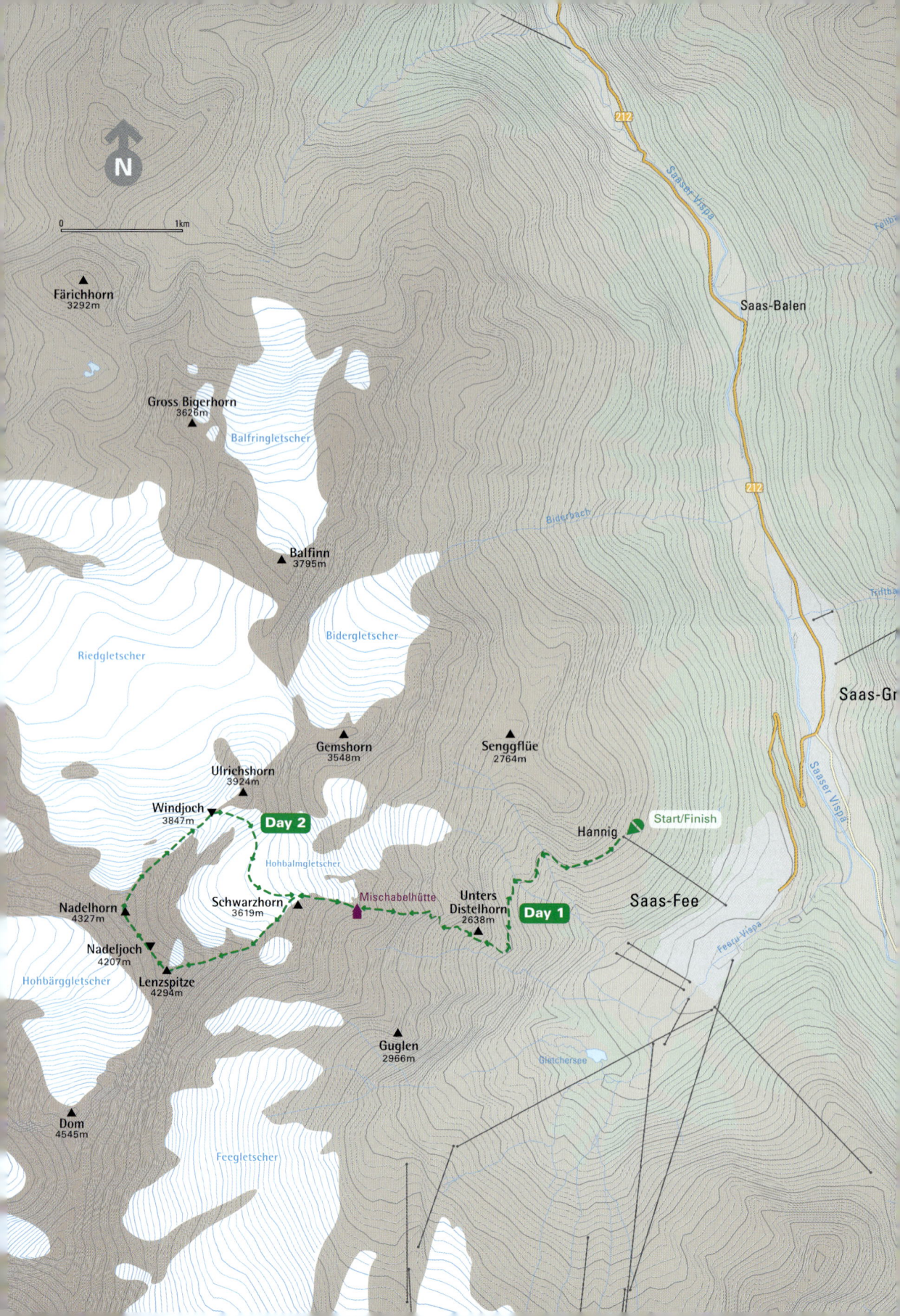

ALPINE CLIMBING

Lenzspitze 4,294m and Nadelhorn 4,327m

The East North East Ridge on the Lenzspitze is best in dry conditions due to its slabby nature. It is an excellent climb. When you reach the summit the best way off is to traverse to the Nadelhorn then descend its north east ridge. This does require a good weather forecast with no afternoon storms as you will be high for a long time. You will be rewarded with one of the best routes at its grade in the Alps.

> **If conditions permit**
> The North Face of Lenzspitze, the Dreiselwand, is one of the most famous easier north faces in the Alps, and in good snow conditions it is a straightforward snow and ice climb of 500m in length. In the early part of the summer, it may still be possible to climb this, but recent hot summers turned the snow to black ice which is horrible to climb and increases the stone fall danger. I will not include its description here, but if you hear the route is in condition the face is nowhere steeper than 55 degrees, steep enough to need two ice tools but shallow enough that you should be able to move quickly.

ENE Ridge of Lenzspitze and SE Ridge on Nadelhorn

Grade	AD+ III+	**Length**	1,100m
Exposure	ENE, SE and NE	**Rock type**	Gneiss
Protection	Leader placed with the odd peg and bolt.	**Descent**	North east ridge on Nadelhorn.
Conditions	Dry rock on the ridge crest then snow on the descent from the Nadelhorn.	**Time**	8-10hrs

Map
Swiss Topo 1:25,000 1328 Randa

Alternative guidebook
The 4000m peaks of the Alps by Martin Moran – The Alpine Club
Valais Alps East by Les Swindin and Peter Fleming – The Alpine Club
Mountaineering in the Swiss Alps by Stephane Maire

Equipment
50m rope, AD rack and glacier travel kit

Hut
Mischabel hut, www.mischabelhuette.ch/kopie-von-home

Rich Parker on the Lenzspitze traverse.

Hut approach
The hut approach is an adventure in itself, climbing steep, interesting terrain with cables and ladders where required. Some people use the cables like a via ferrata but if you are going to climb the Lenzspitze the next day then that would seem overkill. That said, it is probably one of the steepest hut approaches in the Alps.

Saas-Fee is a car free town, you need to park in the large car park at the entrance to the village or arrive by public transport. You now have two options: you can take the cable car to Hannig, which will

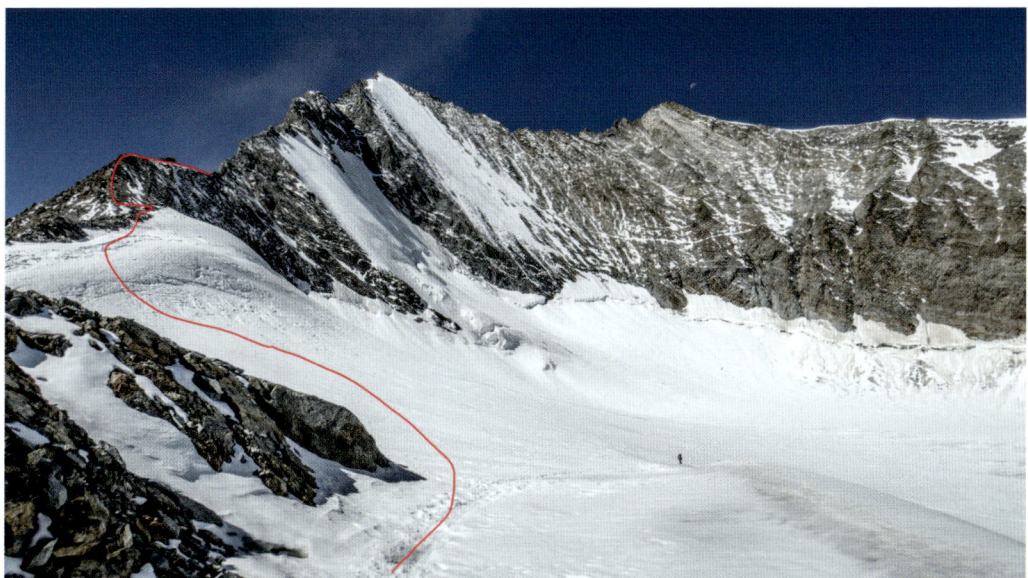

The approach to the Lenzspitze.

save you about 500m of ascent, then traverse south-west following signposts to the hut, to join a direct path coming from the village; or, if you want to save money, walk through the north side of the village where there are a couple of footpath options. The paths meet above Trift / Schönegge at 2,417m.

Follow the path up a blunt rib heading north-west. The path rises into the bowl with steep rocks above, and is marked with blue and white paint splashes. Where the path runs into steep rocks, it zigzags steeply with cables and metal steps to reach a ridge crest. The ridge is then followed west to reach the hut. It is 1,050m from the cable car, around 3 and a half hours.

Route approach

The climbing starts straight out of the back door of the hut. Follow a rock ridge, which may have snow on it earlier in the season, heading in a westerly direction. The ridge leads in 250m to the Hohbalmgletscher. Head south-west and either follow the edge of the glacier or climb the easy rocks on the ridge above the Schwarzhorn to point 3,814m, where the angle steepens.

Route description

Climb the ridge (II+) just right of the crest then downclimb to a notch to reach the foot of the Grand Gendarme. Climb a slab on the left side of the gendarme, then climb two long pitches (III) with bolt belays, to reach a pinnacle. Make a short abseil into a notch – 6m or downclimb (III), the rock is quite slabby. Climb the next step passing a metal spike (III+) and continue to the top of the Grand Gendarme. Make another 6m abseil or downclimb a chimney on the south side of the ridge (II+).

Gareth Hughes climbing on the ESE ridge of the Lenzspitze.

Traverse a horizontal section to reach the foot of a large (60m) buttress. The rock here is quite loose and the cleanest line is in the centre. Move left and follow a groove that leads to a snow crest and then to the top. In good snow conditions you feel more comfortable climbing on the snow right of the ridge, rather than on the crest itself.

The way ahead is to traverse to the Nadelhorn. This 1km ridge has great rock and some fantastic climbing.

Leave the summit and descend the north west ridge, crossing some small towers to reach the Nadeljoch (II+). The route now crosses five towers. The faces are all steep with great climbing and the back sides are easier angled. There are anchors on top of each tower that can be used to abseil the back side. Some of these are quite slabby and are more easily abseiled than downclimbed. The face of the third tower is particularly wonderful with a great 40m pitch (III+). After the fifth tower a narrow ridge leads to the summit.

Descent

Descend the north east ridge of the Nadelhorn, initially on rock; this is solid and there are lots of spikes for protection. The track is usually well worn as this is the classic route on the Nadelhorn. The rock gives way to a snow crest, which can be icy as it is exposed to the wind. Descend this to the Windjoch, then steep snow to the Hohbalmgletscher. Cross this to reach the path that leads to the hut. About 2hr from the summit.

Weissmies 4,017m

The Weissmies is known for its classic PD traverse climbing the SSE ridge on rock then descending the North Face on glaciated terrain, but it is also home to another fantastic traverse at an elevated grade of AD+. Those with the skills to operate at this grade can climb the North Ridge and descend the SSE ridge.

This magnificent undertaking is as good as any other traverse in the Valais. Don't let the ease of access from Hohsaas fool you, as the route is over 2km long and you need to keep moving if you don't want to miss dinner in the Almageller hut.

North Ridge

Grade	AD+ 4	Length	1,350m
Exposure	North	Rock type	Schist
Protection	Leader placed	Descent	South Ridge
Conditions	Dry rock	Time	6hrs up, 3hrs down.

Map
Swiss Topo 1:25,000 Saas 1329, Simplon 1309.

Alternative guidebook
Mountaineering in the Swiss Alps by Stephanie Marie.

Equipment
Alpine AD rack, glacier travel kit, ice axe and crampons.

Saas-Fee

The Weissmies North Ridge and South Ridge in profile.

Hut
Hohsaas hut – A slightly strange hut, in that it is underneath a restaurant at the top of a ski lift. This makes for an easy approach so you can have a rest day on the day of approach and still be in position for a big route the next day.

Hut approach
Take the Hohsaas lift from Saas-Grund, get off the lift, walk one minute, and you are there.

Gareth Hughes at dawn on the Weissmies North Ridge.

Route approach
The traverse starts at the Lagginjoch, the col between the Weissmies and the Lagginhorn. You will be doing this in the dark so make sure you have scoped it out the night before. There has been a lot of glacial recession in this area so don't leave the best route to chance. Leave the hut and follow a path that leads from the hut to the edge of the Hohlaubgletscher. Stay on the east side to avoid two bands of crevasses. The top part of the glacier is threatened by stone fall from the ridge, so it is worth putting your helmet on. A cairn and paint splash mark the easiest access point onto the ridge, and this is a bit loose and scrappy. When you reach the Lagginjoch, turn right. If you turn left this is the South Ridge of the Lagginhorn, also a great route but not described in this book.

Route description
The bedding plane of the rock on the North Ridge means that the terrain is a slab on the west side and overhangs on the east. The route stays almost exclusively on the slabby side which, while you are in balance, does require some careful footwork at times. Like most big ridges in the Alps, the best rock is on the crest. Follow the ridge, crossing a number of small towers (II and III), and at a height of about 3,600m the ridge steepens. The feature ahead of you is known as the Grande Dalle (*the Big Slab*) (IV), climb this using a metal spike and a couple of bolts for protection; these are spaced so focus is required. Continue along the ridge above to point 3,722m.

Rich Parker climbing on the Weissmies North Ridge.

Descend the ridge in a south-east direction to a col. Above the col are a series of slabby towers. Cross the first tower or turn it on the left; the second can be turned on the left as well, or climb direct and make a 5m abseil. The following towers are all climbed directly, and the last difficult section climbs a slim tower via a shallow groove (IV) with a couple of bolts for protection; this can feel quite bold. This takes you to point 3,828, above which the route starts to feel easier. The ridge now takes a more southerly direction and can often become more mixed before the final snow section. Follow the crest. You may need to turn a crevasse on the right before a snow crest leads to the summit.

Descent

If the North Face is in condition, then the fastest descent is down this back to Hohsaas and the lift to the valley. However, in recent years this has not always been the case, so the best descent is down the SSE Ridge to the Almageller hut.

Leave the summit heading south-east. This is initially a superb snow crest that broadens at about point 3,972m, here the ground steepens and becomes much rockier. In most seasons you will want to put your crampons away here. There are a few yellow paint splashes that mark the start of the South South East Ridge. The initial section of the ridge is fun blocky scrambling with the best rock on the crest.

At about 3,700m it is possible to traverse east on a small glacier / snow patch. If this has not turned to ice then it can be much faster to descend than continuing on the rock. If it is icy, continue on the crest of the ridge. You can carry on all the way to the Zwischbergenpass, or you can cut off the ridge and descend a shallow valley on the east side of the ridge before gaining the Zwischbergenpass. At the pass you will pick up blue and white paint markers that lead you all the way to the Almageller hut.

Saas-Fee

Climbers on the Dri Horlini Ridge.

Dri Horlini 3,209m

This is a fantastic rock traverse on magnificent rock in a superb position. It is the perfect follow-on day from the North Ridge of the Weissmies. The route is more akin to a high-quality rock climb than an alpine route in the Valais, though you will need plenty of alpine techniques to climb it. The start of the route also has the beauty of only being about 15 minutes' walk from the hut, and it usually does not need an ice axe or crampons for the approach or descent, so you can climb with a light pack on. Some people walk up from the valley to the Almageller hut to make this traverse or enjoy some of the fantastic rock climbing on its flanks.

SW Ridge traverse

Grade	AD 4b	**Length**	500m
Exposure	South-west	**Rock type**	Gneiss
Protection	Mixed	**Descent**	Scramble
Conditions	Dry rock	**Time**	4hrs round trip.

Map
Swiss Topo 1:25,000 Saas 1329

Alternative guidebook
Schweiz Plaisir West (Band II) by Edition Filidor

Equipment
An AD rack with a few extra quickdraws, 50m rope.

Hut
Almageller Hut, www.almagellerhuette.ch

This can either be approached from above after climbing the Weissmies, (description in the descent from the previous route) or in about 4 hours from Saas-Almagell.

Hut approach
The Almageller hut is a fantastically positioned hut that has been recently renovated and extended. It is situated at the upper limit of summer grazing pastures, so has some grass around it which is really nice. The hut is approached entirely on foot from Saas-Almagell and takes about 4 hours. You have to consider tactics about where you may leave your vehicle.

If you are going to descend from the summit of the Weissmies you need to think about logistics, as you will start from Saas-Grund and descend to Saas-Almagell. Your options are to leave your car in Saas-Grund and get a bus or hitch back along the road; or leave your car in Saas-Almagell and get the bus to Saas-Grund, so that you will descend to the car at the end of your trip.

If you are approaching the hut from Saas-Almagell, the track starts in a car park just as you come into Saas-Almagell, next to a river and waterfall. The hut is signposted, so it is easy to find (yellow signs). The track winds its way up through larch woods to a bridge where the angle eases; you then follow the stream to the Almagelleralp (1hr 30min), where there is a hut selling refreshments.

The path from the Almagelleralp heads uphill more steeply now with great views. Due to the shape of the hillside, you won't see the hut until you are fairly close, so don't despair (4 hours in total).

There is a third alternative where you can park in Saas-Grund, then take the lift to Kreuzboden. From here a path leads over the hillside across a spectacular suspension bridge and through some scrambling sections to reach the Almagelleralp and the other path.

Route approach
Leave the hut and head west following yellow paint splashes that lead to a ramp; scramble up this to the base of the route. This should take about 15minutes. If it is taking longer, you have probably missed the base of the route and are following the yellow paint marks heading for the Rotgrat on the Weissmies.

The approach to the Dri Horlini Ridge.

Gareth Hughes Climbing on the Dri Horlini ridge.

Route description

Start at the toe of the buttress with three really nice pitches of 3a, 3b and 3a to belay on the crest of the ridge. Climb up a slab towards an overhang then turn it on the left. Climb another pitch of 3a to reach the top of the first tower.

Scramble along the crest of the ridge with some moving together and short pitches; this leads to the top of the second tower. You can either make a short abseil from here or downclimb into a notch at the base of the third (Dri) tower. Climb this directly (IV) or turn on the right (II) or left (III). Make an abseil of 15m to reach another brèche.

Climb a series of easy slabs to the summit.

Descent

Leaving the summit, head north-west along the ridge for about 350m until you can scramble down on the south side of the ridge to join an increasingly defined path that leads back to the hut.

Joderhorn 3,035m

One of the amazing things about the Alps is that even in the busiest times of the season it is possible to seek out quieter corners of the range and climb some amazing routes in remarkable locations.

The Joderhorn is such a peak. When viewed as a whole mountain it is easily dismissed, as most of it is granite boulder field. However, this granite pile all comes together into a magnificent 12 pitch route on the South East Ridge. The route comprises some of the best granite you will find in the Alps (one blog described the friction as so good "an eel could not slide on it"). The climbing starts from a notch in

Mike Austin climbing on the Joderhorn with the east face of Monte Rosa in the background.

the ridge then rises in a series of towers, the back drop is incredible with the whole east face of Monte Rosa to the west.

Access is interesting, and there are two key options. You either start from the Mattmark dam at the head of Saastal, or from the village of Macugnaga via a cable car. The approach from the Saastal is significantly longer, about 3hr 15min as opposed to about 45min from the lift. The decision will depend on where you are based. If you are in Saastal, then it's about a 2hr 30min drive round to Macugnaga so it would make sense to keep your base where it is and walk. If you don't mind the drive and want to give your legs a rest, Macugnaga is set in a beautiful valley, and a trip to Italy is always a good thing. You can complete the route in a day with either option, lift or long walk.

If you are coming from Saastal, you can cycle along the side of Mattmark reservoir; this saves at least an hours walking overall. It's gently uphill on the way in (90m height gain), which makes for a very fast descent back to the car. You can lock your bikes to a fence or signpost at the end of the dam, where the track changes from tarmac to walking path. If you don't have bikes, you can hire them in Saas-Grund. If you don't fancy the walk before the route and fancy a night in an Italian hut, you could come up on the cable car the night before or walk in to the hut the afternoon before, ready to climb in the morning.

South East Ridge

Grade	D 5a	**Length**	300m
Exposure	SE	**Rock type**	Granite
Protection	The route is a mix of trad / leader placed protection with a mix of pegs and bolts. Most but not all the belays are in situ. The rock is superb, and it is really easy to find good natural protection opportunities.		
Descent	Easy scramble and walk off.		
Conditions	Dry rock	**Time**	4-5hrs for the climbing. Approach and descent depending on start point.

Map
Swiss Topo 1:50,000 Mischabel 284, 1:25,000 Monte Moro 1349

Alternative guidebook
Schweiz Plaisir West (Band II) by Edition Filidor

Hut
Rifugio Oberto Maroli, www.montemoropass.it tel.+39 0324 65544 valcot.rifugio@gmail.com

The hut can be accessed either by walking over the Monte Moro pass from the Mattmark dam at the head of Saastal, or by a very short walk from the top of the Monte Moro cable car from Macugnaga.

It can also be climbed as a day route from either side.

Equipment
A 40m rope, full set of wires (1-10) cams (0.4, 0.5, 0.75, 1, 2), 8 quickdraws, approach shoes or light boots depending if there is any snow on the ground.

Hut approach
The approach from the lift could not be easier. Come out of the lifts, and walk a few minutes downhill, heading east to come to the hut. If you are coming from Saastal, walk to the Monte Moro pass (there is a large golden Madonna just above the pass), then descend south-west to the hut.

ALPINE CLIMBING

Route approach

The last 45 minutes of the approach are common to both access options.

If you are coming from the Mattmark dam, follow the west side of the dam to the end of the metalled road; here you will pick up a sign and red and white paint markers. These will lead you up through a beautiful high alpine meadow to a steeper rockier section. The route follows a series of large slabs that eventually give way to a boulder field and the pass. The path is a part of the Tour du Monte Rosa, so is very well marked.

When you are at the Monte Moro pass, or at the hut, head east from the path. There are cairns that lead along a broad ridge or bits of path leading from the hut. You are heading for the top of the ski lift to the east of the access lift (San Pietro).

The approach to the Joderhorn, the climb starts where indicated.

Looking south-east from the top of the ski lift there is a small path that leads towards what can only really be described as a block field, as the rocks are too big to be described as a boulder field. You will very quickly lose the path but don't worry, there are some old orange and red poles (old ski piste markers) that lead in the right general direction and some cairns.

The terrain is quite awkward to move through quickly as the boulders are so big. You need to lose about 100m of altitude from the pass to about 2,760m. From this altitude, head east to move round the end of the south ridge of Punta San Pietro. You will come across a big section of slabs and a path; traverse under these, following the base of the slabs until a small path leads you towards a notch in the South East Ridge. There is a short section of scrambling below the notch and a marker pole helps guide your way. At the notch there is plenty of space to gear up.

Route description

The climbing starts right next to the notch described above. Unusually for an alpine ridge, it is really difficult to get a good view of the ridge itself, hence the lack of an overall photograph.

Facing the South East Ridge, the climbing starts a few metres to the left in a corner, where there is a flat spot to uncoil the rope and a bolt to belay on.

Pitch 1 – 4b 10m The route starts up a steep corner; luckily the holds are plentiful, as the steepness is a rude awakening. A few steep moves lead to a ledge and a double bolt belay.

Pitch 2 – 5c 30m Leaving the belay you can step left and climb a steep, awkward chimney, but it is much easier to move further left on easy ground, then come back right into the base of a corner. This corner has 4 bolts in it and is the hardest pitch on the climb. The rock is fantastic and, if you feel at your limit climbing with a rucksack on at almost 3,000m, you can always pull on a bolt. There is a double bolt belay at the top of the corner.

Pitch 3 – 3b 25m Follow the corner above the belay, where there is a peg just at the start. At the top of the corner, move right, then climb another corner with a peg to the ridge crest (double bolt belay on the crest).

Pitch 4 – 5a 25m Above is a beautiful wall, cracks running up the middle. At the base of the wall, move left and make a move up onto a hanging ramp (there is an old, jammed cam

ABOVE: The author climbing on the Joderhorn.
RIGHT: The author on one of the superb crack pitches on the Joderhorn.

	at the start). Move up the ramp to the base of the wall, which is climbed directly with a bolt and some pegs for protection; this is every bit as good as it looks.
Pitch 5 – 3b 12m	A short easy wall leads to the bottom of one of the best pitches of climbing I have done at its grade in the Alps.
Pitch 6 – 5a 30m	Climb the incredible crack. Even where it steepens and looks intimidating from below, the holds keep coming and you can climb the whole pitch in balance.
Pitch 7 – easy 25m	Scramble up a small block above the belay then walk along to the base of a corner, peg and bolt belay.
Pitch 8 – 5a 10m	This is one of those pitches that, although short, has one really awkward move, moving up through a short overhanging chimney. Move up and left to the base of the chimney where there is a thread runner and a good cam slot. Make some steep moves up the chimney on good positive holds, and belay at the top. You may want to consider taking your rucksack off and pulling it up after you.
Pitch 9 – 45m	Climb up the crest of the ridge, it is possible to belay in lots of places.
Pitch 10 – 35m	Follow the ridge crest finishing on a big flat slab below the final wall. This is an amazing place for a picnic and a drink, soaking up the ambience and the incredible views of Monte Rosa.
Pitch 11 – 5a 20m	A flake leads diagonally right to left on the lower part of the wall; there is a peg hidden behind the flake for protection. Step up onto the wall then follow the flake out left, then back right to a thin crack. Clip the peg, then make some amazing moves on positive finger locks to easy ground and a double bolt belay.
Pitch 12 – scrambling 40m	You can shorten the rope here, then move together over easy terrain to the summit.

Descent

You will not need any technical kit for the descent, so you can put it all away and change into comfortable footwear. Head north down a boulder field with cairns to pick up a path. Follow this, intermittently heading slightly north-east until you can head west under some steeper ground and back to the Monte Moro pass, where you can either head back to the lift or towards Mattmark.

ALPINE CLIMBING

The Jegihorn, seen from close to the Weissmies hut.

Jegigrat 3,368m and Jegihorn 3206m
(See map on page 219).

Saas-Grund is famous for 4,000m peaks, as there are 18 of them in the surrounding area. These are great objectives, but you are more likely to meet other people, and these routes require more specific conditions being that much higher. You also need to be acclimatised before climbing technical peaks at that altitude.

At a more modest altitude of 3,368m, the SE Gendarme and traverse of the Jegigrat comes into condition more readily and is perfect to climb while acclimatising for larger things or in its own right. It is worth bearing in mind that, although the maximum height may not be that great, you will spend most of the day above 3,000m.

Jegigrat, SE Spur of Grand Gendarme and traverse

The route is a perfect combination of high alpine rock climb that leads into a superb ridge traverse. It also has the added bonus of finishing over the Jegihorn via ferrata, the highest via ferrata in Europe.

The starting point is the excellent Weissmies hut.

Grade	D 4c	**Length**	670m
Exposure	SE on the Gendarme, SW on the traverse.	**Rock type**	Gneiss
Protection	On the ascent of the Grand Gendarme, the route is a mix of in situ and leader placed protection. On the traverse there is almost no in situ equipment.		
Descent	Join the Jegihorn via ferrata, which is followed over the summit, then follow the classic descent from the Jegihorn, marked with blue paint splashes, either back to the lift or the hut.		
Conditions	Dry rock	**Time**	8-10hrs

Map
Swiss Topo 1:50,000 Visp 274, 1:25,000 Simplon 1309

Alternative guidebook
Mountaineering in the Swiss Alps by Stephane Maire

Hut
Weissmies hut, 2726m, www.weissmieshuette.ch reservations online via the Swiss Alpine Club online booking service www.alpsonline.org/guest/reservations – this has live online availability. You can also call for next day reservations tel. +41 27 957 25 54.

Equipment
50m rope, full set of wires (1-10), cams (0.5, 0.75, 1, 2), 8 quickdraws. It is also worth having at least 2 lengths of abseil tat with you (3m each), as on the traverse of the ridge there are a couple of sections that can be downclimbed, but you may choose to abseil, and the anchors are not always in situ. Approach shoes or light boots, and depending if there is any snow on the ground, early season you may also consider a light ice axe.

The climbing on the Grand Gendarme is more fun in rock shoes. You can then change to more comfortable footwear for the traverse.

Hut approach
The hut is approached from either the lift at Kreuzboden (1hr uphill walk), or Hohsaas (1hr downhill walk, more expensive on the lift). This lift takes you from the main car park in Saas-Grund. Lift times can be found here www.hohsaas.ch. Be aware on the descent that the lift closes surprisingly early, at 1630 on most days. The hut is well signposted from either lift.

Route approach
You can't really see the start of the route from the hut, just approximately where it is. It is also pretty difficult to get a good route photo, so you will have to take me on trust that it's a great route.

Leave the hut and pick up the path to the via ferrata (klettersteig in German) heading north; the path is marked with blue and white paint marks (blue line sandwiched between 2 white lines). Cross a river

The approach to the Grand Gendarme on the Jegihorn.

draining from the Lagginhorngletscher, or what is left of it, on a bridge. There is a faint path leading north from here, but it is worth continuing along the via ferrata path to cross the next stream, draining from the Talligletscher. There is a bridge here whereas if you cut the corner straight after the first bridge, you may start the day with damp feet.

Once you have crossed the second stream, head north picking up the path that follows the crest of the moraine, this finishes at point 2,972. Head north-east crossing a boulder field with the odd cairn; you are heading for the base of the cliffs. Follow the cliffs north-east right round the base of the spur dropping from the summit of the Jegiturm. As you come round the base there are small bits of path linking the patches of scree and boulders.

You are heading for a corner at the bottom left of an area of slabs. The slabs are red in colour with two obvious cracks running up them. There is a big flat area at their base where you can gear up.

The author on one of the lower pitches on the Grand Gendarme.

Route description

Grand Gendarme

Climb easily up and right following cracks in the slabs, where you will run out of rope on easy angled terrain and a belay can be awkward to arrange. Keep heading right. This is walking / very easy climbing following a cracked slab out right, heading for the ridge crest. If the climbing is anything other than really easy you have gone too high. When you reach the ridge, you will find a couple of bolts and a double bolt belay on the north side of the ridge.

Pitch 1 – 4b 30m Follow the arête with the odd peg and bolt for protection, double bolt belay.

Pitch 2 – 4c 30m Carry on up the arête with beautiful, exposed moves to belay on a ledge below an obvious corner with some green moss in it.

Pitch 3 – 4c 20m Step into the corner making really nice bridging moves to end up on a slightly overhanging niche, there is a bolt on a slab on the right and it is possible to avoid the steep wall above you by moving to the right. However, I think this is more difficult than climbing the wall. Clip a peg, then pull up to the right on good holds to regain the ridge. Follow the ridge to a double bolt belay.

Pitch 4 – 4b 40m Move up and left from the belay. Climb the left side of a slab in a stunning position, and then climb a steep black wall on good holds into a niche, belay on a cam and sling.

Pitch 5 – 4c 40m Step right from the belay and make some awkward mantelshelf type moves with limited protection. Climb the wall above and belay on natural gear below an obvious left-slanting corner.

Pitch 6 – 30m 5a Climb the corner crack on excellent holds and you will find a double bolt belay at the top of the corner; you could belay here but it's a very short pitch. It's better to clip in a long extender to reduce rope drag. You will see a wobbly old peg at the start of a horizontal crack. Head across the crack, where the first move feels really committing but the holds improve with every move, and you can place a couple of cams for protection. Belay on double bolts above a small ledge in a spectacular position.

Mike Austin climbing on the Grand Gendarme.　　Mike Austin on the Jegigrat traverse with the Fletschorn behind.

Pitch 7 – 30m 5a　The wall above is more intimidating than it is difficult. Leave the belay and follow excellent holds pretty much straight up, passing a bolt. As you look up you will see a group of two pegs and a bolt where it gets even steeper; clip one or all of these, depending on how you are feeling. Step right and reach up to find 'thank God' holds everywhere. A few big pulls and you are on top of the Grand Gendarme.

Jegigrat traverse
There isn't much space on the summit, so a quick photograph and then you can rig an abseil. Abseil 25m on the north side to a ledge where you can have a drink, some food and change your shoes. A ledge leads round to the left on the north side, with a little bit of downclimbing before you can regain the ridge at the bottom of the Grand Gendarme (south-west side).

The way ahead is to follow the crest of the ridge, where the climbing is never more difficult than 3c, although some of it is quite steep and intimidating. There is very little in situ equipment on the ridge so try not to be drawn onto the sides where the rock is poor (whereas it is generally excellent on the crest). There are a number of downclimbing sections where you may prefer to abseil and there may not be any equipment in situ, so make sure you have some abseil tat with you. The climbing is great fun and some of the towers you need to cross are steep but on amazing holds; so, keep the faith and keep to the crest.

When you reach point 3,350m the climbing is pretty much over.

Descent

At point 3,350m, follow the scree slopes, cairns and small paths in a south-westerly direction to join the Jegihorn via ferrata. The quickest and safest way off is to follow the via ferrata over the summit of the Jegihorn; in some descriptions it mentions that it is possible to descend the Puiseux Couloir (the low point on the ridge between the Jegigrat and Jegihorn) but this looks hideous. If you did need to lose height quickly you would be better descending the first section of the via ferrata, although there is nowhere on this route that would be a good place to be in a storm.

You will almost certainly not have via ferrata kit (which is designed to absorb the impact in the event of a fall), so I would suggest moving together with about 10 metres of rope between each person, clipping into the anchors as you go. This will keep the dynamic element in the system should anyone fall.

When you join the via ferrata you are faced with two options: you can follow the cables down into the notch and out the other side, or cross the Nepalese bridge. In theory the bridge is faster, but I found it significantly scarier.

When you reach the summit, soak in the view then follow the blue and white paint splashes which lead you west then south-east off the Jegihorn and down to a path junction. From here you can either head back to the hut or down to the lift at Kreuzboden.

Dawn, seen from high on the Jungfrau.

Bernese Oberland

The Bernese Oberland is the area of heavily glaciated mountains north of the Rhône valley in Switzerland. This is one of the few places in the Alps that feel like you are in the Himalaya, and Konkordiaplatz, where five major glaciers meet, is a truly remarkable place.

The area is a home to some amazing 4,000m peaks, but due to their remoteness and scale I would suggest that the central Oberland is not the place to venture to in the early part of your alpine career. So, we have focused on some incredible routes on the periphery of the range.

When you look at the Oberland from the north you are faced with a wall of mountains; the Eiger, Mönch and Jungfrau are the jewels in the crown and an incredible sight. I included the classic route on the Mönch in *Alpine Mountaineering* as it is the perfect introduction to moving on exposed snow crests. In this book I have included the Jungfrau, a truly classic mountain with movement on glacier, snow and rock, and the Eiger, the most famous north face in the world. More suited to our needs, the Eiger also has an incredible traverse up the Mittellegi Ridge and down the South Ridge. In my view this is a significantly better route than the Horlini Ridge on the Matterhorn, and a route that should be on any alpinist's hit list.

Jungfrau 4,158m

A magnificent mountain and a great introduction to the Bernese Oberland. While the height gain from the hut may not seem that great compared to some of the other routes in the Oberland, the peak should not be underestimated. The best conditions are in good snow, once the traverse below the Rottalsattel and the upper sections of the South East Ridge become icy the route would not be recommended. A trip to the Jungfrau can easily be combined with an ascent of the Mönch the day before or the day after. This is described in *Alpine Mountaineering* by the same author.

South East Ridge

Grade	PD+	Length	840m
Exposure	SE	Rock type	Limestone
Protection	Some stakes and bolts in place, a light rack might be useful.	Descent	Reverse same route
Conditions	Snow on the glacier and dry rock.	Time	8-10hrs

Map
Swiss Topo 1:25,000 Finsteraarhorn 1249

Alternative guidebook
The 4000m peaks of the Alps by Martin Moran – Alpine Club

Equipment
50m rope, glacier travel kit and a PD rack. You may want to consider a second, light ice tool for the leader.

Hut
Mönchsjoch hut, www.moenchsjoch.ch

Hut approach
As hut approaches go it couldn't be much easier or much more expensive. Take the train from Grindelwald Grund to the Jungfraujoch. The new Eiger express lift from Grindelwald Grund to Eigergletscher, where you change onto the train, makes the journey incredibly fast.

The journey is really expensive but, once you have decided to climb in this area, you just have to park any thoughts of the cost, enjoy the journey, and marvel at the engineering achievement of building a railway through the heart of the Eiger. Being dropped off at 3,454m does have its advantages.

It is worth leaving enough time to have a look around at the station, then follow the signs to the hut. When you get outside onto the snow, follow a marked piste that leads to the hut in about 45min. If you stay inside the markers there should be no worry about crevasses.

Route approach
While the route approach is short, the route is south-east facing and catches any sun, so the snow will soften quickly. Get the earliest start possible.

Retrace your steps past the train station, then SSW descending across the Jungfraufirn to the base of the East Ridge of the Rottalhorn 3,971m (this is a subsidiary top of the Jungfrau). A large rain gauge marks the start of the ridge.

The route on the Jungfrau.

Route description

Climb up and across a snow ramp to reach the ridge then scramble up past the rain gauge to a steep wall. You may want to take your crampons off somewhere around here, as the next section will almost certainly be all rock. Climb a pitch up the wall (bolts), then traverse left on the south side for about 100m. The terrain above you is significantly steeper so you shouldn't be tempted to carry on straight up. Where the angle above eases, climb good rock to reach the ridge crest and snow.

Once your crampons are back on, climb the ridge above then traverse right until you are under the Rottalsattel, you now have to cross the bergschrund and climb up to the col. This can be pretty steep, so it might be worth a having a second light ice tool in the party for the leader.

Follow the ridge then the steep snow, until a traverse left leads to rocks that bound the left, west edge of the steep snow. There are metal posts every 40m to protect the traverse; climb the rocks or the snow next to them depending on conditions. Continue up the rocks to reach the South West Ridge which is followed to the summit.

Descent

Reverse the line of ascent. There is usually an abseil anchor in place at the Rottalsattel to get back over the bergschrund, you will need a 50m rope for this. You can also abseil the steep wall that you climbed above the rain gauge.

In good snow conditions it is possible to miss the ridge and descend the glacier below the Rottalsattel; this is steep and you need to know you can get through the crevassed section. If it is in condition, it is much faster than descending the ridge and you can keep a high traverse around the Jungfraufirn back to the train station.

Climbers on the descent from the Jungfrau.

Bernese Oberland

The Mittellegi Ridge, seen from the hut.

Eiger 3,970m

There are few other mountains in the Alps, or even the world, with the mythical attraction of the Eiger, and few other beautiful mountains are blessed with the same quality of climbing as the classic traverse of the Mittellegi and South Ridge of the Eiger.

Mittellegi North East Ridge

The route starts at the incredibly positioned Mittellegi hut. This small hut, owned by the local guides bureau, organises breakfast at set time intervals so that climbers leave the hut in small waves. This means there are rarely any bottlenecks like those found on the Matterhorn. Most parties continue the traverse down the South Ridge to the Jungfraujoch railway and then to the valley. A nice variation is to stay in the Mönchsjoch hut, which removes the time pressure of catching the train. You can then climb the Mönch in the morning before getting the train back to the valley.

Grade	D 4a	**Length**	650m
Exposure	NE	**Rock type**	Limestone which changes to Gneiss part-way along the descent.
Protection	Mixed	**Descent**	South ridge
Conditions	Dry rock	**Time**	Ascent 4-5hrs, descent 3-4hrs.

Map
Swiss Topo 1:25,000 Finsteraarhorn 1249 and Grindelwald 1229

Alternative guidebook
Bernese Oberland by Les Swindin – The Alpine Club

Equipment
AD rack. A 50m rope is needed for the descent.

Hut
Mittellegi hut, www.mittellegi.ch/en

Hut approach
In many ways this is the crux of the route, as the rock is slabby and loose in places. The first time I did the route my guest said we had to go to the summit, as there was no way he was going back down the hut approach.

Get off the Jungfraujoch train at Eismeer (make sure the train you get on is going to stop there).

Approach to the Mittellegi hut.

Follow the signpost to the hut and walk down a tunnel which pops you out onto a glacier. Head north-east and follow the hanging Challifirn glacier. Traverse the glacier until you are under the Grand Gendarme on the Mittellegi ridge. Just right of this, climb two pitches of III, then easier ground that heads up and right to the hut. An alternative is to climb the ridge that drops from the hut (there are metal posts in place). Although I dislike the idea of following a local guide, as it drives me nuts when others do it to me, I would have a look and see where they go.

Don't be put off by the climbing on the approach, as the route above is much, much better. The approach would be very difficult to find in poor visibility.

Route description
There are few mountains where the route finding is as simple as 'leave hut, follow ridge to summit', but that pretty much covers it.

Leave the hut and climb over some gendarmes. There are bolts on most of them and short sections of fixed ropes on others.

When you reach the summit of the Grand Gendarme make a 20m abseil to reach some steep fixed ropes. These are on the north side of the ridge and can be frozen in early in the season, which can make the climb a bit more challenging. The ambience of climbing with the north face dropping below your feet is incredible. After the steep fixed ropes, another couple of small towers are crossed to a point where the ridge changes from rock to snow.

Crampons on. Then an incredible snow crest with space all round you, the north face on your right, and the other giants of the Oberland on your left, leads to the summit.

Descent
There are two possible descents: the West Flank, and the South Ridge. The West Flank is loose, difficult to navigate, and exposed to stone fall. The South Ridge is objectively safe, and all the difficulties one may face in ascent are abseiled over on the way down.

Bernese Oberland

ABOVE: Climbers on the Mittellegi Ridge.
RIGHT: Andy Ball on the fixed ropes high on the Eiger.

Leave the summit heading south. Stay on the crest to reach a series of short abseils and a downclimbing section on stakes or bolts. When you reach a steeper step, make a 10m, then a 25m abseil to easier ground which leads to the North Eigerjoch.

The rock type changes here to Gneiss and is much better quality, though there was a rockfall here in 2022 that can be passed on the east side (bolts). Climb the ridge direct or on the north-west side, with bolts for protection, to reach the South Eigerjoch.

Gain the glacier and head south to the Mönchsjoch hut and then the train. Allow 5 hours for the descent to the train.

Andy Ball approaching the summit of the Eiger.

Luke Kemp climbing on the Klein Bielenhorn.

The peaks surrounding the Furka Pass.

Furka Pass

If I had to choose one area of the Alps to take to my desert island, this would be it. The quality of the rock, the amazing routes, incredible views, and short approaches combine to provide everything I want in an Alpine holiday. The lack of large glaciers and 4,000m peaks is a drawback for some, but the lack of need to continually race the sun before the snow softens, and quality of the rock more than make up for it. The other consideration is that as the peaks are a bit lower, they clear more quickly after bad weather and are often in condition earlier in the season. It's not all rock climbing; an ascent of the Galenstock 3,584m, the highest peak in the area, is a fantastic alpine outing with movement on rock, snow, and glacial terrain.

The layout of the area allows you to climb most of the routes either in a day from the road or from one of the excellent huts. The huts are generally smaller than the those in the larger mountains and have a more relaxed feel.

Gross Furkahorn 3,169m

A fantastic ridge climb with a bit of everything. There is a small glacier to cross on the approach and you may need an ice axe and a pair of crampons to get to the base of the route on steep snow. Later in the season, when the glacier is dry and the approach and descent are clear of snow, you may be able to get away with approach shoes. If the descent (south facing) is dry, you may be able to leave your ice axe and crampons at the base of the route to be picked up on the way home.

You can approach the route either directly from the road or from the Sidelen hut, depending on where you want to spend the night.

East South East Ridge

Grade	AD+ 4c	Length	350m
Exposure	ESE	Rock type	Granite
Protection	Mix of bolts, pegs and leader placed protection.	Descent	Abseil and scramble.
Conditions	Dry rock	Time	1½hrs for approach from Furka Pass. 4-5hrs for route. 1½hrs back to pass.

Map
Swiss Topo 1:25,000 1231 - Urseren

Alternative guidebook
Schweis Plaiser West Band I – Edition Filidor

Equipment
50m rope, nuts (1-9), cams (0.3-2), 6 quickdraws, ice axe and crampons depending on conditions.

Hut
Sidelen hut, www.sidelen-huette.ch tel. +41 887 02 33

Hut approach
The easiest approach to the Sidelen hut is on the rising traverse path from the Furka Pass. Approaching from Andermatt, this is 2.5km up the road towards the Furka Pass from the hotel at Tiefenbach. Park on the north side of the road, on the pass side of the Furka Refuge (closed). It is also possible to approach from below the hut at an obvious bend in the road where it crosses a stream.

Will Brant on the Gross Furkahorn.

Route approach
If you start from the road, follow the path to the Sidelen hut from the Furka Pass. Where it crosses a river using a metal bridge, head north following a path that parallels the river and leads to what's left of the Sidelen glacier. Walk up the remnants of the west arm of the Sidelen glacier and then trend left, heading for the right side of the toe of the ridge. The route starts at the base of a square-cut slabby

ALPINE CLIMBING

Approach to the Gross Furkahorn.

corner. This route is one of the most popular in the area, so route finding is pretty easy; if you get confused just look for the cleanest section of rock where thousands of previous climbers have passed.

Route description

Pitch 1 – 4c 30m Climb the corner, which can feel a little polished and hard for the grade. Persevere … it gets better. Belay on a ledge at the top of the corner on the left.

Pitch 2 – 4b 35m Move up and left to join the crest of the ridge, follow cracks on the ridge to a good belay.

How you tackle the next section of ridge will depend a bit on the climbing ability of the team. The climbing is between grade III and 4b. It is possible to pitch it all and most of the belays are in situ. However, this is really slow, so I would suggest a mix of moving together and short pitches on the harder sections.

Follow the crest of the ridge until just below an obvious red tower. Move down and left to reach a ledge. Follow this and then make an awkward step down and left to reach a crack just under the red tower; belay here.

Climb a crack to regain the ridge and climb a pitch of 4b along the crest.

The ridge ahead is now pretty much horizontal, follow the ridge (II – 3c) to the base of the final tower.

You can either climb the tower in one longish pitch, or split it with a great belay on the crest. It is easier to do this in one pitch as it saves an awkward change over.

The summit is in a superb position, with great views onto the Rhône glacier on one side and the basin of the Sidelen hut on the other.

Descent

The descent starts with a 15m abseil on the south side of the mountain, and then a scramble down to reach a path. Follow this down and left to a cairn. Keep left and scramble down to an abseil anchor and then make a 20m abseil to a ledge. Scramble down right and downclimb to easy ground. Now follow a terrace that leads under the south face and round the end of the ESE ridge and back to your gearing up point at the start of the climbing. This can feel quite exposed if it is on snow. You can now retrace your steps to the hut or back to the Furka Pass.

Darren Williams on the Chli Bielenhorn.

Klein (Chli) 2,941 and Gross Bielenhorn 3,210m

The Klein and Gross Bielenhorn are situated east of the Sidelen hut, and like most of the routes in this sector they can be climbed in a day or from the hut. The Klein Bielenhorn (also known as the Chli Bielenhorn) is a fantastic half-day route, perfect for one of those days when you have travelled from another part of the Alps then walked in to the hut, or you have a spare morning before having to head off somewhere else, or even just want a chilled-out day. It is usually climbed in mountaineering boots as there are quite a few easier sections which are more comfortable in mountain boots than rock shoes. If you are looking for a longer day, you can climb this as a prelude to the more difficult South Ridge on the Gross Bielenhorn which makes a fantastic day out.

Grade	Klein (Chli) Bielenhorn AD 4c, Gross Bielenhorn D 5c+	Length	Klein (Chli) Bielenhorn 280m, Gross Bielenhorn 300m
Exposure	Klein (Chli) Bielenhorn South, Gross Bielenhorn South East	Rock type	Granite
Protection	Mix of leader placed protection and bolts.	Descent	Down climb and abseil.
Conditions	Dry rock	Time	Approach 2hrs. Route 6hrs up and down.

Map
Swiss Topo 1:25,000 1231 - Urseren

Alternative guidebook
Schweis Plaiser West Band I – Edition Filidor

ALPINE CLIMBING

Equipment
50m rope, nuts (1-9), cams (0.3-2), 6 quickdraws, ice axe and crampons depending on conditions.

Hut
Sidelen hut, www.sidelen-huette.ch tel. +41 887 02 33

Hut approach
Sidelen hut, as for Gross Furkahorn

Klein (Chli) Bielenhorn

Route approach
Leave the hut and head north-east, follow the red and white paint splashes heading for the Untere Bielenlücke pass. The route is the ridge on your right, and it starts below a col at the east side of an obvious tower. The approach should only take about 20 minutes from the hut and often has snow on it well into the season. The route starts in a corner with a piton and bolt for protection.

Route description
Pitch 1 – 4b 35m Start in the corner, climb a few moves then step left past a peg. Climb up into the groove above and then follow easier ground to a bolt belay.
Pitch 2 – 3a 40m Climb up towards the col moving right then back left. Belay at the side of an open chimney on natural gear. Do not climb all the way to the col.
Pitch 3 – 3a 25m Move left and belay on a good ledge at the base of a ramp.
Pitch 4 – 4b 35m Climb the ramp, leading up and left (bolt and piton runners), to belay on a good ledge on a double bolt belay.
Pitch 5 – 100m Shorten the rope and move together to the base of a steep tower.

Approach to the Klein Bielenhorn.

Pitch 6 – 4a 20m	Climb the detached block and step across onto the steep wall above to a good ledge, below a steep wall with bolts and pegs.
Pitch 7a – 6c+ (4b with aid) 20m	The wall above can be climbed direct at 6c+, or 4b with a few points of aid. It is quite awkward so it is worth using some slings to stand in, unless you are strong enough to just pull on the fixed equipment. There will sometimes be some equipment in situ.
Pitch 7b – 4b 25m	Personally, I think this is more in keeping with the standard of the route. Step left round a corner and climb the wall above on good edges to belay on top of the tower.
Pitch 8 – 4a 40m	Climb down onto a flat, slightly broader section, then move together passing a perched block. This is often referred to as the 'turtle rock' which is where the name in German comes from; I can't really see it myself.
Pitch 9 – 3b 20m	Climb the crest of the ridge, past some pegs for protection, to the top of a small tower.
Pitch 10 – 70m	Descend the ridge and then move together, passing a pinnacle on its right side, to reach a ledge. It is possible to escape from here by scrambling down a gully on the hut side of the ridge.
Pitch 11 – 4a 35m	Step left and climb cracks and ledges past some pegs back to the ridge crest – a superb pitch.
Pitch 12 – 150m	Climb down and then move together along the pitch until a final steepening bars the way to the summit.
Pitch 13 – 4a 30m	Climb up a ramp, then straight up to the top of a block.
Pitch 14 – 4c 40m	Step down and across a crevasse-like slot. Then climb steeply up the obvious crack on the opposite side past a bolt; you may want to pull on the bolt as it is quite awkward.
Pitch 15	Move left, and then climb easy moves to the summit.

Descent

Scramble down to the Untere Bielenlücke, there is a fixed chain in place at the most awkward section.

Gross Bielenhorn

Route approach

Gain the Untere Bielenlücke, either by walking from the Sidelen hut or by climbing the previous route. It is also possible to reach the pass from the Albert-Heim hut or the parking above Tiefenbach (Toll route, payable at a machine in cash), although this is a longer approach.

Just north of the pass are two large pinnacles, the Klein and Gross Kamel. Pass the Kamel's on the east side then join sections of path together through a boulder field to the base of the South East Ridge.

There is a good belay ledge at the base of the route, which starts with a crack with some bolts next to it.

Martin Chester climbing the lower cracks on the Gross Bielenhorn South East Ridge.

ALPINE CLIMBING

Gross Bielenhorn approach and route.

Route description

Pitch 1 – 4b 35m	Climb the crack past a couple of bolts to a ledge.
Pitch 2 – 3a 25m	An easy pitch leads to the base of steeper rock.
Pitch 3 – 5b+ (4c with 2 points of aid) 35m	Climb a shallow corner then another amazing crack to belay on top of a block. It is possible to escape from here with three, 20m abseils.
Pitch 4 – 15m	Climb down then move across a ledge to belay below a steep wall. It is possible to run this and the next pitch together, but the rope drag could be awful.
Pitch 5 – 4c 40m	Another amazing pitch. Climb the exposed, tapering slab via the obvious crack, exiting right to a belay.
Pitch 6 – 30m	Scramble across the easy traverse ledge into the obvious notch in the ridge.
Pitch 7 – 5c+ (4c with 1 point of Aid) 30m	Make some physical moves up and left off the belay, climb a wall, and then move right to belay on the ridge crest.
Pitch 8 – 4a 25m	Move along the right side of the ridge, then gain the crest and move along to an in situ abseil point.

Make a 15m abseil onto a big ledge. The take-off is quite awkward as the anchor is low. Just next to where you land is a really deep notch in the ridge with an abseil anchor in it. Lock this into your memory as this is part of the descent.

Scramble along a ledge on the west side of the ridge until you are under the summit block. Climb up to the ridge, where sections of III take you to the summit.

Descent

Just beyond the summit is an abseil anchor. Make a 25m abseil to a ledge and scramble along this to the notch mentioned above. Then make four, 20m abseils on good anchors to a path which leads back to the approach route.

Martin Chester enjoying the cracks on Pitch 5.

Nathan Reeves and team arriving on the summit of the Galenstock.

Galenstock 3,586m

The Galenstock is the highest mountain in the county of Uri. It stands clear of the mountains around it, giving great views of the surrounding peaks and the larger peaks of the Bernese Oberland and the Valais to the west.

The South Ridge is a fantastic route, involving a great blend of alpine skills: movement on glacial terrain, a via ferrata, rock, then snow, followed by a spectacular abseil descent.

As the start of the route is on a glacier and the summit ridge is south facing, you want the snow high on the mountain well frozen; so, it is well worth staying at the Sidelen hut the night before your climb to get an early start. That said, it is easily possible to climb this from the road, you just need to start an hour earlier than you would from the hut. Combining it with one of the other routes in the area is a great way of making the most of your hut night. Walk to the hut, dump your glacier travel kit and overnight stuff, climb a route, stay in the hut, then climb the Galenstock the next day.

South East Ridge

Grade	AD 4b, A0 (or 5b free)	**Length**	500m
Exposure	South	**Rock type**	Granite
Protection	Mixed	**Descent**	Scramble and abseil.
Conditions	Snow on the glacier, dry rock on the ridge.		
Time	3hrs from Furka Pass to the base of the rock using the via feratta. 2hrs from Sidelen hut, 3-4hrs from the base of the ridge to the summit then 3-4hrs back to the Furka Pass.		

Map
Swiss Topo 1:25,000 1231 - Urseren

Equipment
50m rope, ice axe and crampons, nuts (1-9), cams (0.5,1,2), 8 quickdraws

Hut
Sidelen hut, www.sidelen-huette.ch tel. +41 887 02 33

ALPINE CLIMBING

Galenstock South East Ridge route.

Hut approach
As for Gross Furkahorn.

Route approach
Leave the hut and head north on faint paths. Follow snow or small paths north-west under the south west face of the Gross Bielenhorn to reach the Sidelen glacier. Carry on up the east side of the glacier until you are under the gully that drops from the Obere Bielenlücke 3,220m.

At the south side of the gully, you will find some cables that mark the start of the klettersteig (via ferrata). This is marked on the most recent versions of the map, and is on the digital maps.

Climb the klettersteig to reach the top of the Tiefengletscher. Go round the top of the gully then head north-west to the base of the ridge.

The upper section of the South East Ridge.

Route description
Once you have established yourself on the base of the ridge, the way ahead is pretty clear. There are lots of belay options, so you can split the route down into longer or shorter pitches. If you go for the longer options the description is as follows:

Pitch 1 – 3b 40m	Climb the ridge trending left to right on the crest.	
Pitch 2 – 3a 50m	Climb straight up the crest.	
Pitch 3 – 3a 30m	Climb the crest.	
Pitch 4 – 4c 30m	Step right, then trend back left to a large ledge.	
Pitch 5 – 3 20m	Move up and right to the right side of the crest.	
Pitch 6 – 4a 30m	Climb the crest.	

Kris McCoey on the crux pitch of the South East Ridge.

Pitch 7 – 4b 35m Climb the crest, then move right to belay at the bottom of a slab that leads into a steep corner with bolts.

Pitch 8 – 5b or 4b and A0 30m Climb the crack at the left side of the slab (good handholds and technical for the feet). Climb the steep corner via good holds. It is possible to belay at the top of the corner, which allows you to keep contact with your partner.

Pitch 9 – 5a 30m Move diagonally right into a notch where there is a big bolt, so you could belay here. It is also possible to clip the bolt and continue up the wall above the belay. There are a few stiff pulls on good holds to establish yourself on the ridge. Follow the ridge to a belay.

Pitch 10 – 3c 30m Follow the ridge and make an awkward step down and across a gap.

The ridge above lies back and continues at grade II-III to reach the snow below the summit ridge. Put your crampons back on and continue to the summit.

Descent

It is possible to descend the South Ridge, then the Galen glacier to the Rhone glacier all the way to the road, this is incredibly boring and you would then need to hitch or get the bus back to your start point.

A much more enjoyable and practical descent, for those comfortable with abseiling, is to descend the south ridge then down to Point 3251m at the top of the Galengrat. Here you will find a big cairn that leads you to the top of a multi abseil descent. This is rigged so that you can descend comfortably with one 50m rope, the terrain is really steep, so where there are no natural ledges small metal ones have been installed. The abseil line drops you onto the snow that will lead down to the approach route to the hut.

Gletschhorn 3,305m

In a book full of my favourite routes this is one of my favourites, and the fact that it is a bit further from the road means that you are less likely to have to share the route. The line is pure, directly up the south ridge. The approach was on a glacier, but this has retreated so much you can now walk up the side of it on the moraine. The rock is impeccable, and the descent keeps you focussed until you are back on the glacier. You can climb the route either from the car, with an early start to get the snow on the approach in good condition, or from the recently renovated Albert-Heim hut.

South Ridge

Grade	AD 4b	**Length**	400m
Exposure	South	**Rock type**	Granite
Protection	Mainly in situ, but some leader placed protection.	**Descent**	Scramble and abseil.
Conditions	Dry rock, the descent is easier with no snow, but the approach is easier with snow.		
Time	2½ - 3hrs for the approach, 4hrs for the route, 3hrs for the descent.		

Map
Swiss Topo 1:25,000 1231 - Urseren

Alternative guidebook
Schweis Plaiser West Band I – Edition Filidor

ALPINE CLIMBING

Kris McCoey setting off on the South Ridge of the Gletschhorn.

Sam Davidson Webb near the summit of the Gletschhorn with the Galenstock behind.

Equipment
Ice axe and crampons, set of nuts, cams (1,2,3), 6 quickdraws, 50m rope.

Hut
Albert-Heim hut, www.albertheimhuette.ch tel.+41 41 887 1745
Tiefenbach Hotel

Hut approach
Coming from Andermatt towards the Furka Pass, a few kilometres before the pass you come across the Tiefenbach Hotel. Continue past the hotel for 200m then turn right and follow a rough road round some bends to a parking spot. You need to pay for this with coins or via an app.

Leave the car park and follow the signs for the Albert-Heim hut.

Kris McCoey leading the classic corner on pitch 4.

Route approach
If you are coming from the hut, descend a little and take the path heading west. If approaching from the road, where the path splits for the final climb to the hut, head west following a cairned path. At some point, you need to head north and join the large path that leads north-west from the hut. Follow this until you reach some water pipes and an obvious end to this large path. Cross the stream and follow a path that leads north-west on a small moraine and then contours round to a large cairn. Cross a flat area to another well-constructed cairn, below a buttress that drops from the South Ridge. Drop down onto the Tiefengletscher, then head up the east side of the glacier until it is possible to head east up

Furka Pass

Approach and descent, Gletschhorn South Ridge.

some steep snow (scree later in the season and can feel quite involved if dry) to a col below the base of the South Ridge.

You will almost certainly have to use an ice axe and crampons on the approach. It is really tempting to leave these at the base of the route, but the descent does not return to the same point. If you do, you may end up stranded on steep snow.

Route description
The route follows the crest throughout, and you can climb the route using a combination of short or long pitches and some moving together. There are large bolt belay rings roughly every 50m, though climbing the route using long pitches will probably be slower due to rope drag and extended communications.

Pitches 1-3 – 45m, 30m, 40m	Follow the crest. The climbing is steady at grade 3a and 3b.
Pitch 4 – 4b (4a with 2 points of aid) 35m	Climb the clean corner. The crack is the perfect size for a mountaineering boot and bolts are perfectly placed for protection.
Pitch 5 – 3a 40m	Follow the crest of the ridge, climbing down into a notch to belay.
Pitch 6 – 3b 35m	Move left, then climb straight up to belay in a corner.
Pitch 7 – 3c 30m	Step left and climb a subsidiary corner before trending back right to the crest.
Pitches 8-9 – 3b, 3a 22m, 40m	Follow the crest of the ridge to belay in a notch.
Pitch 10 – 4a 40m	Move onto the left side of the ridge, then climb back to the crest and belay on a ledge.
Pitch 11 – 3b 30m	Climb down into a notch and then follow easy ground to the summit.

Descent
Make a 25m abseil from the summit and then scramble down loose ground, following blue splashes of paint (these are initially very faint). A faint track leads right then left to reach an abseil anchor. Make three, 20m abseils back to the snow (this is level with the start of the route).

You can now re-join your line of approach from this morning.

ALPINE CLIMBING

Max leading the south east ridge of the Läckihorn.

Läckihorn 3,068m

Traverse of the Chli and Gross Läckihorn

The area around the Rotondo hut is better known for ski touring than for mountaineering; in fact, the hut guardian described the rock round her hut as 'rubbish'. However, there is a jewel in this sea of mediocrity. It is easy to be distracted by the amazing rock of the Furka Pass and its surrounding peaks, but the traverse of the Chli and Gross Läckihorn give a fantastic mountaineering outing using the full range of mountaineering skills, and you will almost certainly be on your own unlike on the Furka peaks.

This is a brilliant route on which to hone your route finding and alpine ropework skills. It is a perfect blend of a great hut, friendly guardian, and great climbing. There is movement on a small glacier, followed by steep snow, moving together on rock with a mix of pitches and moving together, topped off with a great summit and incredible views to the Furka peaks and the giants of the Bernese Oberland.

Grade	PD+ III	**Length**	560m altitude gain
Exposure	SE	**Rock type**	Granite
Protection	Mixed	**Descent**	North ridge to Läckipass.
Conditions	Snow on the approach gully, then dry on the ridge.	**Time**	6-7hrs hut to hut.

Map
Swiss topo 1:25,000 Val Bedretto 1251

Hut
Rotondo hut, www.rotondohuette.ch tel. +41 41 887 16 16

Equipment
Glacier travel kit for the approach and descent, AD rack for the traverse, an ice axe and crampons. A 40m rope will be enough.

Hut approach
The hut approach from Realp is long and not very interesting, up a tarmac road. However, for a small fee (20chf in summer 2023) you can drive up the road. You can pay using the *'Parking Pay App'*, or in the tourist office in Andermatt, or in the Restaurant des Alpes in Realp (details on the hut website). This reduces the walk from about 3½ hours to 40 minutes.

Whether you are in a car or on foot, leave Realp heading for the Furka Pass and turn left immediately after the Restaurant des Alpes; don't cross the river but follow the road passing through a railway yard. Follow the metalled road until you reach a parking area next to a military looking building at Oberstafel and follow the path heading west (signpost). After about 200m the path splits, both paths lead to the hut the left hand one is probably more pleasant.

Route approach
Leave the hut heading south-west on a good track, which gets fainter as it curves south to the snout of the Witenwasserengletscher. There is a small bridge to cross at the outflow of a small lake; cross the bridge and follow the track to the glacier. The glacier is pretty benign in its lower parts but there are some crevasses as you head up towards the route, so if it has snow on it, put a rope on.

Head up the glacier to about 2,700m. Leave the glacier and head south-west up a steepening snow slope which, depending on the amount of snow around, may feel like a gully. At the top of the gully, carry on up to a flat spot at the start of the South East Ridge of the Chli Läckihorn proper. Apparently, it is possible to climb the ridge direct from the Witenwasserenpass, but it is really loose.

Route description
You will almost certainly take crampons off at the start of the ridge, which is a great place to have a snack. The ridge starts with some short pitches on good rock, with the odd bolt for protection. The rock is generally really good, though the lichen would make it slippery if you were caught in a rain shower.

Approach and ascent of the Läckihorn.

Follow the ridge crest with the odd excursion on the north side to turn any difficulties. When you reach the top of a red coloured tower, have a look for an abseil anchor that takes you into a narrow notch. The take-off for the abseil is pretty tight so you might want to consider lowering the first climber, it's only about 10 metres.

Climb straight up the steep wall above the notch then follow the ridge. Turn an obvious tower on the right. It's easy to miss the right turn but if you end up on top of a steep drop, back track a little then descend down and right, before small ledges lead you round the corner and into a notch. Follow the ridge to reach the summit of the Chli Läckihorn 3,024m.

Leaving the summit, retrace a couple of steps, then head down and right (north side) on some loose ground to reach the edge of a snow patch. In a good snow year this may all be covered in snow. Put your crampons back on, then make a slightly downward and horizontal traverse to reach the col 2,968m at the start of the Gross Läckihorn.

Climb along the crest of the ridge to a steep wall. Climb up and diagonally left on a cracked slab before moving back right to the ridge crest (bolts, 40m 3c). Now follow the crest of the ridge on good rock all the way to the summit.

Ian Loombe on the Läckihorn.

Descent

Head down the north ridge; initially this feels quite exposed with a few awkward sections of down-climbing (bolts). A faint track now takes you down the boulder-strewn ridge to the Läckipass, where you can descend the small glacier (you may want to put crampons back on for this). The end of the glacier has become quite steep, head left / north towards a small lake before following the stream on an improving path to join the approach track from this morning.

The author on the East Ridge of the Diamantstock.

Grimsel Pass

The Grimsel Pass area is most famous for its high-quality granite rock climbs, and it would not be ridiculous to claim that some of the best quality granite slab climbs are in this spectacular corner of Switzerland. Routes like Motorhead, Septumania and Fair Hands Line should all be on any granite climbers tick list. The area is perhaps less well-known for its alpine routes, and the East Ridge of the Gross Diamantstock is one of the finest.

ALPINE CLIMBING

Gross Diamantstock 3,162m

When we first discovered that my wife was pregnant with our first child and the initial euphoria that prospective parents feel wore off, we thought we had better go and do an alpine route together while we still had the opportunity. What better choice than the East Ridge of the Gross Diamantstock.

The route is a mix of moving together and pitching, you need to be comfortable making the decision when to do one or the other, if you try and pitch the whole route you will need a headtorch.

East Ridge

Grade	D 4c	**Length**	850m
Exposure	East	**Rock type**	Granite
Protection	Mixed	**Descent**	Climbing and abseil, SW Ridge then east face.
Conditions	Dry on the ridge, approach is easier with snow on the glacier.	**Time**	9hrs hut to hut.

Map
Swiss Topo 1:50,000 Guttannen 1230

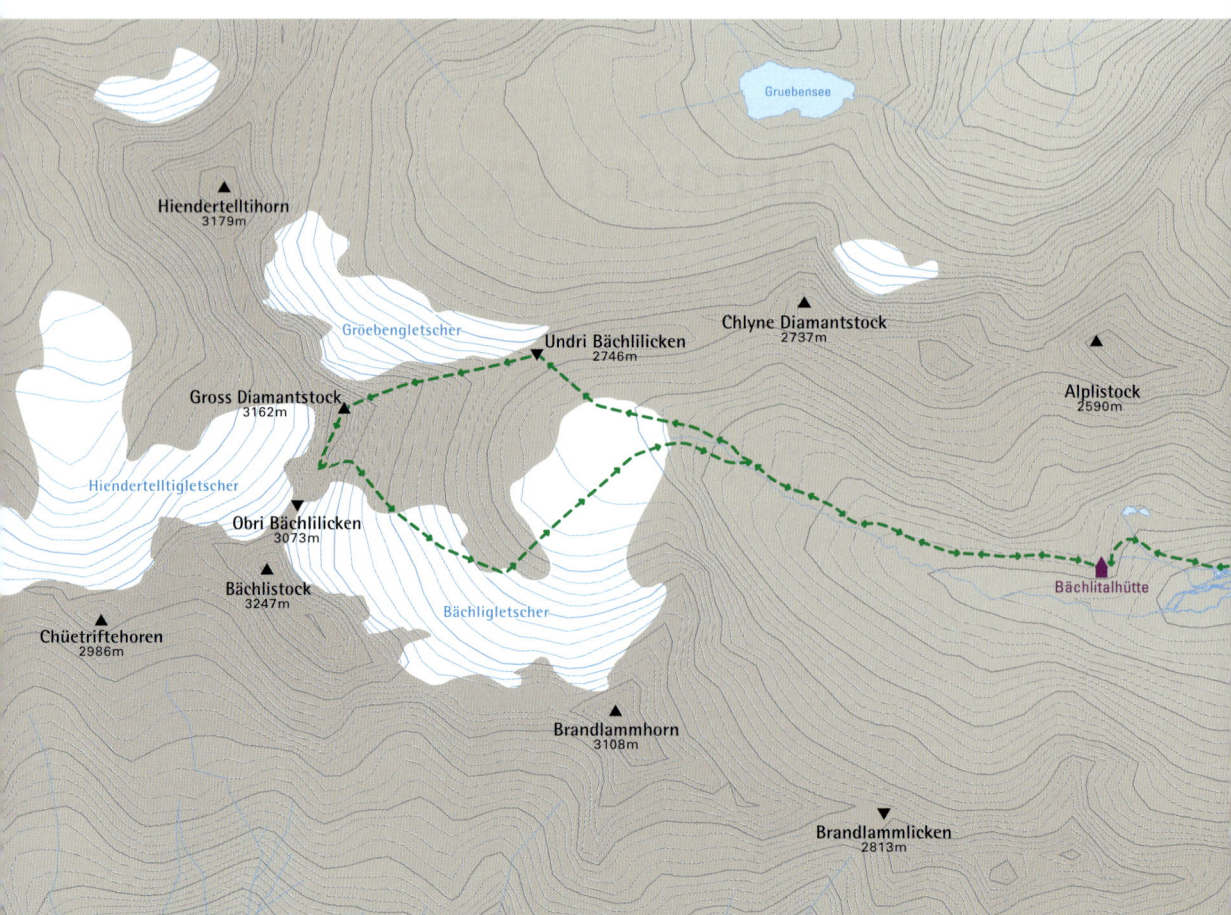

Grimsel Pass

Alternative guidebook
Mountaineering in the Swiss Alps by Stephanie Marie

Equipment
Ice axe and crampons for the glacial approach and maybe the descent, AD rack with some extra small / medium cams. You can climb the route in mountaineering boots.

Hut
Bächlital hut, www.baechlitalhuette.ch

Hut approach
Park below the Räterichsbodensee dam on the north side of the Grimsel Pass. Pick up a path heading west, signposted from the parking. The path follows the north side of a gorge, then cuts south before heading back west to Bächlisboden, an impressive alluvial outwash plain. Stay on the north side of this and the path will lead you up to the hut, which sits on a rocky promontory overlooking the plain.

Route approach
The approach leaves the hut and heads west along a marked path to reach the glacier. If the glacier has snow on it, put a rope on then keep on the right to avoid some crevasses. The lower section of the glacier is often dry in the main summer months and is quite steep at the snout, so it is worth putting

ALPINE CLIMBING

The Diamantstock, approach and traverse.

on crampons. At 2,600m head right, off the glacier, climb up some snow, then head diagonally up and right to the Undri Bächlilicken 2,746m – the col at the start of the route. If there is no snow, there is a track and some cairns to follow.

Route description

The route starts with the crux, so if you are at all nervous about climbing 4c in big boots you can get it out of the way really quickly. Although you may be tempted to use rock shoes for the first pitches (4c,4b), the climbing is positive and well protected with bolts in the right places and you will save lots of time by not changing footwear.

Climb the tower just left of the crest. When you reach the top, move along the crest then make a short abseil into a notch. Leaving the notch, move up and left across a wall, past a bolt, before climbing back to the ridge crest (4a). Follow the ridge, turning any difficulties on the south side.

There is a possible escape along some ledges at the low point in this section of the ridge, should you have got the weather wrong.

The initial pitch above the escape ledge is really nice 3b with a few bolts. Carry on along the crest with sections of II and III, to reach a really obvious pinnacle marked as the Spitz in some other guidebooks (this is a really spectacular feature). Climb almost to its top then

The author making moves on the south side of the Gross Diamantstock.

Kate Scott traversing the Spitz.

traverse left, before downclimbing into a notch in the ridge. The downclimb is easier than it looks. It is possible to escape from the notch in three, 25m abseils.

Climb up and over another small tower to reach another small notch in the ridge. Climb the edge of the slab above on the south side (the original route went up a crack to the right but this is not as good). At the top of the slab move left, then climb the wall above past some fixed anchors (don't be tempted out left by the pegs). It's then back to moving together again across a series of ledges on the south side of the ridge. It is also possible to stay on the crest, which is a bit slower but much more aesthetic. When you are more or less below the summit, climb straight up, then cross the ridge and climb up to the summit from the north side on easy blocky terrain.

Descent

Leave the summit and carry on along the south west ridge to a cairn. Scramble down and right across a series of ledges following a cairned path. If this still has snow on it you may need to put on crampons. Follow this until you find an abseil anchor, then make four, 20m abseils to get onto the snow and a ledge system that leads back to the approach path.

Ross Penver high on the ridge of the Poncione di Cassina Baggio.

The Pizzo del Prévat seen from the walk in.

Tessin and Lombardy

The Val Bedretto and northern Ticino is not really on the radar for many alpinists, but this magical area sandwiched between the Simplon Pass and Lago Maggiore has some great mountains and some excellent weather. The routes we are going to look at both clear quickly after bad weather, have great access and, in the case of the Poncione di Cassina Baggio is one of the nicest huts you will stay in. They also sit slightly south of the main Alpine chain, so will often be basking in sunshine when the higher mountains are clouded in.

The two routes can be climbed in combination to make a brilliant two days. I would suggest climbing the Pizzo del Prévat first using the lift access from Rodi (or you could stay in the Leìt hut the night before). When you have finished climbing, drive for 30 minutes and then walk up to the Piansecco hut in time for dinner. You can then climb the South Ridge of the Poncione di Cassina Baggio the next day.

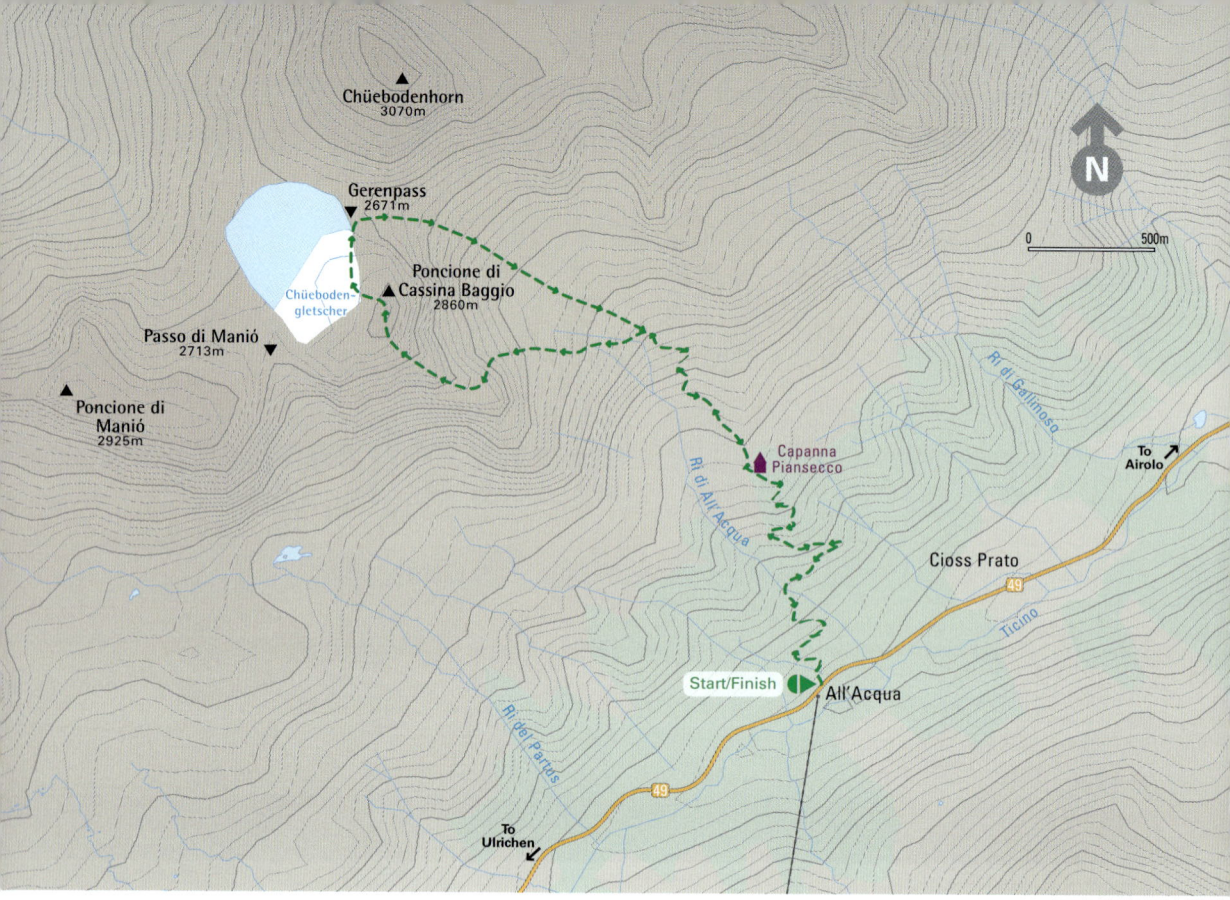

Poncione di Cassina Baggio 2,860m

A south ridge on great granite above a brand new hut with a short walk in. Can it get any better? Well yes, it can. This South Ridge of the Poncione di Cassina Baggio is a bit of an unknown gem, certainly among alpinists from outside Ticino. Outside of the weekend, you are likely to be on your own.

The climbing is really great, being a combination of short pitches, longer pitches, and moving together, and while the only glaciated terrain is the small glacier you need to cross on the descent, the techniques you need to employ are definitely alpine.

South Ridge

Grade	AD with moves of III.	**Length**	920m vertical
Exposure	South	**Rock type**	Granite
Protection	Very little in situ gear, a few pegs.	**Descent**	Scramble down to the Chüebodengletscher and then walk back to the hut.
Conditions	Dry rock	**Time**	7-8hrs hut to hut.

Map
Swiss Topo 1:25,000 Val Bedretto 1251

Alternative guidebook
Mountaineering in the Swiss Alps by Stephane Maire

Tessin and Lombardy

Approach and route on the Poncione di Cassina Baggio.

Hut
Piansecco hut, an extremely comfortable, brand-new hut.
www.capannapiansecco.ch

Equipment
Standard AD rack, it is worth climbing in boots rather than approach shoes as the descent may be partly on snow and a very easy glacier. Early season it may be worth having a light ice axe and crampons for the descent, check with the hut guardian.

Hut approach
The hut approach is an incredibly pleasant hour (370m) through some beautiful larch woodland to the hut, which sits just at the top of the treeline. Drive up the Val Bedretto from Airolo to All'Acqua 1600m. There is good parking just up the road, on the opposite side to the hotel. The path starts just next to the hotel and follows a signpost and red and white paint splashes. The path follows a rising traverse through the shade of the forest before a few zigzags and a blunt ridge deposit you at the door of the hut.

Route approach
You can see the route from the hut, so it is easy to scope out the route for the following morning. The climbing starts at the obvious notch between the first and second towers. It is possible to climb the route from its very base, but the rock isn't as good until this notch, and there is a loose abseil into the first notch which is better avoided.

Take the path that leaves the back of the hut, you immediately have two options.

Option 1
Take the path that heads west and contours toward the obvious stream, the Ri di All'Acqua. Just before you reach the stream and bridge there is a path that heads north up the left bank of the stream. Stay on this until past the cliff band where you will join the alternate path coming in from the east. Follow this path heading for the notch on the ridge. The ascent to the notch looks like it will be steep and loose, but the path is actually quite good and the going easy, though it would be a good idea to put a helmet on for any loose rock.

Kieran Hodgson on the Poncione di Cassina Baggio.

Option 2
The alternate path takes an initially steeper, north-westerly line to join the path previously described above the cliff band. As this is the line of descent, it's quite nice to go up one and down the other, but it doesn't really make any difference time-wise, (this is the route marked on the map in the book).

Route description
Having geared up in the notch, scramble up until the rock steepens. Climb a wall and some ramps leading up and right past a few old pegs. Follow the ridge above to the top of the tower on some excellent rock, and then cross a second tower. Make a 25m abseil into a notch on the west side of the ridge.

Climb the third tower by a mix of moving together and short pitches. As you reach the summit of the third tower, there is a loose looking chimney groove that leads down the west side of the tower. This can either be abseiled or downclimbed (III); it is probably easiest to abseil but be careful as it is a full 25m. At the bottom of the rope, scramble along some ledges to the north to make sure you are not under anything that may be dislodged by anyone following you.

Scramble north back to the ridge to reach a red wall. Climb this up and right (awkward to protect), and cross a red gendarme or turn it on the right to regain the ridge which is followed to the summit. The summit of the route feels like a summit, although the north summit is slightly higher, but there is no need to go there.

Descent
Head down the loose north face to the Chüebodengletscher. Depending on the amount of snow and the exact line you take, you may want to make a short abseil to get off the summit ridge. When you reach the glacier head north-east past the Gerenpass, then pick up a faint path with cairns that heads south-east to eventually join up with the ascent path and leads back to the hut.

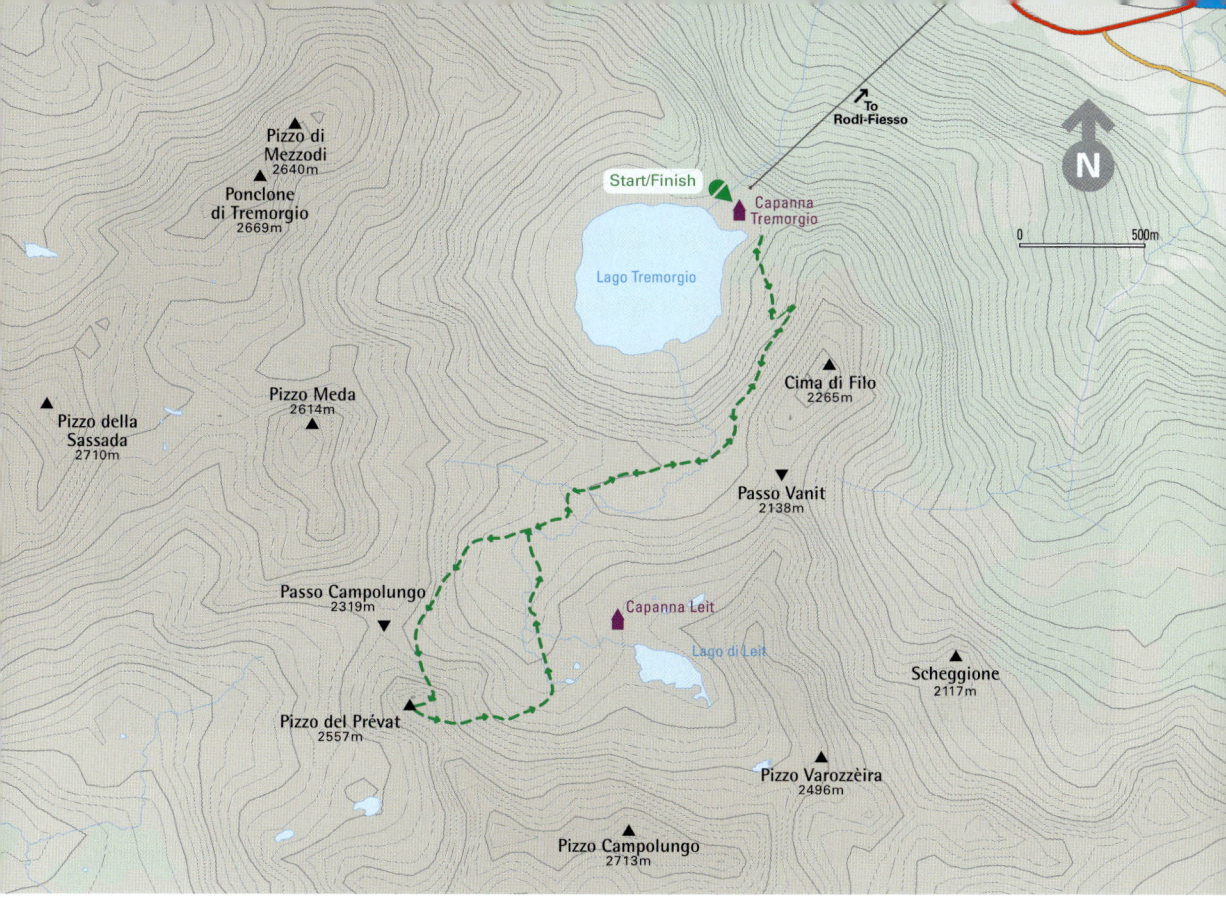

Pizzo del Prévat 2,557m

The North East Pillar on the Pizzo del Prévat is a superb rock climb, on great rock in a pre-alpine setting. It clears quickly after bad weather and offers great climbing in a beautiful position. The route itself is fully equipped and is popular, so it is best avoided at weekends, and it is well worth being on the first lift in the morning if you are not staying at the hut. If it is really busy, or you fancy a technically easier alpine undertaking, then the North East Ridge (AD+ 5a) is a really nice route and can be climbed in big boots or approach shoes. It does need a small rack as there isn't much in the way of fixed equipment.

North East Pillar

Grade	D+ 5c	**Length**	250m
Exposure	NE	**Rock type**	Schist
Protection	The route is fully bolted.	**Descent**	Abseil and scramble.
Conditions	Dry rock	**Time**	Approach 2hrs. 4hrs for route. Descent 1½hrs.

Map
Swiss Topo 1:50,000 Ambri Piotta 1252

Alternative guidebook
Schweis Plaiser Sud Band 1– Edition Filidor

ALPINE CLIMBING

Pizzo del Prévat approach and route.

Equipment
Approach shoes, 12 quickdraws, rock shoes for the climb. A 50m rope is long enough for the climbing and the abseils on the descent.

Hut
The route can be climbed from the Leìt hut, or in a day from the lift that comes from Rodi to the restaurant near Lago Tremorgio. www.capanna-leit.ch

Hut approach
Leaving the lift, climb steeply round the east side of the Lago Tremorgio on a good path. When you're above the lake follow the left branch of the path and the red and white paint flashes to the hut.

Route approach
Start as per the hut approach but when you reach the path junction, turn right and follow the path across the stunning alpine meadow of the Alpe di Campolungo, then climb up to the Passo Campolungo. You get great views of the route all along the walk in. Leaving the col, traverse west across scree under the north face of the mountain to reach the base of the North East Pillar.

If you are coming from the hut there are two options.

Option 1
Descend on the path heading west then north to join the path coming from the lift in the Alpe di Campolungo.

Kate Scott enjoying the flakes on pitch 4.

272

Option 2
This is much faster but rougher under foot. Leave the hut and walk the short distance to the Lago di Leìt, then pick up a rough track heading west and south-west. This track becomes the descent path from the peak. At about 2,350m head north where a slightly improbable looking path leads round the north east ridge to just below the North East Pillar.

If you look above you at the base of the pillar, you will see the line of bolts leading up the first steep wall to a ledge and bolt belay.

Route description
Pitch 1 – 5c 35m I think this is the most difficult pitch of the route. Perhaps because it's the first pitch and you are getting used to the rock after the walk in, or maybe because it's quite slabby and you have to learn to trust your feet. Climb up some shallow grooves passing a ledge and belay; it is possible to split this pitch here but it makes for a very short first pitch. Keep climbing up and right making some slightly exposed moves onto the crest of the ridge, before moving slightly back left and up to a belay.

Pitch 2 – 4c 25m Step left of the belay, then climb up and right on to the crest of the ridge. Follow this before stepping down and left to the belay.

Pitch 3 – 5b 35m The start of this pitch feels committing. Step up onto a blank looking slab. Climb this, exiting left, then climb the groove above to a large ledge.

Pitch 4 – 4c 40m Climb the steep wall immediately above the belay and then step down and left. Step across a gap then climb the left side of the ridge to belay at the bottom of a series of flakes that lead up left across the wall left of the belay.

Pitch 5 – 5b 30m This is a superb pitch. Follow the series of flakes and cracks that lead up and left across the wall above; the holds and the positions are superb. Belay at the base of a steep wall.

Pitch 6 – 4c 25m Move up and left along a crack, then straight up on good holds to a belay below a steep wall.

Pitch 7 – 5c+ 45m Step slightly right, then follow the good holds directly up the wall above. The pitch gets steeper with height, but as it gets steeper the holds get bigger and bigger. Belay where the angle eases.

Pitch 8 – 4c 50m Climb directly above the belay and then into an open chimney / groove. Above this the route starts to lie back and the climbing becomes easier. Follow the easiest line to belay just as climbing comes to an end.

Pitch 9 – 25m Run the rope along the ridge and an easy path to finish next to the summit and a great picnic spot. You can change out of rock shoes here and shorten the rope ready for the descent.

Descent
Leave the summit heading south-east on a well-worn path (this can be really slippery after rain) until you reach a well-positioned abseil anchor. Abseil 15m, then scramble down for another section to where you can make another three short abseils to a notch and the start of the descent path. You can put the rope away, but it's probably worth keeping your helmet on as the initial descent gully has plenty of loose blocks. As you get lower, the path becomes better defined until you reach the approach path to the hut.

Monte Disgrazia 3,678m

Monte Disgrazia is not really on the radar for many non-Italian climbers, which is one of the things that first attracted me to the area. It is the largest mountain sitting south of the Bernina group and is significantly higher than all the peaks around it.

The access road was closed for many years making for a long approach to the Ponti hut. This is now open again making the two-hour hut walk, up a stunning valley, a pleasure. Even with the road now open, outside of a weekend you are likely to experience alpine solitude.

Looking at a map it is hard to work out how this links in with other routes in the book. The first time I visited, we climbed Monte Disgrazia, had a night in the valley, and then went to the Tschierva hut and climbed the Biancograt the next day. This made for an outstanding few days in the mountains.

The closest valley base is San Martino which is also the starting point for climbing on the amazing granite rock of the Valle di Mello. You can enjoy some of Europe's finest granite with one of its finest mountains.

North West Ridge

Grade	AD- III	**Length**	1,100m
Exposure	NW	**Rock type**	Granite
Protection	Leader placed	**Descent**	Return by the same route.
Conditions	Can be climbed in most conditions, mixed is most enjoyable.	**Time**	6-7hrs ascent, 3hrs descent (from the hut).

Map
Swiss topo 1:50,000 278 Monte Disgrazia

Alternative guidebook
Bernina and Bregaglia by Lindsay Griffin – Alpine Club

Equipment
Glacier travel kit and PD rack

Brian O'Connor and Ewan Whittaker approaching the summit of Monte Disgrazia.

Ewan Whittaker and Brian O'Connor crossing the Bronze Horse.

ALPINE CLIMBING

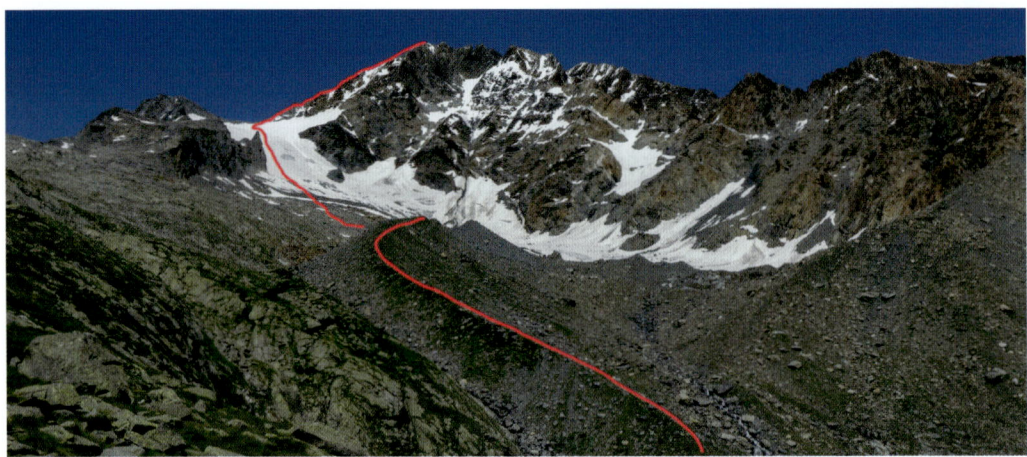

Monte Disgrazia approach and climb.

Hut
Rifugio Ponti, www.rifugioponti.it
A superb comfortable and friendly hut, usually frequented by walkers on the Sentiero Roma.

Hut approach
Drive up the Val Masino and turn right at Filorera and follow the twisty road to Preda Rossa, signposted Valle di Sasso Bisolo. Park at the end of the road at the Piano di Predarossa. It is necessary to pay a toll to use this road. In 2023 the fee was €12 and was payable online. www.valmasino.travel

Leave Preda Rossa and follow a good path on the north side of the river, after a couple of kilometres the path climbs north through a rock band then heads diagonally north-east across a hillside. Above Point 2,391m the path climbs more steeply, before a final horizontal section leads to the hut.

Route approach
Leave the hut and follow the waymarked path ENE across a grassy hillside, interspersed with rock slabs (there are paint splashes and cairns). This leads to a moraine which is followed until you can gain the Ghiacciaio di Predarossa. The exact point of access will depend on the amount of snow (later in the summer the lower part may be bare ice).

Route description
Climb the glacier to the col at its head, the Sella di Poida.

Leave the col and follow the North West Ridge. The first section is relatively steep and is best climbed directly with moves up to III. It is possible to turn some of the difficulties on the right, but the rock is better on the crest.

In good conditions the route now becomes more mixed in nature but is fine when it is just rock. This section leads to a fore summit.

A beautiful snow crest now leads towards the summit. This is interrupted by a large block, often referred to as the Bronze Horse. Climb over this (III), and follow the ridge to the summit. The snow crest may melt out later in the summer, but I have climbed here when there is very little snow and the route is still very worthwhile.

Descent
Reverse your route of ascent back to the hut and the waiting bowl of pasta.

The Biancograt seen from Piz Morteratsch.

Bernina

Piz Bernina is the most easterly 4,000m peak in the Alps. It is a truly majestic mountain with soaring ridges and steep crevassed glaciers. While the Bernina itself is the most famous mountain in the range, the surrounding peaks offer some amazing mountaineering in their own right. They can be climbed individually or as a link up. In fact, the traverse of the Morteratsch skyline is one of the finest alpine outings I have climbed. This links together the Piz Morteratsch, Piz Bernina, and the Piz Palü into a four-day extravaganza.

Sitting at the east end of the alpine chain, the Bernina often enjoys better weather than the western Alps. If you do end up in the area and the high mountains are out, look to some of the routes in the Bregaglia section of the book, which clear much faster after poor weather.

All of the itineraries covered below rely on good snow and ice conditions and are usually best climbed in the early part of the season. They can all be difficult and dangerous when the snow clears from the ridges and leaves hard ice.

Bernina

The Piz Bernina at dawn.

Piz Morteratsch 3,751m

The Piz Morteratsch is a stunning viewpoint situated right in the heart of the Bernina range. Its traverse from the Boval hut to the Tschierva hut is a superb high altitude undertaking and is a perfect introduction to the range, or a great way to acclimatise for what is to come.

Morteratsch Skyline North Ridge

Grade	PD+ II+	Length	1,357m Vertical
Exposure	East, North and West	Rock type	Granite
Protection	A few bolts and a few slings and karabiners.	Descent	Descend the west side of the Fuorcla da Boval to the Tschierva hut.
Conditions	Dry rock, then snow on glacier and summit.	Time	7-8hrs hut to hut.

Map
Swiss Topo 1:25,000 1277 Piz Bernina

Alternative guidebook
Bernina and Bregaglia Selected Climbs by Lindsay Griffin – Alpine Club
Schweiz Plaisir Alpin by Jurg von Kanel

Equipment
Glacier travel equipment, ice axe and crampons and a few karabiners are all you will need.

Hut

Boval hut, www.boval.ch tel. +41 81 842 64 03
Tschierva hut, www.tschierva.ch/en tel. +41 81 842 63 91

Hut approach

Start at the train station in Morteratsch. If you have a car, you can use the train at the end of the trip to get back to it.

Head south on a well-marked path. About 100m after leaving the train track, turn right and head up into the forest. After about 100m of altitude gain the path heads south, paralleling the glacier until a steeper section with a few ropes in place leads to the hut (2 hours).

An alternative route goes along the floor of the valley where the glacier once was, until reaching a marker '1920' (marking where the glacier was in 1920). When you reach a signpost marked Chünetta, turn right and climb steeply to join the path described above.

Route description

Leave the hut and head west on a good path leading towards the Fuorcla da Boval 3,347m; in most seasons you won't need to touch snow to reach the col. The path climbs a grassy spur, then moves across steep boulders and scree; work up left to gain the crest of a moraine. The way ahead is easy to follow as it is marked with red paint. Follow the splashes to reach a large, steep and somewhat intimidating rock wall. The climbing ahead is on excellent granite. Climb up some short steps then trend left to a chimney. Climb this, then move back right on rock that feels steep for the grade (II). There are bolts anywhere you might want one. When you reach a large horizontal ledge head left for quite a long way, until easy scrambling leads to the col.

Leaving the Fuorcla da Boval, drop down on to the Tschierva glacier. It's time to put the crampons on and get into glacier travel mode. Head south, paralleling the rocky ridge that that leads south from

Piz Morteratsch approach and climb from the Boval hut.

the Fuorcla da Boval. Climb the steepening glacier to a shoulder, and then head south-east on a gently rising shelf. This passes under some newly exposed rock. Once past this, head south-west turning an obvious large crevasse / bergschrund on its north side to reach the ridge just south of point 3,610m. The ridge then leads to the summit.

Descent
Leave the summit and retrace your steps to below the Fuorcla da Boval. Descend the Tschierva glacier, keeping slightly right (direction of travel) to avoid some crevasses. Leave the glacier at approximately 3,200m and follow a path that leads down to a large scree terrace, marked on the map as 'Terrassa 3112m'. Work down and left through some steep rock walls to reach an improving path. From here, follow the path that parallels the stream dropping from the glacier through some more steep ground and down to the Tschierva hut.

Piz Bernina 4,048m

The combination of the majestic snow crest, one of the finest I have climbed anywhere, and the mixed climbing above and below make the Biancograt one of the most engaging climbs in the Alps.

The quality of the climbing is combined with the seriousness of the position. When the summit is gained it is a short descent to the Marco e Rosa Hut 3,610m. However, you still have no easy way down. You either have to traverse the snow crests of the Piz Palü, descend the rocky Fortezza and down to Morteratsch, or descend to the Marinelli hut. However, if you choose the latter, you are now in a different country to your car.

Liz O'Connor below the summit of the Piz Bernina.

ALPINE CLIMBING

Biancograt North Ridge

Grade	AD+ IV-	Length	1,500m
Exposure	North	Rock type	Granite
Protection	A mix of bolts and leader placed protection.	Descent	South ridge to the Marco e Rosa hut, then either traverse the Piz Palü or descend the Fortezza Ridge. Any option is AD- to AD in difficulty.
Conditions	Good snow on the snow crest is essential, the rest can be climbed in mixed conditions.	Time	3hrs approach, 4-5hrs for the ridge and 1 ½hrs for the descent.

Map
Swiss Topo 1:25,000 1277 Piz Bernina

Alternative guidebook
Bernina and Bregaglia Selected Climbs by Lindsay Griffin – Alpine Club
Mountaineering in the Swiss Alps by Stephane Maire

Equipment
Glacier travel kit including 2 ice screws each, nuts (1,3,5,7,9), 4 quickdraws, Camalot (1,2). If the mixed section is relatively clear of snow all you need for the route are 4 quickdraws and a couple of long slings. If its snowy, the in situ kit is more difficult to find, so you will want to have the above rack with you. 50m rope.

Hut
Tschierva hut, www.tschierva.ch/en tel. +41 81 842 63 91
Marco e Rosa hut, www.rifugi.lombardia.it/en/sondrio/lanzada/hut-marco-e-rosa.html tel. +39 0342515370

Tschierva hut and Biancograt approach.

Hut approach

If you have climbed the previous route, you will be at the hut. If not, the approach starts at the railway station in Pontresina. You have two options: either walk south along the beautiful, wooded valley that follows the Ova da Roseg river to the Hotel Roseg Gletscher, or alternatively you can take a horse and trap. This may sound decadent, but it saves an hour of pretty boring walking on a four wheel drive track, and gives you the opportunity to soak up the view and save your energy for what is to come. It is worth booking a seat, as at the height of summer this is a popular excursion.

However you get to the Hotel Roseg, head south for a short distance then cross the stream to the east bank of the glacial outwash plain. The path now rises steadily, heading south and south-east, climbing the moraine that bounds the north side of the remains of the Tschierva glacier, before a final few zigzags lead to the Tschierva hut.

Route approach

The approach to the route is quite complicated, so make sure you have time the night before to scope out where you will be going in the dark. Follow the path which is marked with reflective markers like cat's eyes and cairns. At about 2,950m scramble down onto the glacier, which is followed for a short distance before heading east into the glacial bowl below Piz Prievlus. When I first climbed the Biancograt this was all a connecting glacier, but now it is usually dry ice and rubble.

The route ahead now ascends to the Fuorcla Prievlusa. In good snow, this is an easy snow gully, but once this melts out there is serious risk of stone fall. The hut guardians have built a via ferrata on the rocks to the north of the gully; this is strongly recommended in anything but good snow conditions.

Route description

Once you are at the Fuorcla Prievlusa you are on the ridge proper. The next section is usually rock, athough I have climbed it covered in new snow (this is a bit slower but still no real problem). Climb on the right side of the ridge for 50m until you can gain the crest. Follow the ridge until you are forced round onto the east side, where you traverse under some steep rocks to reach the start of the snow

The final approach to the Biancograt, either on snow on the right or the via ferrata on the left.

crest. If the traverse isn't snow it is possible to continue along the crest and descend to the start of the snow crest.

Climb the snow crest. You need to move together on this and the exposure focusses your crampon technique. The ridge is initially quite broad but tapers higher up. You may get an icy section where it steepens, where you may want an ice screw for protection, but this will depend on conditions. This leads to the summit of Piz Bianco.

You can see the summit from here and it is tantalisingly close. The route now becomes rock or mixed climbing and the next section will take a lot longer than it looks. The climbing is superb, in amazing positions, with a great feeling of space around you.

Climb along the horizontal ridge until it starts to descend. Climb down a short distance to an abseil anchor and make a 15m abseil into a notch (you can downclimb this at an awkward IV-). Continue along the ridge and climb over a large gendarme or turn it on the right (III+), then continue steeply along the crest until the angle eases and the summit arrives.

Descent

The descent to the nearest hut is relatively straightforward and quick (a rarity on a 4,000m peak); with no hold-ups you can be in the Marco e Rosa hut in about an hour from the summit, by descending the Spallagrat.

Leave the summit and follow the ridge south then south-east. The exact route will depend on the quantity of snow; you will either be following footsteps under the crest or on well-worn rock on the crest. To get the best conditions on the Biancograt the descent will almost certainly be in mixed conditions, so you will have crampons on.

As you follow the ridge there are a number of steep rock steps; these can be downclimbed but there is also equipment in situ for abseil. The downclimbing is quite tricky, so I would suggest that it is worth changing your rope system and abseiling. Unless there is good snow on the flanks of the ridge, it is worth following the crest all the way to the glacier.

Spread the rope out and carry on down the glacier to the hut.

If you want a really long day, you can grab a drink at the hut and carry on. However, unless the weather is coming in it is much more enjoyable to relax at the hut and enjoy some Italian hospitality (the hut is just over the border), then carry on the next day.

The descent from the hut is either over the Piz Palü, which is a magnificent undertaking in its own right, or down the Fortezza ridge – PD+, which is quite complicated and should not be underestimated. There is no easy way back to the valley.

David Falcus approaching the summit of the Piz Bernina.

The Spallagrat, the normal route on the Piz Bernina and the descent from the Biancograt.

The routes on the Fortezza ridge, right and Piz Palü, left.

Both options involve leaving the hut and heading east under Crast'Agüzza, Piz Zupò and the Bellavista. It is difficult to get the rope system just right on this section as the terrain is heavily crevassed and you are travelling parallel to the crevasses. It is possible to climb along the crest of the Bellavista which looks great, but would add time to already tired legs. Don't be tempted to try and descend the glacier to the north. I did it on skis once and regretted it. We spent hours dancing the line between falling in a huge crevasse or getting avalanched.

If you are going to descend the Fortezza Ridge, traverse under the Bellavista until you are above point 3,589m, and then descend a blunt rib to the north to reach the rocks of the ridge.

Descend the ridge following yellow paint splashes. You can downclimb a lot of it at grade II and III, there are bolts in place for abseiling anywhere you may want to. The ridge leads down onto the small glacier on the north side of the Isla Persa. You now have two options:

Option 1
Carry on down the Isla Persa picking up a path about point 2,719m that leads down to the Morteratsch glacier, then onto the train station at Morteratsch.

Option 2
Head east down the ramp that leads onto the Pers glacier and then head north-east across the glacier aiming for the base of Piz Trovat. Here, you can leave the glacier and pick up a path that leads to the Diavolezza lift station. Go down on the lift and get a train (station next to the base of the lift) to wherever you want to go.

Another alternative is to traverse the Piz Palü to get to Diavolezza. I think this is a much better choice and if conditions are good on the Biancograt they will almost certainly be good on the Palü. See following pages.

ALPINE CLIMBING

Climbers on Piz Palü.

Piz Palü 3,900m

The Piz Palü is a stunning mountain with superb snow crests and solid granite ridge scrambling. I am describing it here as part of the greater Morteratsch skyline traverse, but it can easily be climbed in its own right either from Diavolezza or even from the Boval hut. If you are not quite ready for the more difficult snow crests and mixed routes offered by routes in the AD grade, this can be a perfect stepping stone, having exposed sections but not the sustained nature as found on routes like the Biancograt.

Traverse of Piz Palü

Grade	PD II	Length	300m of height gain from the Marco e Rosa hut to the west summit.
Exposure	West to east traverse	Rock type	Granite
Protection	Natural	Descent	East ridge or west depending on direction of travel.
Conditions	Good snow on the glacier and ridge.	Time	6-7hrs from Marco Rosa hut to Diavolezza.

Map
Swiss Topo 1:25,000 1277 Piz Bernina

Alternative guidebook
Bernina and Bregaglia Selected Climbs by Lindsay Griffin – Alpine Club
Swiss Alps by Stephane Maire

Equipment
Glacier travel gear

Hut
Marco e Rosa hut, www.rifugi.lombardia.it/en/sondrio/lanzada/hut-marco-e-rosa.html
tel. +39 0342515370
Berghaus Diavolezza, www.corvatsch-diavolezza.ch/en/berghaus-diavolezza/rooms – There is accommodation inside the Diavolezza lift station; hotel style rooms or dormitory's of various size are available.

Hut approach
If climbing the Piz Palü on its own, then the approach to Diavolezza is by cable car. For the the Boval hut, see approach in the Piz Moteratsch description. If you are heading to the Marco e Rosa hut then the approach is either by traversing the Biancograt from the Tschierva hut, or from Diavolezza by climbing the Fortezza ridge.

Route approach
If you are coming from the Marco e Rosa hut, leave the hut and head east traversing under the Piz Zupò and the Bellavista to the Fuorcla Bellavista. If you are climbing the mountain on its own and not as a link up, then stay at Diavolezza; you then descend onto the Pers glacier. Climb the glacier to just under 3,000m where you head north-west to gain the Fortezza Ridge. Climb this, short sections of III, with bolts and yellow paint to mark the way. The rock leads to a broad snow ridge which is climbed to the Fuorcla Bellavista.

Dave Smith approaching the start of the ridge from the Bella Vista on Piz Palü.

Route description
When you arrive at the Fuorcla Bellavista the way ahead is pretty obvious; head east along the narrow ridge. The ridge is most easily gained from the south side. Follow the rocky ridge above, where the scrambling is excellent, on solid rock with great positions. The ridge leads to the summit of Piz Spinas. Descend the east eidge, usually on rock, to a col. The way ahead will be on snow so if you have been climbing without crampons, then now is the time to put them back on.

Climb the broad snow slope to the central and highest summit 3,900m. Descend the narrow snow crest to a col, then follow the ridge onto the east summit. Continue down the east ridge which leads onto the upper section of the Pers glacier. When you reach the glacier spread out; don't be shy and use lots of rope, as there are some really big crevasses on the glacier ahead of you. Descend the glacier heading north-east passing under the Fuorcla Palü – Pers and the west face of Piz Cambrena; there is a section of usually open crevasses here with some spectacular glacial scenery. Once you are clear of this crevassed section head north to the Fuorcla Trovat, a path leads up off the glacier then traverses the east side of Piz Trovat, before picking up a path marked with blue and white paint that leads to the lift station at Diavolezza.

You can, of course, make the traverse in the opposite direction starting at Diavolezza heading up the Pers glacier then descending the Fortezza ridge and return to Diavolezza or down past the Boval hut to Morteratsch.

Mike Austin caught by first light on the North Ridge of the Piz Badile.

Will Brant leading the Fiamma, an icon of Bregaglia climbing.

Bregaglia

The Bregaglia is a stunning area of granite mountains situated south of the high glaciated peaks of the Bernina on the Swiss Italian border. Its most famous peak is the Piz Badile, which is an amazing pyramid of perfect granite. The north face of the Badile is most famous for the Cassin Route, a route of legendary status and one of the classic six north faces of the Alps. At TD it is a bit beyond the scope of this book, but the North Ridge is well within the reach of any alpinist with solid rock climbing skills and an ability to move quickly over its 33 pitches.

The area isn't all about the Badile. The climbing around the Albigna dam is some of the best, fast approached granite climbing you will find. There is a cable car that takes you to the dam and drops you minutes from the fantastic climbing on the Spazzacaldeira. There are few finer days out than a route on its flanks or the North East Ridge, finishing with an ascent of the Fiamma (the flame) – a ridiculous needle of rock with an incredible sense of exposure.

The routes situated further from the Albigna dam will almost certainly require an overnight, and the comfortable Albigna hut is perfectly situated for access to the Piz Balzet and the Punta da l'Albigna.

A great combination is to get your multi-pitch skills up to speed round the Albigna then head to the Badile.

Spazzacaldeira 2,487m

The Spazzacaldeira is a fantastic piece of rock. I can't think of any other place where there is granite climbing of this quality, at altitude, with only a 10-minute approach. The route described is the North East Ridge and an ascent of the Fiamma, which is fantastic, but there are a lot of other great routes that can be climbed. My particular favourite is the Via Felici (6a), which follows an amazing series of cracks and flakes to join the North East ridge after 7 memorable pitches. The name is painted on the rock at the base of the route.

North East Ridge

Grade	AD 4c, 5c+ for the Fiamma	Length	200m
Exposure	NE	Rock type	Granite
Protection	Mixed	Descent	Walk and abseil.
Conditions	Dry rock	Time	4-5hrs with the lift to summit, descent 1½hrs.

Map
Swiss Topo 1:25,000 Val Bregaglia 1275, Sciora 1296

Alternative guidebook
Schweis Plaiser Sud Band 1 – Edition Filidor

Bregaglia

Approach and route on the Spazzacaldeira.

Equipment
North East Ridge – 50m rope, cams (1,2) nuts (1,3,5,7,9), 8 quickdraws. Rock shoes are more fun.
Via Felici – 50m rope, cams (1,2) nuts (1-9), 10 quickdraws, rock shoes.

Hut
Valley or Albigna hut www.albigna.ch

Hut approach
Take the cable car to the Albigna dam, cross to the east side of the dam and follow the marked track to the hut. The approach takes about an hour.

Route approach
North East Ridge – Leave the cable car station and take the concrete road that leads up to the dam. A good track leads up a cone of grass and gravel to the base of the route.

Route description
North East Ridge – At the top of the grass, scramble up a short section of III-, then follow a track to the base of chimney. Climb out of the chimney onto a blunt rib on the right to a belay.

Climb the rib (4c, bolts) to a ledge.

Climb through a notch in the ridge and descend, then traverse across a blocky ledge to the base of a crack. Climb up and right to reach the crest of the ridge (4b).

Climb the ridge with a mix of pitches and moving together. The climbing is never more difficult than 4a.

Make a 6m abseil onto a ledge at the base of the pinnacle. The pinnacle is called the Dente (tooth), and can climbed on its south side at 6b. Walk past the pinnacle and climb up to the base of the Fiamma.

Climb the Fiamma via some bolts on the south side (5c+), then make a 25m abseil from the top on the north side. Try not to look too hard at the crack that splits the summit block.

Descent
Leaving the base of the Fiamma, scramble along ledges on the south-west side of the ridge to pick up a path. This leads down to a chimney system that can downclimbed (III max) or descended with a 20m abseil. A path then leads back to the dam.

Piz Balzet 2,869m

As classic routes go this is right up there. A short, one hour approach from the hut, great quality rock, and fantastic views combine to give a great day in the mountains. The routes in the area do not have too much fixed equipment, which adds to the quality of the route, but the belays are in situ so progress can be swift.

South Ridge

Grade	D 4c	**Length**	550m
Exposure	South	**Rock type**	Granite
Protection	Mixed	**Descent**	Abseil and scramble down the east ridge.
Conditions	Dry rock	**Time**	6hrs hut to hut.

Map
Swiss Topo 1:25,000 Val Bregaglia 1275, Sciora 1296

Alternative guidebook
Mountaineering in the Swiss Alps by Stephane Maire
Schweiz Plaisir Sud Band 1, Edition Filidor

Equipment
50m rope, cams (1,2,3), nuts (1-10), 10 quickdraws, more fun in rock boots

Hut
Albigna hut, www.albigna.ch

Hut approach
Albigna hut, take the cable car from Pranzaira to the dam, cross the dam then follow a good path that leads SSE to the hut.

John Orr climbing on the Piz Balzet.

The South Ridge of the Piz Balzet.

Route approach
Leave the hut and head east then north-east, initially on the path that heads to the Pass da Casnil, marked with blue and white paint splashes. Just south of Piz dal Pal the path forks; take the left fork that crosses a flat area. You can spot the south ridge from here. The route starts just left of a narrow gully. Scramble up an easy corner to a ledge and bolt belay.

Route description
Pitch 1 – 4c 35m Climb a slab, then a corner, to belay just below a roof.
Pitch 2 – 3c 15m Step right, then climb past the roof, then pull back left through some steep ground to the belay.
Pitch 3 – 2c 20m Climb easy terrain straight up to belay below a roof. You can easily run pitch 3 and 4 together, if you extend a couple of runners to reduce rope drag.
Pitch 4 – 3c 20m Climb through the roof and belay on a large ledge.
Pitch 5 – 4a 35m Climb the parallel cracks. Easier variation on the left.
Pitch 6 – 4a 35m Climb the crest of the ridge in superb positions.
Pitch 7 – 3a 40m Scramble up on the left side of the ridge then head right along ledge to belay below the tower.
Pitch 8 – 4c 25m Climb a steep, blank-looking wall, then move right and then up to the roof. Turn the roof on the left and then climb up to a good ledge.
Follow the ridge to the summit, mostly easy climbing with a few moves of 3c.

Descent
Scramble down the East Ridge to an abseil point and make a 25m abseil. Follow the most worn path with cairns. Go round a tower on the north side where you will find lots of abseil tat; keep going to reach a chain anchor and make a 25m abseil.

Move back to the south side at a notch and scramble down a gully to reach an abseil anchor and make a third, 25m abseil. At the end of the abseil a faint path leads back to the approach track.

Punta da l'Albigna 2,825m

Via Meuli

The routes on the north west face of the Punta da l'Albigna date back to the early 60's when they were all climbed with leader placed protection; a lot of retro bolting has taken place since then. This is unusual for the Bregaglia, but it does mean that these long routes can be climbed quickly, which is always a pleasure. There are three classic routes on the face: Moderne Zeiten, Via Meuli and the Via Steiger. They are all excellent, and easy to find as the names are marked at the base of the first pitch. Having climbed all three, I think the Via Meuli is the most enjoyable, and this is the route featured here. It has a huge variety of climbing styles and the rock is excellent.

While it is possible to descend after ten pitches, it is worth climbing the extra six on the north west ridge to the summit, which is an amazing viewpoint. This makes for an amazing 16-pitch outing, the perfect warm up for a larger outing like the North Ridge on the Piz Badile.

Grade	D 5a+	Length	600m
Exposure	NW	Rock type	Granite
Protection	Mixed	Descent	Abseil and scramble down the north side.
Conditions	Dry rock	Time	9hrs hut to hut.

Map
Swiss Topo 1:25,000, Sciora 1296

Alternative guidebook
Mountaineering in the Swiss Alps by Stephane Maire
Schweiz Plaisir Sud Band 1, Edition Filidor

Equipment
50m rope, 10 quickdraws, rock shoes

Hut
Albigna hut, www.albigna.ch

Hut approach
As for previous route

Punta da l'Albigna and the Albigna hut.

Route approach
Leave the hut and head south following a path that leads down towards the lake. Cross a stream, and climb up the left side of a scree slope. The route starts in an obvious corner and has Meuli marked at the bottom.

Route description
There are a lot of pitches and being fully bolted it is relatively easy to follow, so if the description doesn't seem to be that detailed, it's because it doesn't need to be.

Pitch 1 – 4a 30m Climb a wide corner and belay. This anchor is common with Moderne Zeiten (at the belay Moderne Zeiten heads right).

The Meuli Route on the Punta da l'Albigna.

Pitch 2 – 4b	Carry on up the corner.
Pitch 3 – 3c	Climb the chimney on the left then move slightly left.
Pitch 4 – 3c	Climb a series of stepped ledges straight up to a belay.
Pitches 5 & 6 – 3c	Follow slabs heading for a corner. Take care here as it is easy to get lost as the bolts are quite spaced.
Pitch 7 – 4b	Climb the corner. I think they forgot to bolt this pitch properly, so it can feel a little bold if 4b is your grade.
Pitch 8 – 3b	Climb a slab, heading diagonally up and left to reach a crest.
Pitch 9 – 4b	Climb a ramp up and right, with spaced protection, to reach a chimney. Climb this, then exit right and climb another 10m to reach a good belay stance.
Pitch 10 – 4a	Climb slabs to reach easy ground.
	Scramble up a gully on the left to reach a boulder-filled gully. Climb up the right-hand side following cairns to reach the base of the north west ridge, then move further right to the base of a bolted slab.
Pitch 11 – 5a+	Climb up and right via a diagonal crack in the slab (well-protected). This is better climbing and has better protection than the left-hand variant which is easier at 4c.
Pitch 12 –	Leave the belay and move right then back left to climb parallel with the edge of the slab.
Pitch 13-16	Climb the crest of the ridge, just right of the crest. The climbing is no harder than 3c and the positions are superb.

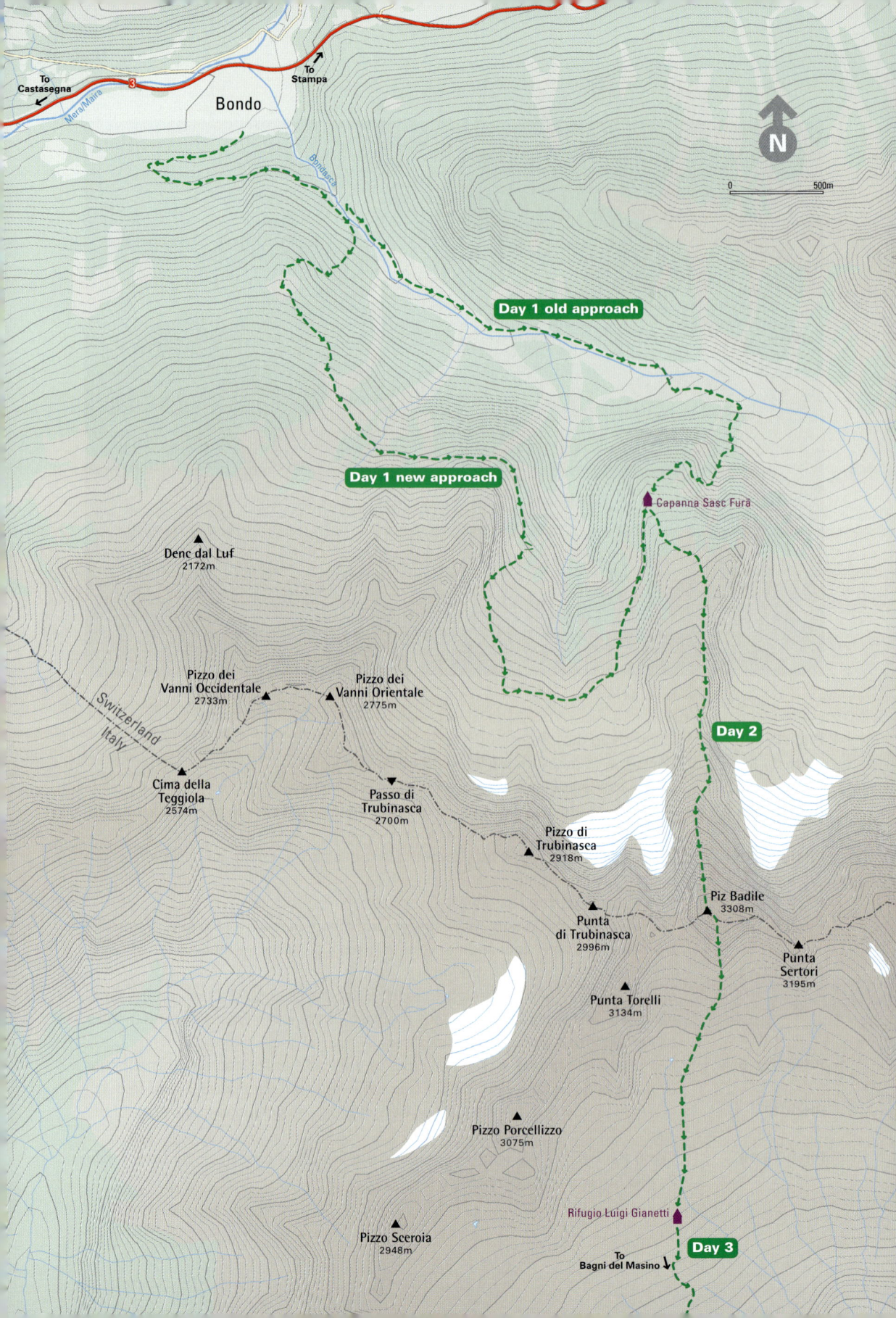

Descent

Traverse the summit ridge over to the south summit, to an abseil anchor and make a 25m abseil on the south face to a large ledge. Follow a cable to a second abseil anchor where you make a second 25m abseil.

Climb up to a saddle (yes up) on a path to the east of where the abseil lands. Then descend into a north-facing valley that is followed using cairns and joining sections of path. This leads down to the stream that descends from the Vadrec dal Cantun glacier. Cross the stream and head back to the Albigna hut.

Piz Badile 3,308m

As iconic Alpine peaks go it doesn't get any more impressive than the Piz Badile, a perfect pyramid of granite that reaches for the sky.

When you look up at the Badile from the north side, your eyes are drawn to the stunning ridge that dances the line between light and shade. This is the line of the North Ridge, one of the most sought-after routes of its grade in the Alps. There are few lines that have the same purity and that drop in 1,000m of amazing climbing from the summit towards the Sasc Furä hut.

North Ridge

While most of the climbing on the route is in the 4's there are more than 25 pitches of climbing, so you need to keep your foot down and keep moving. You should be capable of climbing four or five pitches an hour if you want to complete the route in a reasonable time frame.

The North Ridge of the Piz Badile.

ALPINE CLIMBING

While it is possible to abseil down the route on fixed anchors, I would advise against this, as the route is not particularly steep so the abseiling is really difficult. I have done this after climbing the Cassin, and once after a client asked if we could climb the route with a light sack; I will never, ever do it again!

After descending the Italian side of the mountain to the Gianetti hut and spending the night there, you have two alternatives. You can either walk down to the valley on the Italian side of the mountain and get a taxi back to the car, or walk back to the Sasc Furä hut, crossing the Porcellizzo and Trubinasca Passes, which takes about five hours. Crossing the first pass often requires the use of an ice axe and crampons, so check with the guardian for conditions. The taxi option is much more relaxing, though expensive; the hut guardian in the Gianetti hut will help organise this for you.

Grade	D 5a+	Length	1,000m
Exposure	North	Rock type	Granite
Protection	Mixed	Descent	South face, scramble and abseil.
Conditions	Dry rock	Time	5-7hrs from hut to summit, then 3hrs from summit to Gianetti hut.

Map
Swiss Topo 1:25,000, Sciora 1296

Alternative guidebook
Schweiz Plaisir Sud Band 1, Edition Filidor

Equipment
50m rope, set of nuts, cams (1,2,3), 8 quickdraws. You may need an ice axe and crampons for the approach early in the summer.

Hut
Sasc Furä for approach, www.sascfura.ch
Gianetti for descent, www.rifugi.lombardia.it/sondrio/val-masino/rifugio-gianetti.html

Hut approach
There was a massive landslide from the Piz Cengalo in 2017 which destroyed much of the upper Bondasca valley, destroyed some of the approach path to the Sasc Furä hut, and killed a number of walkers. The new footpath avoids any danger of further landslides but is much longer and more arduous. In 2023 many people, including myself, ascended using the old track as it is two hours shorter, and we felt we were prepared to take the risk. Many of the local guides go by the old route, but the hut is not allowed to give out information about its condition and it is not being maintained. You can make your own decision.

New route
Start in Bondo. Go past the church to the south side of the village, then follow the forest road west where you will find the last possible parking space. Follow the road to point 908m, then head east into the Val Bondasca. Follow the road to where a bridge crosses the river near point 1,023m and turn right / south and climb through the woods to Cugian, 1,317m.

The path now continues south-east to Luvartigh 1,553m, where you will pick up the hut path which is marked with blue and white paint. The path heads south-east then east into the Val Trubinasca, and then climbs to just over 2,130m where it meets the path which leads to the Passo della Trubinasca.

The path now contours round the bowl and descends north to the hut. The approach takes about 5½ hours.

Bregaglia

Mike Austin enjoying the cracked slab pitch.

Old route
Park as above, then follow the route as above to the bridge. Cross the river then turn south-east on a track that parallels the road, carry on up through the hairpins in the road at Pra and follow the road until you come to signs of the landslide. You used to be able to park at the end of the road here. Pick up a rough track that leads down to the river and follow this up to a log bridge crossing the river. Once past the collection of houses at Lumbardui, you will pick up the track and paint splashes that lead south, then west and south to the Sasc Furä hut.

Route approach
Leave the hut and head uphill following blue and while paint splashes and a sign that says 'Vial' (this path used to lead to the Sciora hut before the landslide). Follow paths with paint splashes and cairns, and as you gain height follow your nose looking for the most travelled terrain. As the ground steepens stay on the right side of the ridge. The scrambling becomes easy climbing. Stay on the right, then join the crest and follow it to a flatter area just before the climbing proper begins. There may be a snow patch at the bottom of this steeper ground early in the season.

Route description
The route description for a climb of almost 30 pitches is almost meaningless, so the description below is not that detailed but points out the key places where you may go wrong.

The route is equipped with all anchors, mainly large, door-knocker style bolts. There are also bolts or pegs at key points, so keep an eye out for them as they will help keep you on track. Belays are 30-35m apart, and if one doesn't appear, you have probably gone off route.

The ridge rises steeply above the ledge where you gear up. Climb up, then head left round a corner and climb diagonally left and up to the ridge; this is about three pitches.

Follow the crest of the ridge, where the climbing is amazing and the positions superb. The climbing is all in the III to 4c grade so you can move quickly. The key passage where people go wrong is when the route arrives at a large overhang with white rock at its base. There are pegs and signs of traffic leading left. Ignore this and climb down into a chimney / notch, then move right and climb a chimney to a belay on the left, (the route used to move right and climb an excellent corner / slab feature, but there has been rockfall in this area and it is best avoided). Above the belay on the left, a line of bolts leads up and back to the ridge, climb these then continue on the ridge crest.

Where the angle eases you can move together for sections. Before the summit there is a sub summit, and as you approach this a ledge system leads left. Follow this, then scramble up to the summit cross.

If you are late or exhausted, an insulated bivvy hut is situated south of the summit.

Descent

As intimated earlier, it is possible to descend the North Ridge by abseil, though I wouldn't recommend it. The fastest and easiest descent is on the Italian side. Leave the summit and scramble down an open gully following the best, most travelled track. The ground is steep and exposed but easy. The track leads to an abseil anchor, abseil 25m to gain a track that leads to the Gianetti hut.

The descent on the south side of the Piz Badile.

Index

A
Abalakov (V thread) 114
Abri Simond hut 152
abseiling 108
abseiling, anchors 109
abseiling on snow and ice 113
abseil, protecting 110
acclimatisation 35
active protection 83
acute mountain sickness (AMS) 36
AD (assez difficile), grade 32
AD (assez difficile) route, kit for 86
Aiguille d'Arpette 175
Aiguille de la Cabane 175, 179
Aiguille de la Tsa 194, 196
Aiguille de la Vanoise 146
Aiguille de Rochefort 172
Aiguille d'Orny 175, 176, 177
Aiguille du Midi 151, 152
Aiguille du Peigne 154
Aiguille du Van 160, 161
aiguille (mountain feature) 43
Aiguilles d'Arpette 182
Aiguilles d'Entrèves 166
Aiguilles Marbrées 164
Albergo Ristorante Pian del Re 135, 136
Albert-Heim hut 251, 255, 256
Albigna dam 289, 291
Albigna hut 289, 291, 292, 294, 297
Allalinhorn 217
Almageller hut 217, 222, 224, 225, 226
alpine climbing, styles of 21
alpine day, typical 14
alpine grades 31
alpine season, the 26
alpine terrain 39
alternate leads 102
alternate leads, change overs 104
altitude, effects of 19, 35, 36
altitude sickness 37
altitude, sleeping at 38
anchors, asbeil 109
anchor, snow (setting up) 58
approach, to route 15, 92
Aravis, The 183
Arête du Doigt 183, 184, 186
Arête Laurence 151, 152
Arête Marion 183
arête (mountain feature) 43
axes, ice 77
Ayas hut 213, 214, 215

B
Bächlital hut 263
bandoliers 84
base layer 68
base rack 85
beacon rescue 90
Becco Meridionale della Tribolazione 140
belay devices 82
belays, direct 102
Bellavista 285
Berghaus Diavolezza 287
bergschrund, crossing a 95
bergschrund, feature 42
Bernese Oberland 237
Bernina 277
Bertol hut 196, 197
Biancograt 281, 282, 283, 287
bivouac huts 118
bivouacking / bivvying 118
blending techniques 106
block lead 102
block lead changeover 105
bollard, snow 113
bolts 23
Bon Accueil 179
boot crampon compatibility 75
boot rating 74
boots 74
Boval hut 279, 280, 286, 287
brake knot 50
Bregaglia 289
Breithorn 207, 213, 215
Breya lift 177
Buffs® 72

C
Cabane d'Orny 175, 179, 182
camping 120
cams 83
Cervinia guides hut 213, 214, 215
Chamonix 149, 165
Champex-Lac 177
charging, electrical devices 68
Cheminée Sallanches 187
Cheyne-Stokes breathing 36
Chli (Klein) Bielenhorn 249, 250
Chli Läckihorn 258, 260
cirque (mountain feature) 43
climbing down 108
climbing in blocks 102

climbing, mixed 22
climbing, rock 23
climbing, snow and ice 21
climbing up 91
clothing 68
coils, taking in 51
Col de Bertol 196
Col de la Serpentine 198, 199, 200
Col de la Tsa 196, 197
Col de la Vanoise hut 147
Col des Annes 185
Col des Aravis 189
Col des Vignettes 199
col (mountain feature) 43
cornice (mountain feature) 43
Cosmiques Arête 151, 152
Cosmiques hut 151, 152
couloir (mountain feature) 43
Courmayeur 163, 165
course, taking a 30
crampon rating 75
crampons 79
crevasse, climbing out of 62
crevasse rescue 54
crevasses 48
crevasses, formation 40

D
danger, objective 18
D (difficile), grade 32
D (difficile) route, kit for 87
Dent de Tsalion 191, 194
Dent du Géant 169
descent, from route 16, 92, 107
Diamox 38
Diavolezza 285, 286, 287
direct belays 102
Dix hut 198
Dreiselwand 220
Dri Horlini 217, 225
dry glacier 41, 49
Dufourspitze 207, 210

E
ED (extrêmement difficile), grade 32
edge, preparing (crevasse rescue) 59
Eiger 237, 241
emergency kit 88
emergency, managing a 125
Emosson dam 161
equipment, group 88

ALPINE CLIMBING

F

fall, holding a (crevasse rescue) 54
fast and light 25
features, glacier 40
features, mountain 43
Felix Faure hut 147
F (facile), grade 32
F (facile) route, kit for 86
Fiamma, the 289, 290, 292
first aid kit 89
fixed protection 23
fleece 69
Fontanettes 147
Fortezza ridge 281, 284, 285, 287
Fuorcla Bellavista 287
Fuorcla da Boval 280
Fuorcla Prievlusa 283
Furka Pass 245, 247

G

gaiters 76
Galenstock 245, 253
gendarme (mountain feature) 43
Giacoletti hut 131, 134, 136
Giacomini hut 203
Gianetti hut 298, 300
glacial features 40
glacial retreat 26, 41
Glacier de Bertol 197
Glacier de L'Aiguille 196, 197
glacier, moving on 53
glacier, planning a route on 48
glacier, roping up for 49
glaciers 20
glaciers, understanding 47
glacier travel kit 85
glacier, travelling on 47
Gletschhorn 255
grades, alpine 31
grades, comparison table 34
grades, technical 33
Gramusset hut 183
Grand Bornand 185
granite 44
Grimsel Pass 261, 263
Gross Bielenhorn 249, 251
Gross Diamantstock 261, 262
Gross Furkahorn 247
Gross Läckihorn 258, 260
group equipment 88
group shelter 88

H

half rope 87
Hannig 220
hardware 77
harnesses 66
hats 71
Haute Corde 203, 206
headtorch 67
heavy boots (B2 / B3) 76
helicopter, rescue 124
helmet 66
help, calling for 122
high-altitude cerebral oedema (HACE) 36
high-altitude pulmonary oedema (HAPE) 36
Hohsaas 233
Hohsaas hut 223
horn (mountain feature) 43
huts, staying in 18, 117

I

ice axes 77
icefall 48
ice screws 79
IFMGA (International Federation of Mountain Guide Associations) 31
insulation layer 71
Isla Persa 285

J

jacket, softshell 69
Jegigrat 217, 232
Jegihorn 232, 236
Joderhorn 217, 227
Jungfrau 237, 239
Jungfraujoch 239, 242

K

karabiners 80
kit, emergency 88
kit, group 88
kit, personal 65
Klein (Chli) Bielenhorn 249, 250
Klein Matterhorn lift 213, 215
knot, brake 50
knots, passing (crevasse rescue) 60
Kreuzboden 233, 236

L

Lac d'Emosson 161
Läckihorn 258
Lagginhorn 223
Lago di Telessio 141
Lago Tremorgio 272
L'Arête à Marion 188
La Vanoise 145
layering, clothes 68
leading in blocks 102
leads, alternate 102
Leit hut 267, 272
Le Miroir d'Argentine - Alpes Vaudoises 201
Le Miroir d'Argentine (direct route) 204
Le Miroir d'Argentine (Haute Corde) 202
Lenzspitze 217, 220
Les Perrons 160
Les Perrons de Vallorcine 159
L'Été Indien 183
lightning 20
limestone 44
Lion d'Argentine 203
load, transferring (crevasse rescue) 59
Lombardy 267

M

Macugnaga 229
Malvassora 140
Marco e Rosa hut 281, 282, 284, 287
Marinelli hut 281
Mattmark dam 229
mechanical advantage (crevasse rescue) 61
metamorphic rock 44
Mischabel hut 220
Mittellegi hut 241, 242
mixed climbing 22
Mönch 239, 241
Mönchsjoch hut 239, 241, 243
Mont Blanc de Cheilon 191, 198
Mont Blanc Massif (Chamonix) 149
Mont Blanc Massif (Courmayeur) 163
Monte Disgrazia 275
Monte Rosa hut 210, 211
Monte Viso 131, 135, 136, 138
moraines 42
Morteratsch 280, 281, 285, 287
moulins 41
mountain features 43
Mountain Guide, using 30
moving together 29, 96
moving together on a descent 108

N

Nadelhorn 217, 220, 222
navigation tools 90
North Eigerjoch 243
north faces, conditions 40
nuts 82

O

Oberto Maroli hut 229
orientation, of a mountain 40
Orny hut 175, 179, 182

P

Panoramique gondola 165
passive protection 82
PD (peu difficile), grade 32
PD (peu dificile) route, kit for 86
Pian del Re 131, 134, 136
Piansecco hut 267, 269

Index

Pigne d'Arolla 198
pitching, descent 108
Piz Badile 289, 297
Piz Balzet 289, 292
Piz Bernina 277, 281
Piz Bianco 284
Piz Morteratsch 277, 279
Piz Palü 277, 281, 284, 285, 286, 287
Piz Spinas 287
Pizzo del Prévat 267, 271
Plan de l'Aiguille hut 155
Pointe de Chombas 183
Pointe de l'Ifala 160, 162
Pointe de Tsalion 197
Pointe Graham 171
Pointe Percée 183, 184, 186
Pointe Percée hut 185
Pointes de la Blonnière 188
Pointe Sella 171
poles, walking 76
Pollux 213
Poncione di Cassina Baggio 267, 268
Pontese hut 140, 141
Ponti hut 275, 276
Pontresina 283
power bank 68
progression, alpine 115
protection 80
protection, fixed 23
pulley system (crevasse rescue) 60
Punta da l'Albigna 289, 294
Punta Udine 131, 133

Q

quickdraws 83
Quintino Sella hut (see also Sella hut) 135

R

racking 84
racks 85
randkluft 95
Räterichsbodensee dam 263
Realp 259
rescue beacon 90
rescue, crevasse 54
rescue helicopter 124
rescue services, information required 124
rescue services in the Alps 122
ridge (mountain feature) 43
Riffelhorn 211
rimaye (see also bergschrund) 42
Rochefort Arête 170, 172
rock boots 75
rock climbing 23
rockfall 18

rock types 44
Rodi 267, 272
rognon (mountain feature) 43
rope, carrying on rucksack 73
ropes 87
rope, spacing on (glacier travel) 49
ropes, tying together 109
rope systems 87
roping up, glacier travel 49
Rotenboden 211, 213
Rotondo hut 258
Rottalsattel 240
route approach 15, 92
route, descending from 16, 92, 107
route finding 91
rucksacks 72

S

Saas-Almagell 226
Saas-Fee 217, 220
Saas-Grund 223, 226, 233
Saastal 229
Salle à Manger 170, 171, 173
San Martino 275
Sasc Furä hut 298, 299
Scottish grades 33
scrambling boots (B2) 75
screwgates 81
season, alpine 26
Sella di Poida 276
Sella hut 131, 135, 136
seracs 20, 41, 48
sheet sleeping bag 68
shelter, group 88
short rope techniques 29
sickness, altitude 37
Sidelen hut 247, 250, 253
Silbersattel 212
single rope 87
situational awareness 45
skills check list 11
Skyway Monte Bianco 165
sleeping at altitude 38
sleeping bag liner 68
sleeping tablets 38
slings 84
snow anchor, setting up 58
snow bollard 113
Solalex 203, 204
South Eigerjoch 243
south faces, conditions 40
spacing on the rope (glacier) 49
Spallagrat 284
spares kit 88
Spazzacaldeira 289, 290

stoves 119
sunglasses 72
sun, protection from 67
sun shirt 69

T

tag lines 88, 112
TD (très difficile), grade 32
technical tools 78
techniques, practising 30
techniques, short rope 29
Teodulo hut 214
terrain, alpine 39
Tessin 267
thunderstorms 20
Tiefenbach 251
Tiefenbach Hotel 256
Torino hut 163, 165, 167, 170, 173
Tour St Robert 137
travel, to / in the Alps 28
trousers, softshell 69
Tschierva hut 279, 280, 282, 283, 287
twin rope 88
Tza hut 194, 197

U

UIAA (Union Internationale des Associations d'Alpinisme) system 31
umbrella 73
Untere Bielenlücke 250, 251
USA grades 34

V

Val d'Hérens 191
Valle dell'Orco 139
Via Meuli 294
Vignettes hut 198
Voie de Trou, the 183
V thread 114

W

water bottle 67
waterproofs 70
weather 20
Weissmies 217, 222, 223, 225
Weissmies hut 232, 233
wet glacier 41, 49
when to climb 26
where to stay 28
windproof 70
winter rooms 118
WI (water ice) grading system 33

X, Y, Z

Zermatt 207